W9-DGZ-989

India and the United States

by SELIG S. HARRISON

India: The Most Dangerous Decades
India and the United States

Conference on India and the United States

INDIA AND THE UNITED STATES

Edited and with an Introduction
by SELIG S. HARRISON

New York The Macmillan Company 1961

© The Macmillan Company 1961

All rights reserved—no part of this book may be
reproduced in any form without permission in writing from the publisher, except by a reviewer who
wishes to quote brief passages in connection with a
review written for inclusion in magazine or newspaper.

First Printing

The Macmillan Company, New York
Brett-Macmillan Ltd., Galt, Ontario

Printed in the United States of America

Library of Congress catalog card number: 61–5473

E
183
.8
I4
C6

Editor's Preface

In the years since Indian Independence several rather inbred fraternities have grown up among the increasing number of Americans concerned with separate aspects of the new relationship between India and the United States. The scholars have communicated, by and large, with the scholars; businessmen have discussed investment opportunities in India at conferences with other businessmen; returning foreign aid practitioners have developed a language of "Five Year Plans" and "Village Development" all their own. Expertise has rarely been transmitted from one set of experts to another, let alone to the many politically literate Americans who have sensed the importance of India and would like to know more about her problems and prospects, and what they imply for American policy.

The Conference on India and the United States held at the Mayflower Hotel in Washington on May 4 and 5, 1959, brought together for the first time eighty-eight of the two countries' most distinguished authorities on internal Indian affairs and on the major issues of Indo-United States relations. Sponsored by the Committee for International Economic Growth under the chairmanship of Mr. Eric Johnston, with the Stanford Research Institute, the MIT Center for International Studies, the Asia Foundation, and the National Planning Association as co-sponsors, the Conference was attended by 724 registrants from all parts of the United States. Businessmen and officials of national organizations made up the largest representation. Appendix A lists in detail the format of the Conference program. It should be noted, however, that in editing and adapting the proceedings, at the invitation of The Macmillan Company, the original format has in many instances been disregarded to avoid repetition as well as for the sake of greater coherence and a more meaningful presentation. Two thirds of the original raw transcript of some three hundred thousand words has been eliminated. What has been kept has been regrouped and re-integrated in a chapter plan which does not necessarily conform to the plan of the Conference panels, though care has been taken, in so doing, to retain intact the original immediate context of those excerpts presented.

Chapter Five ("The Slowly Simmering Story") is an adaptation of an earlier panel discussion over which I had presided at the San Francisco Conference on United States-Asian Relations in November, 1957, sponsored by the United States National Commission for UNESCO. This previously unpublished discussion remains, so far as I am aware, the only attempt of its kind by working newspapermen to consider the place of the press in our relations with Asia. It was my feeling that this made an appropriate companion piece for the Washington panels.

I am grateful for the cooperation of the Committee for International Economic Growth, in particular George Barnes, Willard Johnson, and finally, Sally Ann Sessions, who most competently typed the manuscript.

S. S. H.

Washington, D.C.
July 21, 1960

Contents

For table, "United States Aid to India, as of June 30, 1960," see page 65.

INDIA AND THE
UNITED STATES: THE LONG VIEW

by Selig S. Harrison

Facing the complex world of the sixties, the United States scans the landscape of the past decade in foreign policy and searches, hopefully, for some guideposts imposing enough to establish a new national sense of direction. In the case of our relations with South Asia the Eisenhower good will mission of 1959 was an unmistakable landmark and what the President said on his return might well help us to see our way into the future. His mutual security message on February 16, 1960, amounts to something of a foreign aid Eisenhower Doctrine. He informed Congress that India among all the developing countries holds singular promise: the Nehru government will now get a "major share" of United States development loans. This was simply the concrete application of a broad new policy calling for greater selectivity in the allocation of aid, for emphasis on "those areas where the determination and the will to progress are greatest and the capacity to use such resource effectively is greatest."

Whether by design or by a happy accident of phraseology Mr. Eisenhower made the principal criterion for aid a country's political temperature-reading, attaching to "determination" and "the will to progress" a natural order of priority over strictly economic tests. Is this self-evident? Is it obvious that political health decisively conditions the ability of a country to make economic progress? If it is, the record of the fifties shows how easy it was to overlook the obvious in the fits and starts of an aid program growing up as a by-product of the cold war. Countries got aid for reasons having little to do with political health—because they were, or were not, willing to sign up with Washington, or merely because they were too big

1

and "strategic" to be left out. India compels consideration by virtue of size alone. And yet India also sticks out a mile from the rest of Asia, Africa, and the Middle East in the more critical sense that the Nehru government commands the broad nation-wide support and confidence of the Indian people.

The United States properly assigns pride of place to India in foreign economic policy for the fundamental reason that in these first years of freedom India still trusts in the Congress leadership and does indeed show a remarkably unified national determination and will to progress. By the same token, however, India in another ten or fifteen years may for domestic Indian political reasons of the moment seem to offer a much less promising opportunity for the effective absorption of aid than, to take a random example, a re-vitalized Indonesia which has picked itself up from political dis-array, or some new federal combination in Africa led by some new charismatic hero. Mr. Eisenhower has alerted us to the probability that one country's time of doldrums and political transition may be another's high point of progress and common cause. He has fore-warned us that the United States in its aid program may frankly have to favor what are at any point in time the areas of greatest opportunity, and that only through the exercise of such discrimina-tion will the United States necessarily prove able, in fact, to direct adequate resources to the right place at the right time.

India, as the discussions recorded in this book make amply clear, is still the right place. Now is still the right time. But one cannot read these pages without wondering what it will be as a practical matter to apply any set of aid criteria in the years ahead. The problems confronting Indian leaders are so oppressive and so com-plex that no one can say what political solutions will be attempted or what relation a given level of aid in 1963 or 1968 will have on the course of events. Already India shows signs of political despond which were not present when Chester Bowles as Ambassador in 1952 first proposed a $1 billion annual United States contribution to Indian development. American sympathy has grown in direct proportion, or so it often seems, to the decline of India's own self-confidence and political *élan*. Those in the West who wish India well might temper good will with caution, recognizing how risky it is to base long-term friendship on an assumption that "democracy," as defined and experienced in the West, will necessarily survive on

Indian soil. The challenge to American policy lies precisely in anticipating the possibility that the present political order will not survive, which is to say, in preparing through study of the Indian scene to make exceedingly sophisticated judgments as to the political health of this or that new order. It is to be hoped that the following pages will serve as a useful source of facts and ideas relevant to such balanced study and assessment. Most of these discussions center on areas of opportunity and challenge—on certain urgent and immediate problems, such as the food and foreign exchange shortages, in which the United States has a decisive role to play. They focus on what might possibly be achieved if we try, rather than on the chances of success. Here and there, however, in the candor and spontaneity of discussion, some of the awful truth sneaks out.

Chapter Four, for example, tells the hopeful story of the "Community Development" program, unparalleled among the developing countries, which is the focus of nearly all plans for progress in rural India. Yet we also learn here that the men who gave life to this program in its early stages have profound doubts concerning the possibility of multiplying quickly and on a national basis what was successful only after years of intensive work in a few "pilot projects." The Ford Foundation's Carl Taylor speaks of how "terribly diluted" standards have become in the process of multiplication. Against this background one can appreciate why Sherman Johnson, Chief Economist of the United States Department of Agriculture, advocates a more far-reaching "emergency" effort to bring food production abreast of population growth. The demographic projections set forth by Ansley C. Coale of the Princeton Office of Population Research underscore the concern expressed by Johnson and, in Chapter Three, by Senator John F. Kennedy, who cites the rate of population growth to support his argument for increased United States aid. Coale points to 1966 as a deadline for what he believes to be necessary action. Should India fail to initiate a downward trend in the birth rate by 1966, a trend which progresses to a 50 per cent decline no later than 1981, Coale says, in effect, that the situation will be past control and already-low living standards will thenceforth go on a steady slide.

India's interrelated food and population problems lead one logically to weigh the political weapons now available to the national leadership against the weight of the problems and the force of the radical action that may be needed. In Chapter Seven, B. K. Nehru, cousin of the Prime Minister and India's Commissioner General for Economic Affairs in Washington, characterizes democracy as a kind of obstacle course which Indian leaders must run. They do so by choice, but they might in time decide that the choice is too exhausting unless the West recognizes its stake in the success of India's free institutions and provides enough assistance soon enough. Frank Moraes, editor of the *Indian Express* newspaper chain, doubts that India was ready in the first place for the direct election of a national Parliament. He can see the day when India may have to surrender personal freedoms to a central government sufficiently strong to assure the maintenance of national freedom. Socialist leader Asoka Mehta believes that if need be India would rally around a military government to preserve her national existence. Professor Richard L. Park of the University of Michigan maintains, on the other hand, that Indian political institutions have adequate "staying power" and adaptability to survive the stresses imposed by population growth relatively unaltered.

In the address which initiates these discussions Barbara Ward Jackson observes that the developing countries find themselves in their present desperate race with runaway population not as the consequence of "any inherent defects in the Asian social order" but because the West in the colonial years "helped to send up the birth rate but did not modernize Asian economies to match." If this stands up as historical analysis, it is patent, also, that the "Asian social order" does have defects and that these severely handicap Asians today in the solution of their problems. In the case of India one may go so far as to say that it is the uniquely rigid compartmentalization of the social order that makes population pressure so dangerously disruptive to political stability. Revolutionary social upheaval builds up in intensity with the spread of the economic revolution, and the powerful social rivalries central to Indian life become a basis for the new competition over the spoils of progress. Population pressure not only places a premium on limited resources but in so doing heightens the issue of who gets how much. National leaders call for common sacrifice—to increase the size of tomorrow's national cake, as it were—but each region and each region's interest groups prefer taking what they can today.

Perhaps the most critical challenge to the present Indian Con-

stitution and the one least understood in the West is the stress and
strain of the centrifugal forces resident in the demarcation of India
on the basis of her ancient linguistic regions. With the exception
of the sprawling north Indian Hindi heartland, which subdivides
into five states, the boundaries of each of India's political units are
the boundaries of the separate linguistic (and political) territories
which were conglomerately known as "India" in the long centuries
preceding Mogul and then British unification. Regional patriotism
rivals all-India loyalty in these disparate segments with their proud
histories and highly-developed literary heritages. Linguistic dif-
ferentiation is sharpening with each passing year as schools and
colleges and the institutions of state government are conducted increasingly in the popular languages of each of ten distinct regions.
Many Indians are continuing to learn English, but they are not
learning it as well as they used to and the number learning it is on
a rapid decline. Real political power appears to be passing into the
hands of new regional leaders whose horizons are hardly the cosmopolitan horizons of the present English-educated generation and
who are often, as a consequence, found in the ranks of sectional
movements making mutually conflicting demands on an embattled
central government.

Regional alignments are reinforced by the phenomenon of a
Hindu caste system divided not only "vertically" into high-born and
low-born but "horizontally" into regional caste units. The Brahman
in the Tamil linguistic region does not normally intermarry or inter-
dine with Bengali or Marathi or Assamese Brahmans. As the oper-
ative unit of social life, the regional caste unit becomes quite
naturally a vehicle for the clash of political and economic interest.
The most conspicuous exception to this regional delimitation of interest groups is the cosmopolitan character of the Marwari entrepreneurs whose business interests span linguistic regions. The
Marwaris—members of three kindred trading castes native to the
Marwar area of Rajasthan—compete with regional interests who are,
at the same time, in competition among themselves.

Even if there were no Communist Party to egg on regions and
regional caste groups, the political problem of resolving the conflict
between rival social groups would be an acute one for leaders functioning within the restraints of a democratic Constitution. The
framers of the Indian Constitution deliberately set up an uneasy

balance of powers between the states and the central authority. As a consequence, the state governments retain control over education (which means that they can decide the language to be used in the universities) and over the taxation of agriculture (which means that powerful rural lobbies at the state level can prevent the effective taxation of India's wealthy village gentry). In Chapter Three, H. V. R. Iengar, Governor of the Reserve Bank of India, alludes to the inadequacy of agricultural taxation when he states that there is "every reason for increasing" the so-called "land revenue" tax now levied on Indian farm property but that this carries "political implications." Some authorities on Indian taxation such as Matthew J. Kust have questioned whether, even if Indian leaders could, politically speaking, compel the exaction of greater resources through the "land revenue" tax, this would prove to be enough. More basic agricultural tax reforms are said to be necessary, and these imply a more centralized Constitutional scheme giving to the national government new power to tax the affluent upper stratum of the peasantry.

Although India might be able to make quite fundamental political adjustments within the framework of her present institutions, the odds are close to fifty-fifty, in the view of this writer, that she will prove unable to do so. Yet even if one rates the odds much more favorably, is it not advisable to look to what might very well happen, as well as to what, hopefully, will happen? What if, to pose a specific possibility, India should in the post-Nehru period become a shambles of feuding regional ministries held loosely together by a government in New Delhi whose writ in economic development clearly does not extend to much of the country? In such a period, should our aid be kept stable or even increased? Should we prop up a weak central régime? Or would large-scale aid in such circumstances merely serve to prolong a period of political agony and do an injustice to aggrieved regions? What if, to avert the real or imagined threat of political collapse, a combination of political, bureaucratic, and military leadership should set aside the existing Indian Constitution in the name of strong, confident government and the eternal importance of Indian nationalism? "Democracy" having failed, would such a new authoritarian or quasi-authoritarian order necessarily be disqualified from receiving substantial Western economic support?

It runs against the American grain even to imagine the worst because we are emotionally committed as a people to the Can-Do spirit. Mirroring as it does a historic experience "in which our conscious efforts to 'make' history coincided with and were aided by the movement of history," observes Robert L. Heilbroner, optimism, as a national philosophy of historic expectations, "has given us the notion that history is only or largely the product of our volitions. . . . The optimistic outlook has taught us that the impetus of popular political aspiration leads naturally to the development of democratic governments as it did in the cradle of history in which it was nurtured, but has failed to alert us as to the turning which those self-same aspirations can take—and have already taken—in an environment in which the preconditions of Western parliamentary democracy are totally absent." The obsolescence of optimism in this respect need not imply, however, and in this Heilbroner is emphatic, that we should go to the other extreme of a cynical pessimism. What it does mean is that we should take care to avoid getting in over our heads in situations basically beyond our control. Given the possibilities of an unstable alternation between regional disarray, on the one hand, and authoritarian or quasi-authoritarian rule, on the other; given the enormous, autonomous force of the social, economic, and political revolution in India, the United States should in extending increasing help to the Nehru government avoid such deep and inextricable involvement that we become committed to the support of each of a procession of possible successor governments.

The perils of involvement inspired some anxious reflections on the part of *The Economist* as it pondered the implications of a Western commitment to provide the foreign exchange component of India's Third Five Year Plan. Suppose that such a firm commitment were given: if the contributing parties in time come to fear that the beneficiaries "have thereby gained an exaggerated sense of security . . . can the contributors tighten their purse strings without seeming to go back on their word—and if so, how? If they seem at any point to be giving orders about how the money is to be spent, they are liable to arouse an indignation that will erase all memory of their original generosity. And what if, having pledged their help for a fixed term of years to an effort designed to make the recipient country's economy self-sustaining, they find that that goal is nowhere in sight at the end?"

Experts disagree on when to expect India's passage into self-sustain-

ing development: a majority would agree, however, that if this is the
goal, it is, indeed, likely to be nowhere in sight at the end of the
Third Five Year Plan. Some would say that the goal will still be
distant in 1981 on the completion of the Sixth Plan. This suggests
two guiding principles for our policy. First, the final responsibility
for success—and failure—should remain clearly with India. It should
be cause for alarm rather than satisfaction when an underdeveloped
country throws its arms too enthusiastically around our necks. The
faint hint is that we are being looked to for miracles which we are
not likely to perform. Limited responsibility is implicit in the mere
act of extending aid, any aid at all, and most certainly so when the
amounts are those of the United States aid program in India. But
the location of ultimate responsibility can be kept clear so long as
the amounts do not loom too large in a relative sense—next to the
resources mobilized by the country itself and, in particular, next to
the aid given by other powers. An American aid commitment out of
all proportion to the commitment of others would lead to an inevitable confusion of responsibility and would become, in the long run,
politically insupportable in New Delhi, sensitizing latent anti-West-
ernism and weakening the very government it is intended to bolster.
This suggests, in turn, a second guideline. The United States should
consciously try to spread the burden of assistance, and thus of responsibility, on as broad a basis as possible among other governments.
To some extent the State Department has already sought to diffuse
the responsibility for assistance to Indian development through its
initiative in establishing the joint Western study mission to South
Asia headed by Sir Oliver Franks. Out of this mission and its recommendations will come, let us hope, the multiplied Western aid effort
envisaged in Chapter Three; but only West Germany, of the European powers, is in a position to make a contribution remotely comparable to that legitimately expected of the United States. Here we
are brought face to face with the conclusion that, if we seriously
mean to broaden the aid burden, the Soviet Union may in time
seem to be less of a threat in the aid field than an actual if un-
acknowledged ally.

"We have been chiding the U.S.S.R. since the end of World
War II for not doing its share in helping to eradicate sickness and
poverty in the world," declares George V. Allen, former Ambassador
to India and now director of the United States Information Agency.

"But now that they are beginning to show some activity in this direction, there is a tendency on the part of many Americans to view the development with great alarm. I for one do not take this approach." Nor, he might have added, does Charles de Gaulle, who has repeatedly urged joint U.S.-U.S.S.R. efforts in aid to the developing countries. Among United States authorities one increasingly hears the suggestion that there is little to fear, in the case of India at least, from a bigger Soviet aid program. The Stanford Research Institute's Senior Economist, Eugene Staley, declares in Chapter Three that "on Russia and the Communist countries and assistance, it seems to me we might . . . ask the question whether it would not be a good policy for the United States to encourage more of it." Richard L. Park, in a report on United States policy in South Asia commissioned by the Senate Foreign Relations Committee, proposed specifically, on the eve of the President's New Delhi visit, that "considering the extent of the economic need in India . . . one policy worth considering would be the negotiation of an agreement between India, the United States, the U.S.S.R. and other interested countries such as Japan and West Germany . . . to support given segments of India's Third and Fourth Five Year Plans on the basis of long-range (10 year) commitments."

One might argue that the Soviets have no intention of extending large sums of loan capital indefinitely and that their assistance to the Nehru government is only a passing political gesture. One might well wonder also what effect continuing Indian tensions with China would have on Indo-Soviet relations. The effect on Indo-American relations would no doubt be to strengthen domestic United States political support for aid to India, but one can only speculate on the implications for Soviet policy. The fact remains nonetheless that Soviet aid disbursements to India are now scheduled to reach $803.3 million during the Third Five Year Plan. The Soviet Union, like the United States, will probably discover that it is easier to start an aid program than to stop one and that the aid-receiving countries have a way of asking, as the constituent in Alben Barkley's anecdote did, "But what have you done for me lately?" Some sort of Soviet aid program in India seems a reasonable certainty. It is to be expected, however, that for some time to come the totalitarian Soviet state will choose to extend large-scale aid on a bilateral basis, within its own administrative and political control, rather than through United

Nations or other multilateral programs. And this means that the United States, for its part, will probably make its major contributions to Indian development bilaterally, increasing its support of U.N. aid efforts, at the same time, in the hope that the Soviet Union will eventually join in a fully internationalized effort. The pattern of the short-term future will thus find the Soviet Union, the United States, and to a lesser extent, the West Germans, the British and the Japanese, necessarily dividing the responsibility for a task of development too big and too full of political perils for any one of them, and doing so through separate aid programs which are, in the nature of things, competitive in greater or lesser degree, each rated by its sponsors largely in terms of the political and economic advantage gained as against the rest.

This is a very different pattern from the familiar one in which, it is assumed, a politically placid India will at some point opt for either the United States or the Soviet Union, one or the other of which will "win" exclusive Indian allegiance. The competition between the United States and Russia will be a real one, but it is perhaps inappropriate to speak of a "winner" when we contemplate the "prize" to be won. One is reminded of that perennial quip heard among foreign correspondents in New Delhi during the cold war: the best way *really* to fix the Russians, it was said, would be to "let them have India." This might be funny were it not for the grim reality contained within it; and it might be appropriate to the American-Soviet confrontation in India were it not for the fact that in reality the United States could no more be sanguine about the prospect of India coming under Soviet domination than the Russians could be in the face of impending United States hegemony. Neither can afford to assume responsibility for India's overpowering problems. Neither can risk the chance that the other will. Both must compete, willy-nilly, in helping the Indians to find their own destiny.

What are the strengths and weaknesses of the United States in such a competition with the Soviet Union? The essential strength of the United States lies quite simply in the fact that it could, if it would, extend much more capital to the developing countries than the Soviets with much less of a domestic economic pinch. Still, no matter how much more than the Soviets we do, the political impact of their aid may well continue to be disproportionately great if we fail to identify ourselves with India's aspiration for national industrial independence. The Third Five Year Plan reflects India's increasing accent on the development of heavy industry. In the light of this shift in emphasis the United States should rectify the present imbalance of its aid program toward agriculture and, in increasing assistance to industry, should not restrict its aid to *private* industry. Nearly all Soviet aid given or promised to India has been directed to such publicly controlled strategic industries as steel mills and thermal power plants. United States aid, on the other hand, does not on the whole promote industrial growth. And to the extent that it does, United States aid goes to private American or Indian interests or to the new Indo-American combinations, analyzed in Chapter Five, which hold so much promise as the pattern for greatly increased United States private business participation in Indian development. The weakness to date of United States aid to industry, let it be emphasized, is not that much of it goes to the private sector but that none of it goes to the public sector.

To appreciate why this makes all the difference one must return to the social rivalries, described earlier, which one invariably finds to be a highly supercharged factor in the politics of the developing countries. Control of the indigenous "private enterprise" sector in these countries normally rests with certain small, tightly-knit social groups who happened to get a head start during colonial rule—often through questionable methods. In India it is control by the Marwaris; in Ceylon, as Howard Wriggins has pointed out, by the Kuravas, Salagamas, and Duravas; in Indonesia, by the urban trading families centered in the Masjumi Party; in Ghana, by the "Mammy traders." In the case of India the Marwaris are unusually vulnerable to political attack because of the extent of their monopolistic power (565 directorships in industry, banking, and insurance are held within eight families) and because of the near-contempt for mercantilism in the traditional Hindu scheme of values.

Actually, many Marwari entrepreneurs who made their first millions in the black market now exhibit a measure of industrial statesmanship, and the younger Marwari generation tends increasingly to imitate modern Western industrial practices. But in popular Indian political symbolism the Marwari remains the very caricature of the avaricious robber baron. Like the Viennese Jew of the Austro-Hungarian Empire, who was a scapegoat for all the grievances of the

Balkan nationalist middle classes, the cosmopolitan Marwari is an evil demon to emergent regional business groups in India. Indian "socialism" may have had its birth in the ideological atmosphere of the London School of Economics but it has been nurtured by the anti-Marwari bias of the high-caste civil servant and the back-country *nouveau riche*. In marking out certain areas—e.g., iron and steel, heavy electrical machinery, heavy castings and forgings, industrial machinery—for public rather than private development, the Indian government, in its Industrial Policy Resolution, seeks at one and the same time to initiate the fastest possible economic growth and to forestall monopolistic control by entrenched social groups over the new Indian economic structure now rising. "When we increase production through our plans," Govindan Nair, India's Economic Minister in Washington, comments in Chapter Three, "we would like at the same time to prevent too great a concentration of wealth in the hands of those who might already hold it."

What may appear in Western terms to be aid for "private enterprise" may be in some Indian eyes, one can now see, not this at all. A loan from the World Bank or the United States Development Loan Fund to an Indian entrepreneur is more than economic intervention in behalf of development. It is also political intervention on the side of one social group as against its rivals. The critical question in the eyes of any particular Indian is whether the intervention is inadvertent or part of some new crypto-imperialism. D. R. Gadgil, the eminent economist, gives us the reaction of one Western-oriented Indian whose regional attachment is to Maharashtra, near Bombay, and whose Maharashtrian caste-fellows are the Chitpavan Brahmans—numbering many of the newer entries into the Bombay business world and rivals of the Marwaris. Dr. Gadgil in pleading for a potent Indian government role in economic development has often intimated that only in this way can the Marwaris be kept from running off with the Indian economy. "Private enterprise" in India, he wrote in the September, 1959, issue of the Indian journal *Artha Vijnana*, "belongs in the main to those whose position and practices would be clearly labelled as monopolistic in other countries. Even so, the cry . . . for 'economic liberty,' for scope for individual initiative, is fully taken up by many forces in the Western world. The international organizations betray a marked bias in favor of these interests when any loan, etc., programmes are considered. The activities of the joint investment groups inevitably result in strengthening the position of their counterparts in the new States."

To Dr. Gadgil the West is guilty of unpremeditated bias traceable to its own economic experience. But in Communist propaganda the persistent theme is that the Americans have a more deliberate and insidious design. Mr. Khrushchev in his speech at the Soviet-built Bhilai steel mill on February 15, 1960, contrasted Western aid—"the weapon of a new colonial policy"—with Soviet aid, "which promotes economic independence." "The U.S.S.R. was the first to agree to build a steel plant in the public sector in India and thus break the boycott of the West against the public sector," claimed the Indian Communist monthly *New Age* on the eve of the Khrushchev visit. It is true enough that the United States alone has not given public sector aid: British and German firms, respectively, are building the government-controlled Durgapur and Rourkela mills. "And now it seems that the major part of the strategic plants under the Third Plan will be built with Soviet help."

Bhilai is the showpiece of Soviet aid in India not only because it is a steel mill, a spectacular, visible accomplishment, but because it symbolizes the Indian aspiration for national progress equally shared. Responding in part to the propaganda triumph at Bhilai, the Development Loan Fund explored in 1960 the possibility of a United States-built steel plant at Bokaro which would, it was hoped, steal some of the Soviet thunder. There were flying trips to New Delhi by representatives of Kaiser Engineers and other United States firms interested in an Indian steel enterprise. But the D.L.F. clearly had in mind a privately-controlled steel plant and the Government of India, which was divided within itself on the priority to be given steel expansion, did not in the end include the Bokaro plant in the Third Five Year Plan. The government had made clear its distaste for circumventing an Industrial Policy Resolution in which steel is explicitly marked out for development by Hindustan Steel Limited, a public corporation. This case exemplifies in almost classic fashion the disability of the United States in its competition with the Soviet Union. Had the D.L.F. offered to loan funds to Hindustan Steel—or to Hindustan Steel as majority partner in a combine with a private American firm—India's Third Plan might have allowed for a new plant at Bokaro and the United States might have built its own Bhilai within the four corners of the Industrial

Policy Resolution. The Third Plan might yet conceivably be modified to permit construction of the Bokaro mill should the United States alter its attitude. As matters stand the United States role in the development of India's steel industry is limited to a worthy but relatively unspectacular steel technicians' training program and the expansion of the Tata steel plant by Kaiser. The Kaiser project appears to most Indians as a strictly business transaction and wins little political benefit.

A new opportunity now on the horizon is the expansion of facilities for the manufacture of heavy electrical machinery in India. One such plant is now under construction by British contractors, but a second could very well be built for the Indian government by Westinghouse or another United States firm. Backed by credit from the D.L.F., it would clearly carry the American label. But this, too, will probably be left to the Soviets because heavy electrical machinery is in the public sector and the D.L.F. loan needed to support such a project would have to be made to a public enterprise.

This is not to say that loans should be withheld from private Indian and American entrepreneurs. The reason prominent Marwaris obtain much of the loan capital extended to Indian industry by United States agencies is that on strictly economic tests the big established operator is often a better risk than the newcomer and promises to do a better job than a government enterprise which might (or might not) be bureaucratically encumbered and inefficient. The American firm going into an Indian partnership may find its most appropriate partner in a large established firm. In general, loans encouraging American firms to go to India are all to the good because the technical services needed by new industries can be provided, in the case of the United States, only by private firms; the United States government must have the private sector as its agent in competing with the Russians in aid to industry. But it is for the very reason that United States government loans to private firms are in economic terms so clearly justified that the political problems inherent in them should be given due importance and mitigating action taken. Care should be exercised to identify the United States aid program with some public sector heavy industry projects, and special attention should be given to the dispersion of private sector loans among rival social groups—favoring neither the Marwaris nor their current as well as would-be competitors. Aid to small entrepreneurs may offer the best chance to accomplish this dispersion and might well be given increasing priority. The case history of United States machine tool aid to Indian small industry in Chapter Three suggests that it is in comparatively small localized establishments that the rising social groups new to business activity are to be found and in these that many of the untapped possibilities exist for United States-Indian partnership ventures.

Economic development, in short, should not be an end in itself, and economic tests should not be decisive in making United States policy choices in India. On many occasions the United States might for political reasons have to withhold assistance from projects offering clear economic promise and extend aid, conversely, where the economic justification is weaker but the political requirements appear overriding. This is not the exasperating prospect it might seem once one discards the easy nostrum that economic growth can act as a cure-all for the ills of the developing countries. The more economic growth the better, and the more the United States is identified with the aspiration for progress the better. But our policy should be addressed to the aspiration as well as to the arithmetic of growth itself, to the hundreds of millions of human beings who are in the midst of what is a social and political as well as an economic revolution. The assumption that economic development automatically promotes political stability glides over the accumulating evidence that the revolution of rising expectations is just that: expectations progressively rise as economic standards do, so that the case for development, and thus for aid, has to rest on some more solid basis than the statistical discovery of, say, a per capita income increase from $60 to $67 in the course of a Five Year Plan. The case for aid, meaningfully stated, lies in the fact that only a sense of development taking place gives men hope for a better future, and that only this hope holds men together in political and social unity. Take away the hope and it is each man—each group—for himself. In this sense the United States makes as much of a political as an economic contribution when it aids India and should, therefore, apply political quite as much as economic tests in deciding the nature as well as the extent of its aid at any given time. To make this distinction today might smack of an academic exercise, but in an unstable India ten or fifteen years from now it may hold the difference between a clumsy policy and a dexterous one, between a defensive posture in the face of a growing Soviet presence and the posture of confidence becoming to a great power.

I / AN ACCIDENT OF HISTORY

an address by Barbara Ward Jackson

I am convinced that the relations between India and the West lie at the core of the free world's drama in our day. And I am convinced that this is the field where we have to apply all our gifts of intelligence and understanding and more than that, our gifts of vision and generosity as well, because I do not believe that the human race is going to survive simply on "the dismal science." It is by our imagination, by our passions, by our capacity for larger vistas, that we shall be able to master the crisis in which we live. And here, in the core of that crisis, lie the relations between India and the free world.

What I should like to discuss are some of the issues which are faced not only by the United States, but by all of us in the Western world—all of us who live around the North Atlantic ocean—who by so many fortunate chances of environment, resources, and history, have been changed almost without our noticing it into one of the great privileged minorities of the human race. We are all in this together and I hope that you will not mind if I speak from this background of common fortune and common concern.

Now, what is happening in the world is basically something we can all understand, because it is something through which we have already been ourselves. One third of mankind, the Western third, has passed through the "sound barrier" of modernization, technical change, and industrialization. We have contrived to find ourselves the institutions needed for the modern economy and for the modern creation of wealth, and we are blessed indeed that we have been able to do so within the frameworks of free institutions. But let us, for heaven's sake, not forget that when we began this process a hundred years ago, it was a turbulent time. The transition to the modern economy brought trouble even in the fortunate West.

If you look back to the history of the early Industrial Revolution in Britain, the times about which Dickens wrote in such great novels as *Hard Times* and *Bleak House*, you will realize that for us, too, the process of transfer from the static agricultural economies of the past over to modern dynamism were times of immense strain and difficulty. And the reason for this is a quite simple one. It is that in this period of transition, when you are moving from a static economy on to a dynamic and growing economy, you have to be able to save. You have to be able to find the capital necessary for this transfer. And, although it is sometimes hard for us in the wealthy West to remember the fact, saving means "not consuming." It means "postponing consumption." Now, if you already have a high standard of consumption, to postpone a little of it is not too difficult. In fact, if you want the absolute figures, each year we save comfortably on the average in the West about the entire per capita annual income of the people who live in India and other parts of the less developed world. In other words, our margin of saving, which is what we can take out of our consumption, is the equivalent of the entire resources that they have to consume and live on year by year.

But, in the early stages of our economy, when we, in Britain, for example, were emerging from our agricultural past, there was no such cushion of adequate consumption. The agricultural workers were streaming into the big cities, and the fruits of their labors were very largely being devoted not to raising their standards, but to creating the capital equipment of the new economy. And those times were hard—do not let us make any mistake about it. In fact, they were so hard that they provided Karl Marx with practically the entire material upon which he based his theory of communism. Communism in some measure reflects the conditions of early capitalism in Britain before we had learned to live with this monster, to tame it, to transform it, and to make it into an instrument of the public good.

Back in 1848, in fact as late as 1860, the massive transfer of capital was still going on. Some economic historians estimate that during that period, in spite of the massive creation of new wealth, popular standards actually fell. The wealth was being transferred to the new industrial sector. Heaven knows, in those years, we British faced our hard times. But we were relatively fortunate because we got through it quickly and we were fortunate for another reason: in our own Western communities the arrival of modern sanitation and a modern medical health system coincided with and did not precede the growth of technology and the coming of a fully fledged industrial system. So, when our population began the spurt of growth which follows from a sharp reduction in the death rate, our economy could grow and was in part spurred forward by the growth of population that was going on at the same time. We grew, as it were, with relative balance.

But now consider what happened in Asia, and remember, I pray, that we have some responsibility in this development. In the late eighteenth century there was still a favorable trade balance between Asia and Europe, and the balance was all on the side of Asia. At that time the commodities which people wanted to buy, muslin and silks, brocades, spices, all the things which were the luxuries of European life, could be secured in Asia, but they had to be paid for in bullion for the simple reason that Europe, in those preindustrial days, had little that Asia wanted to buy. I may say, the East India Company's attempt to sell Yorkshire woolens in Madras before the monsoon had understandably little success. So the shipping of gold and silver to Asia was the alternative. Thus there was a bullion gap—not a dollar gap—but still it had the same causes. And the balance was entirely in favor of Asia.

Then what happened? What happened was a complete reversal of roles because of the Industrial Revolution. Cheap industrial manufactured products—above all, textiles—swept out from Europe into Asia; colonial control was extended, markets in China were forced open by Western trading interests; above all, there occurred a partial introduction of modern methods and particularly the introduction of the beginnings of sanitation and medical science. But I would plead with you to remember that this whole process was partial. The result was a spotty, patternless modernization. And one of the consequences was to put the Asian economies into a state of unbalance from which they have not yet fully recovered.

On the one hand, modernization in sanitation and medical services set in progress a vast increase in the birth rate, but at the same time the tremendous influx of Western industrialized goods not only failed to stimulate economic and capital development in Asia; it actively stopped the development that was there. In other words, at the time when the normal processes of modern sanitation and health were beginning to get the population into a state of rapid growth, one result of the Western impact on Asia was to hinder the processes of rapid economic growth in such countries as India and China. This unbalance must be understood by anyone concerned with the history of colonialism in the past (and any Briton who is *not* should have his head examined). I do not mean that the lack of balance was part of a cold-blooded plan of economic imperialism. It was in some measure a haphazard consequence of the impact of Western industrialism upon the East. But its consequence—partial modernization—is central to an understanding of India today.

The birth rate went up, but economic growth did not go up in any commensurate way. The stimulus given by the West, which was a trading stimulus, directed almost entirely to Western trading interests, was one that could not, except in a fairly marginal way, encourage and hasten local capital development. It stimulated the production of local raw materials, it built up the avenues of trade, and I do believe that in India, where there was a direct political responsibility, quite a bit of the essential substructure of the modern economy was also introduced. But China was battered and disorganized by this trade drive. Industry largely under foreign control was built up only in the treaty ports, for instance, while behind it the great peasant countryside sank back into a crisis of bankruptcy and debt, made all the worse by the fact that European manufactures were wiping out the peasant handicrafts which might have been the basis of a new industrial system.

If one wants to see the full impact of partial modernization, one needs only to look at Japan. After the sixteenth century, Japan rigorously excluded all Western traders and all Western interests, and did it for 250 years. Half way through the nineteenth century, the Japanese realized that isolation could not continue and they recognized that the old maxim, "If you cannot lick them, join them," was the soundest advice. Under their own steam and under their own impetus they industrialized themselves, and the result was that in the late nineteenth century Japan was the only Asian country in which population and dynamic growth in the entire economy to some extent kept pace. They were able to secure this balance because their modernization was not partial and was not simply induced from abroad in a haphazard way; it was done by themselves.

Now, the great drama of today is that India and China, facing the consequences of this partial modernization, are now trying to complete the full process. But they are doing so with the inherent difficulty that their birth rate is 'way ahead of their general economic development. As I say, this is not their choice; this was the result of the terrific battering-ram of the West's impact upon Asia in the nineteenth century; and, if I may add the parenthesis, although it is perfectly true that the colonial powers of Europe were most responsible for this impact, believe me, every great trading nation had a part in it. American traders in China, for example, were one of the elements in the immense impact of the West upon the East. An American Commodore opened Japan's harbors to the West. So let us, on this economic plane, accept responsibility together.

But what is the consequence? The consequence is that Asia now faces the great challenge of getting through the sound barrier into a modern economy under conditions of what I would call maximum difficulty. This challenge of the growing birth rate, coupled with the fairly static patterns of an old agricultural society, means that they face the greatest obstacle just where their need is most urgent.

You cannot grow without capital, capital is saving, saving is "not consuming." But how do you "not consume" when people already are so nearly not consuming that if they did "not consume" a bit more they would not live? This is the dilemma. You cannot grow without saving but once the birth rate has shot ahead, saving is the hardest process to bring about.

This dilemma is not due to any inherent defects in the Asian social order; it is due above all to this tremendously powerful accident of history in which East and West became interlocked and in which we blindly, unknowingly, affected the whole pattern of Asia's future advance. Their dilemma is that they must save; their difficulty is that it is very difficult indeed to save when your per capita income is only $60 a year. It is all very well if your income is $2,000 a year to cut it down, shall we say, by $10. But try doing that when it is down to $60. This is the dilemma and it was brought about in large measure by Western traders and colonizers who introduced the beginnings of modernization in health, helped to send up the birth rate but did not modernize Asian economies to match. Today many of the worst difficulties obstructing Asian capital formation can be traced back to this source.

Now in this situation I need hardly say the Communists say they have an answer and it is "Operation Bootstrap." Its underlying technique is direct political compulsion and even terror. They give up the carrot and they use the stick—the stick of total political discipline, reinforced in some measure by political enthusiasm but underpinned by force. The discipline does have the effect of transferring an increasing amount of capital from the agricultural sector which can then be dedicated both to the modernization of farming and to the development of the whole industrial sector. And the reason why in the last ten years India has been outpaced by about 3 to 1 by the Chinese effort is because the Chinese have used methods of forced saving which already, in the Russian context, have produced a sensational rate of increase. Yet these are precisely those measures which India is pledged not to use—and heaven knows, when you think of how easy it is to get into a political strait waistcoat and how damnably difficult it is ever to get out of it again, for any society to wish with all its strength and with all its possibilities of imagination and capacity to keep out of that kind of political discipline is surely one of the most worthwhile of objectives.

To keep an open society, to preserve the various, the infinite possibilities of the human mind and spirit, to leave them channels through which they can grow, to spare men the indignity of talking ideological poppycock every time they open their mouths—this surely is one of the great aims which we should set before the human race. Anything more dreary than the kind of bureaucratic jargon that gets talked when people are committed to a total political and economic ideology is hard to conceive. Perhaps one of the worst sins of the totalitarian system is not even terror. It may well end up by being an inhuman boredom of the spirit. To spare the human race from this is surely a worthy and legitimate aim of human policy.

What, then, are we going to do about it? Is there anything relevant in our own Western experience to this tremendous crisis of saving, of capital, which we have helped to force upon Asia? Well, I would like to turn back once more to our own history and ask ourselves how it was that we emerged from our times of trouble? How did we survive our turbulent early days of industrialization? How did we prove that Marx was wrong when he said that under modern capitalism the rich would get richer and the poor would get poorer—a conclusion which it was not unreasonable to draw from the scene he and Engels observed in the 1840's.

The Western democracies made a monkey out of Marx because he basically misunderstood their political system. He said that political liberty, constitutional rights, the whole dream of the rights of man, the free vote, the rights of labor to organize, and above all, the Christian and humane conscience of the West, were all window dressing, that they were all illusion and nonsense and simply used to deceive the workers who were being exploited. Then what happened in the West? What happened surely was an immense reversal of this. The window dressing turned out to be the article itself. The right to vote, the concept of free association applied to trade unions, the sense of obligation within a community felt by the rich for the poor, by the healthy for the sick, by the fortunate for the unfortunate—these were the forces that helped us to humanize our great industrial machine, to remake our society, so that our industrial system could become, at least in some measure, not the monopoly of the few but the servant of the many.

Now, I know there are some words I am not supposed to use in this country. "Progressive taxation" and the concept of "welfare" do not universally excite cries of enthusiasm. Yet these were the means by which we in the West learned to express institutionally our concern for our less fortunate brothers. These were the policies that proved Marx wrong. These were the great instrumentalities whereby Western industrialism was tamed, humanized, and transformed. And this is part of our direct political experience.

Now we must ask ourselves whether these concepts are relevant today. Make no mistake about it, there are signs in the world at large that the paradox of Marxism, the claim that modern capitalism would lead to the rich getting richer and the poor getting poorer—a claim which has been triumphantly disproved in the West—is showing signs of reappearing on the world's stage. Now you know quite well that in this country we talk happily and confidently about a $500 billion economy. In my own country we talk equally confidently and happily about doubling the standard of living in the next twenty-five years. The same is true of the new ideals set before the European Community. Not only do we set ourselves these ideals, we know jolly well we are going to get them. In other words, we confidently expect to get richer.

But have we looked at the other side of the coin? Which is that if the Asian countries cannot save, they will inevitably and infallibly get poorer. And so, the Marxist vision that we chased out of the Western world by our political imagination, our humane conscience, and our Christian sense of responsibility is back with us again, and in a much more acute form. While we are certainly going to be able to raise our already fantastically high standards of living in the West, in Asia, without concerted, sustained, imaginative action on our part, the opposite is likely to occur. Not more wealth but growing poverty is their present fate.

Faced with this situation, I suppose we could say blandly: "Too bad—but of course our wisdom only applies to ourselves. We are brothers, but we are brothers just exactly up to the shores of the ocean, and then see how quickly we stop." We can, conceivably, argue that the Western ideals for which we believe our civilization stands are confined to the white Christian minority that lives around the North Atlantic. Yet, did I somewhere hear in my Christian teaching some word about the brotherhood of man? Or is this just one more projection of the idle imagination and not, repeat *not*, essential to the whole tradition of Western man? We could possibly, barring accident, go on getting richer while everybody else gets poorer. We could sit back, just as we could perhaps have sat back in the days of Marx and allowed his dreadful prophecy to develop in the core of our own society. Well, looking back, we can see that the wisdom that led us to change the direction of our economic institutions then was what has saved us politically as well. It was because our society became more just and more humane, because its wealth was in large measure, by political decision, more widely shared, that we survive as free societies in the West. And I profoundly believe that this is the great challenge to us in the crisis that faces us today. It is, by accepting a sustained and generous transfer of wealth from West to East, to repeat in the world at large the reversal of Marx's prophecy: and by doing so to prove that the insights and the institutions which saved our freedom within the Western world are not confined to our geographical limits, but are valid for this human society which is struggling to integrate itself into something like a moral community.

We have a community of destruction because, if you can lob a hydrogen bomb into somebody's back yard, he is a neighbor, whether you like it or not. We are also something of an economic community because our modern economy stretches from one end of the world to the other. We are all meshed together in webs of trade and investment. Indeed, at the moment the Western nations show every sign of becoming more and more dependent upon supplies coming from outside their own borders. But we are not a moral community because we are not a responsible community. This seems to me the greatest challenge that faces us because, if we merely remain a community of potential destruction and blind self-interest, I maintain we are hardly a human community at all. We can become human only by creating the habits and institutions of mutual solidarity and general welfare. And if we want to know where to begin, I suggest our great opportunity is Asia's need to grow and invest and prosper—and in this context, India stands at the head of all the rest.

The reason is partly that India has the equivalent population of all Africa and Latin America combined. We are not considering simply a country. We are picking out nearly half of the free world. Again, India has the institutions and the technical capacity to be very nearly at take-off point in its economy and, therefore, a big effort done with generosity and with imagination can have the kind of quick results that Asia needs. Then again, India's link with a tolerant and a humane tradition goes back through the millennia. While my ancestors were running about virtually still covered with woad, the great King Asoka was proclaiming on carved pillars from one end of the continent to the other the principles of humanity and tolerance which are as valid today as they were in his peaceful reign. In other words, in this great tradition, we do not play the lead; we repeat themes rooted in India's past.

And then I also like to think that—although many of the things that the British did, as I tried to point out, were blind, led to exploitation, and created the economic unbalance of which I have previously spoken—some of the things we did, maybe all too inadvertently, were truly constructive. In other words, we could not leave all our liberal ideas at home when we went out to India, and some of these ideas I think were congenial to the Indian spirit. And one reason, perhaps, why one can now feel a real sense of kinship between the British and the Indians is the generosity with which they have taken this whole link with Britain into their historical experience and have learned, as it were, to live with it at its best level. Because of this, there is a kinship which I believe we feel and which may perhaps be a special contribution the British can make in this postimperial phase.

But more than all this, here in India is a country determined to keep the open society, and determined to keep open the avenues of man's growth, man's imagination, man's capacity to create and discover and not to be fixed into the closed ideological system of the day. And this is an immense stake for us in the West. I think that economically, for the time being, the greatest contribution is going to come from West to East because by the lucky chance of our early industrialization, by the lucky chance that we achieved it without an agonizing problem of overpopulation, because we enjoyed a background of such generous resources—for all these reasons, today, we do enjoy an economic surplus. We could easily contribute jointly the billion and a half dollars each year for the next five years—or however long—which are needed to give a tremendous impulsion outward and upward to the Indian economy. We can do this. I reckon it is about the equivalent of two packets of cigarettes per person a week. Do not tell me we cannot afford so much.

But if you look at more than the economic issue, you can see at once that our stake in successful relations with India is fully as great as any stake India may have in the outcome of our policies. Look at the possibilities of destruction around us, look at the extreme difficulty the human race has in living together. May it not be that the West's chief political need today is a working experiment of how to live with our fellow men? May it not be that after the generation of imperialism, of colonialism, after all the time spent in the pursuit of blind economic interest, in the attempts at isolationism, in the excesses of extreme political sovereignty—may it not be that a working relationship with a great people whose culture, history, and racial background are different from ours, is of first political urgency for ourselves? We have been so privileged. We have been so comfortable. We have had it all our own way. This has indeed been the century of Western man. And out of it we have come, I think, with certain enormous, arrogant assumptions about ourselves and about the world in which we live. And I think we have to be taught how to get rid of some of these assumptions.

Well, as you say, we learn by doing. I would like to feel that the great stake we have in a long-term creative plan with India would be to learn how to live with the human race. Believe you me, we white people are not very good at it. We have a lot to learn. I think that in an association of this kind, which would be a working association, which had behind it the ideals of creating a partnership on a truly human basis, we would be the gainers, because we would learn about something more than simply economic growth. We would learn our full stature and dignity as men.

And so I say, let us have an India program. Let us give this tremendous push that could provide India the extra capital it needs in its time of transition. But let us also feel that beyond all ideology, beyond all race, beyond all cultural differences, and beyond even the accidents of history, we can, all of us together, build a home for the family of man.

II / THE ROOTS OF
INDIAN FOREIGN POLICY

"Americans who live in India," A. M. Rosenthal once reflected in *The New York Times,* "come to recognize, flinchingly, a certain glint in the eye of Indian friends, a certain preparatory raising of the finger. The glint and the finger mean that the Americans are about to be called upon to explain why we don't kick the French out of Algeria, why we give guns to Pakistan, why we are unkind to the Communists, why we don't scuttle Formosa, why we build military bases and why John Foster Dulles says those things." Send these same Americans home, he went on to say, and before they have had a chance to fill themselves up on steaks they will be pleading ardently that India is not pro-Communist, that Indians really do like Americans, and that there are significant reasons for the Indian position on most international issues. The ambivalence is simply a measure of the gaps in understanding between India and the United States, and the ardor a testimony to the near-unanimous verdict of Americans who get to know India that the gaps can be spanned.

But most Americans do not get to know India, and most Americans, even in the wake of the President's New Delhi visit in 1959, still had a long way to go in understanding Indian foreign policy. One may doubt, in fact, whether when Eisenhower in India was inspiring a surge of mass confidence in United States *bona fides,* the majority of Americans returned the compliment. "Neutralism" in many American minds comes down to a willingness to compromise with the forces of communism—if need be—at the expense of the United States. In this uncomplicated image India today is disengaged from her whole past and the nonalignment policy with its profound basis in history becomes indeed almost beyond comprehension. Former Ambassador to India *Chester Bowles* and *Barbara Ward Jackson* explain "neutralism" almost wholly in the perspective of the past. Congressman Bowles likens India to the United States in its own postindependence period, reminding us that although it was the British fleet in the Atlantic that "kept the world away so we could grow . . . we never thanked them, and they never asked us for thanks." Lady Jackson's analysis of the "total intermixture of European intervention with local civil wars" as a root factor in the Indian world view is followed by *Averell Harriman's* defense of Indian policy.

NEUTRALISM IN PERSPECTIVE

Chester Bowles. I have always believed and believed very deeply that there can be no real stability in the world unless India succeeds and the United States succeeds. The dual success of these two great democracies is essential if we are going to be living in any world that we can remotely call rational. Yet, India and America have never found it particularly easy to understand each other. We have a sort of stereotyped view of India and India has an extremely stereotyped view of us. India is inclined to look upon American foreign policy as overly militaristic, as negative and purely defensive against communism. We impatiently look upon India as a neutralist nation, unwilling to stand up and be counted in a struggle throughout the world which clearly in our mind is between the forces of freedom and those of servitude.

I would like to cite briefly the course of history of the last 150 years, which I think might be helpful in analyzing why this gap in understanding exists. I would like to begin with a reminder that the American people were born in revolution. It would seem rather unnecessary to comment on that but we too often forget it. We were, moreover, born in a period of intense change. At that time warfare was general throughout the world. Sometimes they were cold wars, more often hot wars. All of Europe was seething with struggle and revolutionary change. The French Revolution occurred just shortly after we had won our own independence.

During the war we were greatly helped by our friends, the French. I think you might say that without the technical military assistance that we received from the French people, from General Von Steuben, Lafayette, and others, we might never have become a nation. Without military support programs which came to us in a variety of forms, clothes for George Washington's soldiers, all kinds of muskets and cannon from the French government, I am quite confident that we would all be living as part of the British Empire. Our British friends might say that the world would be better for it, but certainly at least it would be very different. So, European, foreign

Point Four and even military support was essential to us in those very early days. But we felt no particular sense of gratitude for this and shortly after our own war for independence was over, we started to pull away from Europe very hard. We began to wonder if there was anything good in Europe after all.

You will remember the words of George Washington. On September 19, 1796, he said: "Observe the good faith and justice of all nations. Cultivate peace and harmony toward all. An attachment for one nation or another produces a variety of evils. It is our true policy to steer clear of all foreign entanglements." Of course, Prime Minister Nehru could have easily uttered those words.

There were all kinds of forces alive in the world trying to pull us one way or the other. The French were trying to pull us their way, the British were trying to pull us theirs. During the Napoleonic Wars in the beginning of the nineteenth century, Britain, a democratic nation struggling to try to maintain her power and her very existence, struggling against totalitarian Napoleon, found the Americans quite unsympathetic. We lectured both nations rather freely, told them what was wrong with them, but went about our business. Indeed, when the British got into a particularly bad scrape in 1812 we tried to take Canada away. We attacked Canada in the War of 1812 on the theory that we could possibly appropriate Canada when Britain was in rather serious difficulty. I think we should remember some of these things as we look on the world situation today.

In 1820 John Quincy Adams wrote to our Minister in St. Petersburg to relate that he had just been approached by the Russians who were seeking an alliance with the United States. They wanted to involve us in a close association with the Holy Alliance of Austria, Prussia, and Russia. Mr. John Quincy Adams cautioned our representative in St. Petersburg, reminding him of George Washington's good advice that we should have no truck with all these Europeans who were constantly trying to draw us into their struggles and their conflicts.

Just three years later, in 1823, George Canning, British Foreign Minister, came to our Minister, Richard Rush, in London and in effect said, we have a wonderful idea. The Holy Alliance is going to try to establish itself in South America. It's going to try and turn back the revolutionary changes that have occurred there. We would like to have Britain and America stand together in opposition to this upsetting of the South American revolutions. We want to see that we maintain free trade with that part of the world.

Well, we thought this over and it did not sound good to us because we remembered what George Washington had said—no foreign entanglements of any kind. At the same time, we thought it was rather a good idea. We didn't want the Holy Alliance meddling in South America any more than the British did. So, after a good deal of thought and many cabinet meetings, we announced that we would keep these foreign imperialistic forces out of South America and we announced our Monroe Doctrine. That night in his diary, John Quincy Adams wrote, "Why should America be a cockboat in the wake of the British man-of-war?" In other words, we were prepared to do what the British thought was right, but we weren't prepared to do it with them. They were a colonial power, we had just thrown them out, and we wanted no part of this association.

At this point, however, having proudly announced that we were going to keep the imperialists out of South America, we also understood we did not have the power to do so. We had almost no navy and a very small army, so it was the British fleet in the Atlantic for something like a hundred years that enabled America to grow behind a protective military shield. Now, we never thanked them for it and they never asked us for thanks. Indeed, if they had ever reminded us that they were saving us from European imperialism, they would have had a very angry and embittered nation on their hands. We might even have again attacked Canada. Nevertheless, we sat here for a hundred years behind the shield of the British fleet and we built the United States of America without an army and without a navy. You almost might say without a foreign policy. We didn't need one because Britain kept the world away so that we could grow.

Barbara Ward. One of the reasons, I think, why Indian neutralism is so misunderstood is that a particular phase of the history of Asia is insufficiently understood in the West. We get our images deeply and profoundly from the past just as I believe the psychiatrists tell us we get so many of our individual reactions deeply and profoundly from our childhood. I don't think we can understand neutralism unless we see a very, very particular phase of Asia's experience in relation to the West and it is this.

In the eighteenth century, when the European traders were going out with the firm intention of monopolizing the entire carrying trade between Europe and Asia and in addition between the Asian countries themselves, they had two problems. One problem was to have sufficient law and order when they got to the ports and the harbors to be able to trade, and the second was to keep the other rascals out, the other rascals being my definition of the other European nations in this context.

Now wherever Asian power was weak there was quite a problem of law and order because it does interfere with trade if your warehouses are burned down or if your people's throats are cut or if they scuttle your ships. Moreover, if the local authority was weak, it was very tempting to get in and show what law and order really looked like. But at the same time, you had the problem of making sure that the Dutch, or the French, or the Portuguese weren't doing the same at the same time; because if they put in their law and order, one thing was for sure—your traders wouldn't get a look-in. So wherever authority was weak, and it was weak straightaway in the Dutch East Indies, what happened? In went the Europeans. They began backing various local sultans and rajahs; they began creating their own notions of law and order, and one way in which they made absolutely certain that the other European nations didn't get in was by making certain that the rajah backed by the other Europeans didn't win. In other words, you had total intermixture of European intervention with local civil wars and as a consequence, a deep sense, on the part of Asians today, that if you are asked to take sides you are inviting the return of old conditions. Asians believe, on the basis of their own history, that if they are asked to take sides, this is the first step toward some loss of local autonomy and local authority. And it is no good turning round and saying, "Look, it is perfectly unreasonable because you know the West is good and the Communists are bad." "Well," they say, "yes, but you know we've been through all this before and you kept telling us that the French were good and the British were bad, or the British were good and the French were bad, or vice versa. And all we do know is that every time we did take sides, one thing happened. We lost out."

This was repeated in Africa; one set of chiefs wouldn't give you the monopoly of ground nut and the monopoly of palm trees, okay, you went to another chief who would, and in the process you kept out the French or brought in the Germans. And out of this came the fantastic frontiers of Africa today. The present boundaries are simply those that were fixed in Berlin, Paris, and London sixty years ago. The fact that they may cut tribes into three and four different bits—that was the coincidental result of the fact that they were fixed at the point at which a particular military expedition happened to run into the mud.

You have the feeling in Africa, too—"Oh, don't let's start this again, because if we do, where will it end up?" Some of them I think perhaps are being a little foolish in the way in which they are letting it begin again by accepting gifts of arms from dubious sources, and this is the beginning of trouble. But in general, the feeling of not wanting to take sides is not irrational. In their context it's profoundly historical and I pray we can remember it. This is reinforced by one other factor which I think we can all understand; I wonder if, living in countries that possess the hydrogen bomb (and the British just do marginally possess this one large egg), do we understand the feeling of total helplessness that overcomes people that don't? There is an African proverb that was quoted to me by Dr. Nkrumah and I have never forgotten it—"When the bull elephants fight, the grass is trampled under." Every country in the uncommitted world has a sense that it is no more than grass if the bull elephants really begin fighting because they know that any addition that they might make in military strength is meaningless. They don't believe that to add one battalion of Ghana soldiers to the fighting forces of freedom is really going to affect what the Russians do, and I can't really argue with them that they are wrong.

Averell Harriman. I know that some Americans are puzzled by the foreign policy of the Indian government, particularly as it is expressed by Mr. Nehru. This question of nonalignment. Well, India is not neutral. Anyone who thinks India is neutral doesn't understand India. There is no country, there is no group of men, those in the government and those in the Socialist Party, who are more determined to preserve the fundamental principles on which our own nation is founded than you find in India. And if that is neutrality, I don't understand the word. They are vigorous allies of ours in the attainment of the fundamental objectives which we, our nation and our people have. That is, independence for themselves and independence for other peoples. Noninterference from any quarter—they've been very energetic in ridding themselves of the colonialism of one nation and are determined not to come under the colonial influence of any other nation, whether it be Russia or whether it be China. The fact that they are unwilling to sign military alliances is a matter that we should leave to their judgment. There should be no undue influence brought upon them. I believe that all peoples are with us until they've proved to have taken a position against us, and that to me is the true American position. I don't know any country that ought to be more understanding of nonalignment than the United States which, for nearly a century and a half, went on a course of its own. India has enormous problems, staggering in their dimension, and it is the opinion of the Prime Minister and all of those associated with him that it is not for them to take sides at this time in any alliances, military or otherwise.

To be sure, we don't always like everything that Prime Minister Nehru says about the Soviet Union or about ourselves. But I think it is only fair that we should be understanding of the motives that lie behind what he says. He told me himself that it was the Gandhian philosophy to see the best in others, even your enemies, and you see the results of that in India. You see the British today respected and even beloved, in spite of the bitter struggle through which they went, in spite of the many years which many of the leaders of India today spent in British jails. We should understand that things don't always look exactly the same from the Indian perspective. They don't look the same in New York as they do in San Francisco. We have very vigorous differences of opinion, not only between our two parties but between people who live in different parts of our country. And so we should be understanding, I believe, of what is said about others and what is said about us.

"Neutralism" is a relatively recent intrusion into the complex imagery described by veteran foreign correspondent *Harold R. Isaacs*, author of *Scratches on Our Minds*, a study of the "mental baggage" which encumbers Americans as they view India and China. It is nonetheless a critical factor. For as Cowles Publications reporter *Clark Mollenhoff* and *Lawrence E. Spivak* of "Meet the Press" insist in an exchange with Editor *Frank Moraes* of the Indian Express Newspapers, moral and political neutralism are not the same. India's political nonalignment would be tolerable in this view if Indians did not equate the values of both power blocs.

Harold R. Isaacs.   This business of attitudes and opinions and prejudices is something like money, you know. There is a lot of it around, but some people have more than others. I cannot pretend to deal with "American" notions, attitudes, opinions, stereotypes about India. All I can hope to do is simply to run down as briefly as I can some of the principal ingredients that appear to go into our thinking about India and Indians.

Roughly speaking this can be done under three headings. First is the fact that we Americans have a peculiarly scanty past in relation to Indians, much less so than with many other countries with whom our present relations are important. Comparatively little has entered from India into the mainstream of American life, in contrast, for example, to that part of our legacy which is Chinese. We have one set of notions about exotic, opulent India. These go back all the way to the European quest for the Indies, and are carried forward to our time by the images of the gem-encrusted maharajahs and their gem-encrusted elephants. These were very powerful images indeed. They are part of almost everybody's mental baggage about India. Every person carries them around, and they are evoked for him again and again in a hundred different forms in radio, television, in advertising, even today when the reality of the maharajahs and their gems and elephants has so largely faded in India itself.

We also carry from the past, the past of these scanty fragmentary images, another set of notions which are perhaps best suggested by the phrase "the benighted heathen Hindu." We acquire this in part from our missionary tradition—which was one of the least scanty elements of our relationship to India over this past century or more. This figure of the heathen Hindu occupies a very special place in our minds. It has a lot to do with real and pervasive differences in American and Indian culture, differences which are not to be minimized. Part of this image also came from Kipling, and I suppose that for most people whose bits and pieces about India are from this source, it would still mainly be those tribesmen around the fringes of India against whom those Bengal Lancers kept charging across our Hollywood screens generation after generation.

There is a second more recent collection of images which are of quite a different order, and these have to do with the ideas we acquired out of the Indian freedom movement of this century. Here again, I suppose most Americans would know of this in two forms;

the first would be the vague general notion of a people struggling for freedom, especially against Britain. This is something that automatically aroused certain traditional affinities and sympathies. But secondly, aside from this more generalized reaction, there are two figures who emerged from this movement who exist as rather vivid images in most of these American minds. The first is Nehru, the philosopher-statesman-king type who has made an enormous impact on certain kinds of American minds if only because he has written more about himself than any other man of comparable world stature. Anyone who has read Nehru's self-explorations and self-discoveries in the volumes he has written has knowledge of a world figure hardly matched by any other case I can think of. Churchill has written lots more, but much less about himself, than Nehru has. The other great figure, of course, is the most commanding figure of all, and that is Gandhi, and here again I can but mention it and leave it, reminding you only that from the puny, little, rather ridiculous figure that was shown to us in the cartoons we all saw twenty-five or thirty years ago, he grew into a giantesque sort of figure, the only man to be bracketed in the imaginations of many with such figures as Jesus and Buddha and the great saints of the great religious traditions. This too has created its current among our notions about India.

Finally, there is the whole set of ideas about India and Indians that has come into being since India emerged as an independent nation barely a decade ago. This is a quite new and different set of ideas, although all the old ones live in it, are part of it, and co-exist with all the new. For one thing, more Americans have met more Indians and more Indians have met more Americans in the last ten years than in all the previous history of the two nations. For another thing there has been an extraordinarily complex, miasmalike cloud of difference and confusion over world tensions and policies, a positive fog of misunderstanding that has dogged every encounter between individual American and individual Indian. On the whole, with certain exceptions, these encounters have been calamitous. Let it be said immediately, however, that while this American-Indian meeting has some unique features, most encounters between peoples across cultural lines have or tend to have their calamitous aspects. Americans make a special business of wanting to like and to be liked. This is why we fail so badly. Very few people like other people, regardless of race, creed, or color. It just doesn't work out and when you expect this and are frustrated in your expectations, then you suffer and you have problems.

I would say finally that in all of this, to divide myth from fact would be a very delicate and difficult operation. As you know, everybody's myth is somebody's fact and almost anybody's fact at some point or other is somebody else's myth. Somebody else's heathenism is in some way related to the nature of your holiness, and since we have different kinds of heathenisms and different kinds of holinesses, Indians and Americans are between them running into considerable difficulty. Indians may not use the word "heathen" but they use its equivalents, and of course Western, and especially American traditions are full of negative irritants on this score. So when the wrong combinations meet, the results can sometimes be shattering. If one could venture any kind of a generalization at all, it might be to say that both Indians and Americans tend to be in some measure apostles of righteousness, and when two apostles of righteousness meet it is not generally the beginning of a beautiful friendship.

Clark Mollenhoff. I think much of the American image of India as being "pro-Communist" would reflect an impression from Krishna Menon when he comes over here and appears on television panel shows. Now, I am wondering, is India aware of the kind of impression that this man makes?

Frank Moraes. I will answer you. I think Krishna Menon is an obsession here and if Mr. Dulles were not ill, as he is—well, the last time I came to the States when I was asked about Krishna Menon, I used to say he is our Mr. Dulles.

Harold R. Isaacs. I think the kernel is here, and let us take it away from individual personalities. At the bottom of the confusion and ambivalence that has hung over American-Indian relations and beclouded individual encounters there is something that has to do with our mutual conceptions of our *bona fides*. American backs have been put up time after time over the last six or seven years—this is changing under the stress of current events—by assumptions made by Indians, questioning our motivations, seeing us as warmongers, and that sort of thing. To be sure, we contributed to this by the military accent in our policy, so there was a combination of things coming together. With respect to our view of the Indian on the level of foreign policy attitudes and Cold War relationships, I think that what we have to deal with here is the matter of equating the values of contending powers in the Cold War. To Americans this is a peculiarly objectionable idea, and when it proved impossible to break through it, there were tensions of many kinds.

Lawrence E. Spivak.   Nonalignment and neutrality have been mentioned but perhaps the concern of American opinion is not with neutrality, not with nonalignment, but the very opposite—the feeling of Americans has been that India has been aligned because of the actions of Mr. Krishna Menon, because of the votes in the UN, and frequently because of some of the things that Mr. Nehru has said, up until recently over Tibet. I mean, haven't you found a great many Americans have been worried not about neutrality and nonalignment which they are ready to accept, but about what they think is alignment and nonneutrality and possibly a leaning toward communism—hasn't that been the tendency?

Harold R. Isaacs.   I think that is a fair statement of what has occurred. Many Indian leaders, by the attitudes they have taken in a series of crucial events, including I am sorry to say the events in Hungary, and many others, have given grounds for this impression. There are always two sides to this kind of collision and encounter, and I think it is necessary for our Indian friends to understand that they have contributed at least as much to the difficulties as the Americans have and the things that you referred to are parts of the ways in which they have contributed. When I say the test of events, I mean events which change that kind of orientation, such as the recent events which have made the nature of Communist China a little clearer right on India's frontiers.

Lawrence E. Spivak.   Along this same line, does India today think that it is a part of this struggle between what we call freedom and communism, or does it still feel that it is not a part—and I am talking now about the morality of the issues, not the power blocs that are involved? I think this is a fundamental question.

Frank Moraes.   Yes, I think it is extremely vital. I do not think there will be any change in our policy of nonalignment and I think with the Chinese on our northern borders we can have no other policy. We will be even more deeply committed to nonalignment, but I think there will be a shift in emphasis in the direction that we will be prepared to give the benefit of the doubt to the democracies.

MORALITY OR NATIONAL INTEREST?

The fact that India does have its "apostles of righteousness" explains to a great extent why Indians in morally equating the two blocs so irritate many Americans. Insult is added to injury. The reflex on the part of Indian spokesmen to present their policy in terms of morality rather than of national self-interest may be less noticeable in 1960 than it was in, say, 1950, but it continues to exacerbate Indo-United States relations. *Quincy Wright*, Professor of International Relations at the University of Virginia, and *Ross Berkes*, co-author of *The Diplomacy of India*, discuss the motivations of Indian policy as reflected at the United Nations. Professor Wright emphasizes a traditional Indian national attachment to peace. However, *Michael Brecher*, author of the political biography *Nehru*, joined by Professor *Norman Palmer* of the University of Pennsylvania, argue that India bases its foreign policy decisions not on principle but on national self-interest. It is Nehru's good fortune, says Brecher, that national interest and traditional Indian moral principles have often coincided. He cites India's UN position on the Hungarian rebellion as an exception, necessary, in the Indian national interest, to forestall a plebiscite which could become a precedent for Kashmir. This brings a rebuttal from *A. K. Mithra*, political adviser to the Indian UN delegation. In the view of *Phillips Talbot*, author of the definitive study *India and America*, the controlling factor in the interplay between morality and national interest is that India's interests have proliferated with each year of expanded diplomatic activity. "There are now more cross-lines of interests," and India, like all major powers, confronts increasingly the same necessity to compromise national self-interest and principle which faces all major powers.

Quincy Wright.   India is traditionally for peace. The great national figures of India are the emperor Asoka and Gandhi, both of whom were notable for their policies of peace. One can say that although India's history is not free from war and violence, in theory India is committed to the maintenance of peace.

India hopes that the United States is also for peace, but is not quite certain. There is a great deal of criticism of what is called

American militarism in Indian circles. India's method for pursuing peace is at least different from that of the United States.

The essential element of the Indian conception of a policy of peace today is ending of the "cold war." Indians are convinced that the rivalry of the two great power blocs in the world is extremely dangerous and that it is not necessary.

India feels that the reason for the "cold war" is mutual fear and that this ought to be capable of solution, given the spirit of tolerance called for by the United Nations Charter and reasonable good will and intelligence on both sides. This policy, of course, is associated with India's policy of nonalignment. India does not wish to add fuel to the "cold war" by joining either side, but seeks rather to maintain a position of impartiality which might facilitate mediation between the great factions in that "war."

India believes in conciliation rather than in the strict application of international law.

The United Nations is looked upon as a key institution for the practice of conciliation and the gaining of acceptance of the great principles of peace which are in the preamble and the first articles of the Charter, as well as in the Panch Shila.

I may say that the attitude of India toward the United Nations is very different from its attitude toward the League of Nations. India was, of course, an original member of the League of Nations, but was represented largely by appointees of the British viceroy of India, and the attitude of Indians in the Congress Party and of public opinion as expressed in the press was bearish toward the League of Nations. The feeling was that it was committed to the maintenance of the *status quo*, including imperialism.

India's attitude toward the United Nations has been quite different. It is believed to be a more practical institution, more committed against imperialism, more in favor of human rights. The great principles that India has supported in the United Nations are anticolonialism and antiracialism. India has been very glad to have the United Nations pass resolutions opposing the South African attitude on the racial question, and also to have the development through the United Nations of the independence of many new states, breaking up colonial empires. On this point, of course, India has favored the independence of Algeria in the United Nations, as well as the independence of other Asian and African states. On the

Kashmir problem, however, India's special interest seems to get in the way of its application of the principle of self-determination of peoples.

In regard to collective security, the attitude of India may seem to conflict with its policy of nonalignment, but Nehru in his introduction to the Australian book, *Paths of Peace*, makes a sharp distinction. It is one thing to favor collective security against aggression and another to enter an alliance on the assumption that the state against which the alliance is directed is going to commit aggression in the future. Nehru believes that a government ought not to brand any state as an aggressor potentially, but only when it actually commits aggression. That is, one should assume that every state is innocent until it has been proved guilty.

Ross Berkes. India's attitude toward the United Nations may not be quite as simple as some of us sometimes think. I feel that they have looked upon the UN as two different institutions over the past ten years, that a transition has taken place, and that the Indian attitude toward the United Nations in the present and in the future will even be different still. The first of these United Nations related to the emphasis on conciliation noted by Professor Wright, their concern that the United Nations not become an instrument of one of the great powers in the Cold War, indeed their hope that the United Nations could be used as an agency whereby amelioration of these great power disputes could come about.

In this last ten years and up to the recent past there has been something of an automatic majority—I hesitate to call it that—but certainly a built-in majority on the part of the Western powers, which the United States, much to the concern and dissatisfaction of India, has seized upon to prosecute the Cold War against the Soviet Union—and vice versa, although the Soviet Union was not in a position in those days to be in the majority. Consequently, the fear that the United Nations would become an instrument of the Cold War has led India to deemphasize the coercive features of the United Nations, the collective security system, which otherwise I think the Indian government would be perfectly willing to subscribe to. Indeed before the Cold War became a primary concern of the United Nations, dominating nearly everything, the Indian Prime Minister was insisting that the United Nations do something very strong and forceful against some of the colonial powers. In particular during the time of Indonesian efforts to obtain independence, he made loud and complaining statements about the failure of the United Nations to do something very actively and in a forceful way to assure the world that it was on the side of right and justice.

That's the one side of the United Nations, this fear of India that the great powers would merely use it as a means of pursuing their rivalry and therefore this hesitation in supporting any collective security system whatsoever.

The second United Nations and the one that I think India is mainly concerned with is—and I say so in all courtesy and respect—not one enshrining high principles so much as one offering the possibility of the advancement of the welfare of the African-Asian world toward equality, economic, political, and otherwise. I say that not in any sense of disparagement. High principles mean something in terms of specifics to most countries and most peoples.

As for the future, I think these old differences between our two countries in the United Nations may be disappearing. This is largely due to victory on the part of India in that in these days the "automatic majority" which has for so long been available to the West no longer can be assured and the United Nations has become an instrument of power for the Afro-Asian bloc. India is now serving in a manner of restraining rather than in the former position of encouraging the demands of the Afro-Asian powers. These things will make quite a difference in the United Nations.

Michael Brecher. It is one thing to speak up in favor of such general principles as antiracialism and anticolonialism, but it seems to me that the Indian government can no more act exclusively on the basis of principles than other governments.

The fact of the matter is that Nehru with all his moralizing has been among the most acute exponents of what we call political realism, and as early as 1947, when he assumed the prime ministership, he stated quite bluntly and boldly that in his view it was national interest rather than moral principles which ultimately would have to guide India in its foreign policy.

I think there is an ambivalence in the Indian attitude to the United Nations which has come through very clearly on two questions—Hungary and Kashmir. Both Professor Wright and Professor

Berkes have pointed out that the Indian government has long sub-
scribed to the view that the United Nations has an important role
to play as an instrument of conciliation, but largely because of the
feeling of intense dissatisfaction with the way the United Nations
conciliated or did not, in fact, conciliate its own very significant
dispute with Pakistan over Kashmir, there intruded an element of
distrust which, in fact, influenced India's attitude to other aspects
of the United Nations. On the question of Hungary we have seen
this very clearly. When questions of vital interest, as viewed in
Delhi, were involved, India found itself voting in support of a position, namely the Soviet position on Hungary, which Mr. Nehru
on the basis of much of his moralizing in the preceding eight years
would never have been expected to endorse.

Now I am not arguing that the morality of Indian foreign policy,
both as it expresses itself within the United Nations and outside,
is insincere. I think it is sincere, but I think it has the great merit
of coinciding very effectively on most issues with what are in fact
Indian vital interests as they are defined by Nehru and his closest
colleagues.

Quincy Wright. I don't think it is quite fair to say that Nehru's
attitude was on the Russian side in the Hungarian matter. It was
not as vigorous in condemning the Soviet Union as many people
thought it ought to have been, but I think it is clear that India
took a different position in regard to Hungary and Suez. I think
this was because they identified Suez with colonialism, and they are
both against aggression and in favor of anticolonialism.

Michael Brecher. What I was referring to specifically was the fact
that in the United Nations India voted in such a way as to protect
what it considered to be a vital interest in Kashmir. Now here was
a clear case where the moral principle involved would have dictated
an Indian vote in favor of a plebiscite held in Hungary under the
United Nations' auspices. India deserted from this, surely not on
moral grounds, but only because of the precedent that might be
created for Kashmir which it was reluctant, shall we say, to accept.

Norman Palmer. I could cite, and I am sure all the rest of you
could, a great many statements by Nehru himself, saying very, very
plainly that he doesn't pretend to take the moral position, that this

is not his intention whatsoever. Possibly we read into the Indian position an effort to operate on a higher moral plane because India thus far has not had quite as great a role in world affairs. Usually, a less important nation, just speaking in the power political sense, is able to give a certain sweetness and light to international relations which the big, bad powers don't seem to be able to give.

Phillips Talbot. Well, isn't this precisely the point, that India's role has changed? In the early years, for instance, world problems were for India a quite simple dichotomy between the imperial powers and the colonial people who had to gain their freedom. Indeed, outside of the Indian subcontinent it is hard to find an instance in those early years in which India's national interest was directly and vitally affected by any activity, say, perhaps before the Suez and Hungarian issues came along.

I think it is central to this discussion that since India became independent in 1947 its interest in the world has rapidly expanded, its contact with the world, which in 1947 was limited mainly to Britain and Britain's neighbors and to some extent the United States, has subsequently expanded until they have become very close with parts of the Middle East, with parts of Southeast Asia, with parts of East Asia. Indeed, even two years ago one would have said India and Japan were fairly distant. Now one would say they know more about each other. One can see, too, new points of contact between India and Latin America.

The role of India in speaking for colonial people, first in Asia, and then when there came to be almost no colonial peoples left in Asia, under old Western domination, now in Africa, has been pretty well publicized. India has played a role, not only in the formation of the organization of the Bandung Conference, but in contact with a good many of the newer states of Africa. By and large, there has been a very strong, active trend toward greater and greater involvement in world affairs. This has meant, I believe, not only that India's expression of the rights of the case in various issues has been heard around the world, but also that increasingly India's direct interests are involved. In 1947 and 1949 and 1950 or 1951 one could have talked of India's foreign policy in a clear-cut fashion. Now there is more complexity, there are more cross-lines of interests—which is nothing to be surprised at, it seems to me, because this certainly is the historical parallel in American foreign policy and British foreign policy, and the policy of any major power with widespread interests in the world.

Ross Berkes.   I feel that the distinction to be made on this point has less to do with the general moral principles involved, although I can see their close relationship, than with the tactics employed by the West in pursuit of those moral principles, and particularly the tendency on the part of the Western powers to use the United Nations to register condemnation of what the West would call the immoral acts on the part of some of the Communist powers.

Now when you look over the record of the United Nations, you will find that India has its own cross to bear on many subjects and brings them to the United Nations with high moral principles behind it, but the resolutions it sponsors and the resolutions it supports are not condemnatory. Even in the case of South Africa or the racial situation in general, they take a stand which has been fair, which has been consistent, that condemnation simply increases the difficulties in the problem.

A. K. Mithra.   About Hungary, I think Professor Brecher said that the voting of India was in support of the Soviet position. Yet the difference in the position of India with regard to Hungary and to Suez is precisely that every resolution about Hungary used the word "condemn" or "deplore." The resolutions about Suez did not.

Michael Brecher.   Do you really think that was the only reason?

A. K. Mithra.   I think many reasons figure in these matters, sir, and let me remind you that when we were negotiating the resolution about South Africa, we had a passage in it which said, "regrets the action of the Government of the Union of South Africa." We were requested officially to change that to "notes with regret" by the same people who two weeks later came to us with the resolution about Hungary, which used words like "denounced" and "deplores" and "condemns." Now this is it.

Michael Brecher.   If I may just make this one further comment about the difference between Suez and Hungary, however, it is that the United Nations, without using any terms such as "condemn," called upon Great Britain, France, and Israel to withdraw, and they agreed to withdraw—whereas they called upon the Soviet Union to withdraw from Hungary, and they refused to withdraw, and therefore. . . .

A. K. Mithra. Quite right, sir. Now if I may add, as to your point about holding a plebiscite in Hungary, the position of the Indian government in this instance is that the United Nations is unfortunately not an organization which can hold plebiscites in different parts of the world. There are a lot of members of the United Nations, very respectable, some of them members of the free world, which I am sure would hate to hold plebiscites in their own countries, or in various territories under their control. For example, I would like to see a plebiscite in Portuguese East Africa, or. . . .

Michael Brecher. My friend, surely you are not arguing that the Indian position on Hungary in the United Nations was one to be terribly proud of. There are people in the Indian government in Delhi with whom I have talked who were not at all proud, and I am talking about senior officials. The fact is that Mr. Nehru himself denounced Israel and later Britain and France on the basis of a newspaper report of the invasion of the Sinai Peninsula by Israeli troops on October 29. He denounced them on the 30th, but it took something like three weeks in the case of Hungary.

Now I know for a fact that Mr. Nehru is not particularly proud of this, but this is not the point surely. I was merely trying to suggest that in the case of Hungary Mr. Menon took a position at the United Nations which was at least in part dictated by the concern that a plebiscite in Hungary would create a precedent for a United Nations-sponsored plebiscite in Kashmir.

A. K. Mithra. I am saying that the main fact is that the United Nations is not an organization to hold a plebiscite and has never been so designated. You read the charter of the UN, which I know you have; you cannot hold plebiscites through the UN. This is not a UN function. The UN is not a territorial appertaining body. It's not that kind of an organization. This is the same reason, incidentally, why we always had a difficulty about Cyprus, because self-determination can be invoked by a minority, too. If we permit self-determination by a minority, tomorrow the *colons* in Algeria may demand self-determination, and what happens to Algerian freedom then?

"HINDI-CHINI BHAI BHAI"

Not all its American critics charge Indian foreign policy with a Janus-faced duplicity. To many, Indians are simply "soft" on communism, wishful thinkers and therefore unreliable, if well meaning, as partners in world affairs. India's China policy has most often been cited as a case in point and the Chinese border incursions in 1959 were, accordingly, counted on to alert New Delhi at last to Communist intentions. Discussing India's relations with China at a time following the Tibetan repression but prior to the border incidents, Professor *Norman Palmer* pointedly notes the absence of emotional bonds between the two countries in the past. Still, he questions the likelihood of basic change in Indian policy toward China. This view is shared by *Michael Brecher* and *Quincy Wright*. Professor *Palmer* suggests that the United States nonrecognition policy and India's consequent fears of United States intervention on the mainland have helped push India closer to China during the past decade.

Norman Palmer. It seems to me notable that in modern times there have been relatively few contacts between India and other parts of Asia, and this is particularly true of that part of Asia which we call the Far East.

Southeast Asia, to be sure, is in a somewhat different category. It is a fact, of course, that historically speaking, the ties of India with Southeast Asia, through Indian colonies and Indian kingdoms, were close for several centuries, and that at the present time a rather substantial number of Indians live in various countries of Southeast Asia, especially Burma and Malaya. It is also a fact that today India is beginning to pay more attention to the Southeast Asian area. For example, Nehru himself, when he went to China in 1954 and stopped, going and coming, in all sections of what had been French Indo-China, in both North and South Vietnam, in Laos, and in Cambodia, was reported to have been impressed with the evidences of the impact of Hindu civilization to the west of the line dividing Vietnam from Laos and Cambodia.

But if you take China and the Far East generally, it seems to me to be a very impressive fact that there have been relatively few contacts until quite recently. There is, to be sure, the tradition of what some have called one thousand years of intimate contacts between China and India, dating roughly from the first thousand years of the Christian era. A lot of people have made a great deal out of that, as when Mr. Nehru was in China in 1954. But these contacts were after all very few and mostly due to the influence of Buddhism. There was also a certain amount of trade and other contacts both over land and over sea. However, after approximately 1000 A.D. India and China were cut off almost completely. Even during the British period, in what K. M. Panikkar has called the Vasco da Gama epoch of Asian history, the contacts between India and China were still relatively few, and they were, for the most part, indirect.

So it has been largely in the present century that India and the Far East have really got acquainted with each other.

When I was a visiting professor at Delhi University some years ago, I was asked, among other things, to give some work in Far Eastern politics and history. My first reaction to this proposal was that it didn't make sense for an American professor to offer work on the Far East in India, but I soon learned that my graduate students at Delhi University knew very little, surprisingly little, about that part of the world. They knew that American policy toward China was all wrong. This was Q.E.D.—and they had a certain general orientation toward China, but that was about the sum and substance of their "knowledge" of Far Eastern affairs. With all due respect to the fine work that is now being done at the Indian School of International Studies in New Delhi, it seems to me that even today, if I may base my impressions on the last visit which I made to India in the fall of 1958, there is still relatively little serious attention either on an official or unofficial level to China and to the Far East generally, although there is now a great interest in India in what is going on in the "New China" and a widespread conviction that these two most populous states of the world have got to learn how to coexist.

That is by way of general background. Now. . . .

Quincy Wright. May I interrupt here? In his speech yesterday [May 4, 1959], as reported in *The New York Times*, Prime Minister Nehru said something like, "We will hold to the policy of co-existence, even if no one else does."

Norman Palmer. That will be a feat of Indian legerdemain which we should appreciate very much.

I think the recent Tibetan developments have again illustrated the fact that in a sense the relations of China and India have been on a relatively superficial plane.

In the past, you might say that the Indian impact on China, through Buddhism and other sources, was much, much greater than the Chinese impact on India. At the present time, you might say it is just the reverse, that the Chinese impact on India seems to be much greater than the Indian impact on China. Indeed, to some extent the Chinese Communists, it seems to me, have been supremely and rather surprisingly contemptuous of India. They have been very, very much remiss in even keeping India informed of certain things which you would think would be to their mutual interest.

Now we know that on at least three major occasions relations between India and China have been less than satisfactory. I am referring to the situation in 1950 when Chinese troops went into Tibet and to the recent developments in Tibet and their repercussions in India, but I am also thinking of the exchange of harsh words between Russia and India and then eventually Communist China and India in the fall of 1952, when India made some serious and carefully thought out efforts to be helpful in trying to work out a cease-fire in Korea. Now I think these are the three big examples.

Now about Tibet, one result of the present Tibetan business is that some Americans are rubbing their hands with glee and are proclaiming that suddenly the scales are falling from the Indians' eyes, that the Indians are waking up, and that now they realize that all that we said about the dangers of China and communism are true. There are, to be sure, some evidences that the Indians are quite aroused by the Chinese move in Tibet. Nehru seems to be using stronger language every time he makes a statement. Statements in the Indian press certainly suggest that there is a great stirring of indignation in India with respect to Chinese actions in Tibet. I wonder, however, to what extent this is a tempest in the teapot situation, and to what extent this is something which will really make a lasting impact on Indian minds and on Indian foreign policy. Let me call your attention to a clipping from *The New York Times* which contains the following observations: "Nehru now sees China in different light. Peiping's sharp replies to protest on Tibet shock Indian Premier. Observers think the Indians who had been friendly admirers of Communist China have now suffered fall from the high idealistic plane on which they thought these affairs were being conducted."

This is not dated 1959. The date is November 4, 1950!

Quincy Wright. In a recent speech in Parliament Nehru said his broad policy was governed by three factors: Preservation of the security and integrity of India—he puts himself into it first; the desire to maintain friendly relations with China; and deep sympathy for the people of Tibet.

It seems to me that India in its relations with China has been caught between two ideals of admiration and fear. I found that many members of the Indian foreign office believe that China is making more rapid economic progress than India. This gives them great concern. They realize that if China does forge ahead economically, with its rather brutal methods, that there are going to be a lot of people in India who are going to say that we should do the same thing, and I don't think the Indians—the government certainly doesn't want that.

Furthermore, there is a certain fear of China, which I think has been manifested right along. They realize that China is a great neighbor, and it is becoming powerful rather rapidly.

So the combination of that admiration-fear seems to characterize the Indian position. I found that there was more criticism of the United States policy in regard to the nonrecognition of China than anything else except the giving of arms to Pakistan. That came first.

But second to that they think that the American policy of nonrecognition of China is beneath contempt. The idea was often expressed that you don't socialize people by ostracizing them. There are reasons for fearing China; the best way to ameliorate them would be to have China in the United Nations and have it generally recognized by the United States and the world.

Michael Brecher. I think we have to be perfectly clear in our minds that for good or ill the Indian approach to world affairs which we define as neutralism or nonalignment is very, very deeply rooted. It is deeply rooted in Indian thought; it is deeply rooted in Indian national interests. Professor Wright has cited Nehru's own enumeration of three guiding considerations here, and vital interests came first.

Mr. Nehru has been perfectly clear as early as 1950 that any attempt to intrude into Nepal or the border states of Sikkim or Bhutan would, of course, immediately call for direct Indian response, that this is of vital Indian interest, that India would not, in fact, accept any threat or any claim by the Chinese. Similarly on the MacMahon line—that is to say, on the undemarcated border between India and China—he has stated a number of times that as far as India is concerned the Chinese maps which include part of Assam are, of course, utterly objectionable, and he has rejected them. On one recent occasion, when he was asked in Parliament whether the Chinese had been told about this, he said, "Yes, on a number of occasions, but they seem to respond that they have not had time to change the maps." To which he felt compelled to add that they have had time to change a great many things, but not the maps. He is quite clear in his own mind that India will stand on the MacMahon line and on the northeast frontier as India views this.

Now he may be annoyed with Tibet, he may be unhappy, he may be distressed that the Chinese acted, shall we say, using Cold War tactics, and I think he feels somewhat slighted. But I don't think he has reached the point yet where he is prepared to use anything stronger than the kind of language that has come into the press unless the Chinese push him to the wall. True, they are pushing him very far at the moment.

Norman Palmer. Superimposed upon all of this pattern of relationships between India and China might be added the fact that so many Indians, including the government, were subconsciously or unconsciously forced on the side of the Communist régime out of the fear, which I think they were quite sincere about, that the Korean War was going to be used—or at least the threat was there, that it might be used as an instrument by the United States to reopen the Chinese civil war and perhaps a general war would result.

Out of that came also a tendency to come closer to the régime in China than otherwise might have resulted.

As India has stiffened its posture toward China following the 1959 border pressures, the juxtaposition of a democratic India arrayed against a Communist China has taken on greater apparent validity than ever and has figured increasingly in the argument for United States economic aid.

Yet to some Indians—and some Americans—this is an unfortunate basis on which to rest the case for aid to India. *Frank Moraes* sees in this a suggestion of blackmail, and *Henry R. Lieberman,* assistant to the foreign editor of *The New York Times* and former correspondent in China, warns that an American effort directed to the increase of Indian state power as a counterforce to Chinese power—a policy inspired primarily by United States rather than Indian strategic design—is destined in the end to fail. *Hans J. Morgenthau,* author of *Politics Among Nations* and other books, reports that in Asia he has found little sense of a Sino-Indian rivalry and that this is largely an American creation.

Frank Moraes. I think what Tibet has done for us in India could not have been done in a hundred years. I think we have suddenly been awakened to the danger along our northern border. India has the longest Communist border just next to her, extending over 2,000 miles, and Tibet has had, I think, a very important and a very significant reaction, a very deep reaction in India. This is because for the first time we realize that colonialism need not necessarily mean, as we always thought, the domination by a white race of the black, the brown, or the yellow. I think for the first time we realized this, in a very dim way, when Hungary was attacked—that there could be a type of colonialism of a white race vis-à-vis another white race. However, I think now, though we may have realized it also during the Sino-Japanese War, we realize sharply that an Asian race can dominate another Asian race.

But the unfortunate fact is this, that today India is caught in a sort of double vise. We have China along our northern border, a very aggressive China, and we have a hostile Pakistan on our eastern and western flanks, supported by the Western powers. So we are in the curious position of being threatened by the Communists on the north, and on the east and west by somebody supported by a Western power. I do not say that critically; it is a matter of fact. I do not know in what way you should reorient your policy or not, but there it is.

Let me also say frankly that we don't come to the United States to beg. This is what is suggested when one speaks of aiding India because it is opposed to China. Opposing China to India is political blackmail, and I do not think that this is the right thing, that any decent nation or any decent country or any decent individual would accept this as the premise of assistance. I do not want to ask help on those terms. If you believe in us, and only if you really believe in India, then help us.

Henry R. Lieberman.   I would like to comment on this question of the competition between China and India. I'm not qualified to speak on the sensitivity and sensibilities of Indians about this competition. As an American, though, I might be able to—I have a moral right at any rate, to talk about this in terms that are meaningful to us and are important to us. I think that we can go astray in India with an aid program if we think of it in terms of competition between India and China. This program must be useful and usable, in India. If we think, for example, that China is getting too powerful and seek therefore to make India powerful in the same terms, we're going to fail. This must be an Indian program, dear to India, and it must be carried out by Indians. We must find our place in such a program, and this place must be assigned to us by the Indians.

Hans J. Morgenthau.   I fully agree with the statements which have been made as to the fallacy of looking at the relations between the United States on the one hand, and China and India on the other, in terms of a competition between China and India in which we must, perhaps against our preferences, support India. When I was in Asia I did not find any considerable trace, if any trace at all, of this competition. I have the suspicion that this competition is really the invention of some Western journalists who have coined a phrase to which hardly anything corresponds in reality. The Indian experiment is a great experiment of a very great fraction of the human race, and it so happens that the success of that experiment is in the vital interest of the United States. I think nothing more is needed to justify an effort of the United States which is commensurate with the magnitude of the task and the nobility of that experiment.

NEW DELHI, KARACHI, AND WASHINGTON

In India's own world image Pakistan looms as large as China or the Soviet Union or the United States. *Michael Brecher, Phillips Talbot, Quincy Wright,* and *Norman Palmer* discuss Indo-Pakistan relations in general and Professor Brecher's proposal, in particular, of a "package deal" for the settlement of differences between the two principal South Asian powers. Mr. Brecher, author of *The Struggle for Kashmir,* proposes a Kashmir solution in which the central object of dispute, the Valley of Kashmir, would be internally autonomous and "jointly guaranteed."

Michael Brecher. There are a few general propositions I would like to put forward. The first one is that India's position in South Asia is not really dissimilar in one important respect from the position of the United States in relation to the rest of the world; that is to say, it is the Great Power of South Asia, a Great Power by virtue of its size, its geographic position, its population, its economic potential, its status in the world community, and its leadership. Its immediate neighbors, Ceylon, Burma, Nepal, and even Pakistan, are by comparison pygmies.

They are not satellites of India. Indeed, this is one of the main problems, because I think that just as the United States incurs, I think, envy as well as fear and suspicion from many parts of the globe, so too India has, I think, brought upon itself the fear of its neighbors, partly because of its own actions and partly because it is the great power of the area. This is particularly true of Pakistan, and to a lesser extent of Ceylon.

I can't get into all of the regional problems here. Suffice it to say that in India's relations with Pakistan, we have a picture of cold war, on occasion hot war, which again is not dissimilar from the relations between East and West. The relations between India and Pakistan since the partition of 1947 have been characterized by extreme tension much of the time, tension almost all of the time, economic blockade on occasion, one case of military hostilities—in the latter part of 1947 and all of 1948 in Kashmir—periodic threats of war, and continuous ideological and political warfare, which have produced, to put it mildly, a shambles in the relationship between these two countries.

The key issue, of course, has been Kashmir. This is almost the Achilles' heel of Mr. Nehru's foreign policy, because with all of the support for the right of self-determination for Algerians, in fact for anticolonialists everywhere in the world, he looks very weak when he appears, and I choose my words advisedly, to deny the right of self-determination in Kashmir at least by a given deadline.

The reasons for that policy, I think, are many. My own feeling about all these problems is that they are not insoluble, but that they require a kind of boldness and vision and imagination which have not yet been forthcoming from Karachi or Delhi, or indeed from any outside Powers. It seems to me that as in any other diplomatic dispute, despite the adherence to moral principles, there's got to be a good deal of give and take.

I think the lines of a solution are well understood in both Delhi and Karachi, but both of these have to save face or prestige. The real problem is to cut through in such a way that neither side gives way in a manner which would weaken its position with its own people or would suggest that it is, in fact, making a major concession of principle.

Of the five areas of Kashmir, the five distinct geographical regions, there is no problem regarding four of them. Two would go to Pakistan in any fair plebiscite, Gilgit and Poonch; two of them would go to India, Jammu and Ladakh. There remains, of course, the major issue of the Valley, which both parties want very badly for a variety of reasons. My own feeling is that a plebiscite at this time would cause greater harm than the benefits which would accrue.

I am not at all convinced, I might add, that there is an absolute quality to self-determination. I think there are other principles which may be invoked and that self-determination in the pure sense of a plebiscite in the Valley of Kashmir is not the only consideration. My own feeling is that the Valley of Kashmir could become an internally autonomous State whose territory would be jointly guaranteed by India and Pakistan, with the remaining parts of Kashmir divided between the two of them, and with both having access to the Valley for tourists and for trade. The result would be that neither would lose face, the Kashmiris would be happier, and the Indians and Pakistanis could persuade their own peoples that they haven't really given ground. But in order to make this kind of concession, it seems to me that both sides would also have to make concessions on other issues.

The real problem, of course, is mistrust. The disputes are soluble, but the trouble is that the mistrust has become so deep that a new approach is needed. To use a phrase which has now become very general in the West, I would say a package deal, in which you include all of these disputes, rather than separating one from the others and incurring all kinds of responsibility on one issue without the counterbalancing compensations in regard to other disputes.

Phillips Talbot. Professor Wright once taught me that as these difficulties accumulated between Britain and the United States over the past century, about once a generation there was a package deal that resolved the crises.

Quincy Wright. Yes, if I may say a word, I think maybe Brecher would agree that there is a certain similarity between the relations of India and Pakistan and relations of the United States and Canada.

Michael Brecher. Not as bad, though—not yet anyway.

Quincy Wright. No, Benjamin Franklin at the beginning of negotiations for peace in 1782 said to the British, "Well, it would be a good thing for you to cede Canada to the United States. It will make a lot of trouble in the future." The British saw it a little differently, and we thought the relations with Canada were settled after the War of 1812, but I think it is clear that Canada felt that the United States still had its eye out for Canada as late as the reciprocity agreement of 1912 over a century later.

Michael Brecher. I would just add that some Canadians think this is still true in 1959.

Quincy Wright. But I am not sure—somebody said that India doesn't have her eye out for Pakistan. I am not sure but what the Pakistani does feel that India does have its eye out for the reannexation, if you like, of Pakistan, and it may be that this in the background is one of the great difficulties in solving that problem. And actually, I am not entirely sure a package deal is the best approach. Most issues between Pakistan and India can very soon be settled, but I don't think the Kashmir issue can be settled until you have a better atmosphere.

Now usually a changed atmosphere, where you have a high tension, results because both of them are scared of somebody else more. There was a package deal between Great Britain and the United States in 1898 because the British were getting afraid of Germany and they thought they ought to settle things all over, and so we made a new deal in regard to the Panama Canal. The British and the French had been rivals for centuries and made a deal about the same time because they were both scared of Germany. I suppose if Pakistan and India both became scared over the developments in Tibet that you might have this better atmosphere.

What can the United States do to help India and Pakistan moderate their relations? *Chester Bowles* and *Averell Harriman* doubt that one can succeed while the other fails and believe that the United States should avoid playing favorites. This, say *Frank Moraes* and *Hans J. Morgenthau,* is the difficulty—the United States has through military aid to Pakistan followed a policy in which the left hand (Karachi) did not know what the right hand (New Delhi) was doing.

Chester Bowles. The reasons for the conflict between India and Pakistan of course go very deep. Many people, I think, on both sides of the border wish this decision might have been a different one, but everyone knows that the decision is taken and it will not be reversed. I have never heard anyone on either side of the border argue that it should be reversed, or even that they desired it to be reversed. Pakistan is a permanent, free nation, and so is India; and our task lies in helping these two nations to whatever extent we can to understand each other's common ground and to work together.

We have made considerable progress during recent years in the Indus Valley problem. David Lilienthal was there in 1951 and 1952 and spoke about the possibility of international control between India and Pakistan of the waters of the Indus, modeled on our own association with Mexico, over the Rio Grande, and with Canada, over the St. Lawrence and the Great Lakes—an international agreement for the control of all these waters. The international aspects of that have been rejected by both nations. I hope this isn't final, because if the two nations could form a commission to develop the waters of the Indus together, I think it would be more constructive than trying to do it separately where there will always be the possibility of conflicts and difficulties. But in any case the United States can do a great deal in these coming years to make possible the peaceful development of this Indus Valley. A good part of the problem is to get the necessary capital and I hope we will do our part.

I would hope that we might see during these coming weeks or months a kind of a "Summit Meeting" between Mr. Nehru and the new President of Pakistan, who has spoken so reasonably, it seems to me, of the need for *rapprochement* between these two countries. The point of it all is that if India succeeds, Pakistan's hopes for success are going to be infinitely greater. If India fails,

Pakistan's road is going to be particularly rocky. I believe it might become an impossible one—and vice versa.

Once we have an understanding on the waters of the Indus, we may begin to make progress even in such difficult subjects as Kashmir. We're not going to settle that problem in Washington or London, or I doubt, very likely in the United Nations. It's only going to be settled by a closer coming together of these two great countries who belong together in spirit even if they can't share, and will never share, I believe, a common government.

Averell Harriman.   I feel that we have not been very helpful in the relations between India and Pakistan. I think that we have in fact contributed to the ill will that unfortunately exists between those two countries through the policy of giving arms to one without attempting to understand the attitude on the other side. By the same token, the Pakistanis have strong feeling against our aid to India. Now, we have an opportunity in connection with the efforts of the World Bank to support the Indus waters program, the development of the canals between the six tributary rivers to tie together the waters of that great Himalayan watershed so that it can take care of the requirements of both India and Pakistan.

In general, I think we could give more thought to what we can do to help to bring those two countries together and I think we should review our policies and see how we can avoid some of the mistakes that I'm afraid we have made in the past. Certainly both countries deserve our full support, both countries deserve our fullest understanding and we have a tremendous stake in the success of both countries.

Frank Moraes.   I think that as the result of what has happened in Tibet we have for the first time realized how near and how close is this threat of Communist China. But I should like to reiterate what I have often said and without meaning any offense to my American friends: that in addition to an aggressive China on our northern frontiers, we have also on our western and eastern flanks another country, possibly hostile to us, supported by the West. We are caught in a double vise, with a Communist country strung along our northern frontiers and with a country aided by the West on our eastern and western flanks. I think that is extremely important and I think that is where the policy of India as a nonaligned country really begins. I hope it will not end there because I think if a responsibility rests on the Communists, I think a greater responsibility rests on the West for our being caught in this double vise. I do not say anything critical because I can understand why that has happened but I think you also should understand our position today. Caught as we are in this situation we feel that we have a certain demand, if I may say so, on those who back countries who are hostile to us.

Hans J. Morgenthau.   Our policy with regard to India has been of a rather half-hearted and somewhat less than enthusiastic nature. It is not for me here to point to the possible contribution which Indian policy and Indian attitudes have made to that lack of enthusiasm and to that half-heartedness. But certainly, regardless of that contribution, and because of our own limitations, we have not realized how completely identical the interests of India and our own interests are. This identity of interests has been obscured by our alliance with Pakistan. The facts are beyond dispute, but I am not under the same hesitation which Mr. Moraes quite naturally finds himself under, when it comes to criticizing this policy. Criticize it I shall. For I am sure, as sure as I can be of anything, that future historians will look with amazement at this policy which forces the United States to engage in a kind of armaments race with itself. For with one hand we build up the armaments of Pakistan, for a purpose which nobody can really see, and while we are doing this, we force India to divert a considerable fraction of its productive resources into armaments in order to keep up with Pakistan. Since in our saner moments we realize that we cannot afford to let the Indian economic and social experiment fail, we must, with the other hand, shore up the Indian economy at least to the extent that its resources have been diverted to armaments for which we are indirectly responsible. If this is a rational policy, I would like to know what an *ir*rational policy is.

THE JEFFERSONIAN IDEAL

Despite all past errors—on both sides—the United States and India were undoubtedly closer than ever in 1960. Member of Parliament *Asoka Mehta,* Chairman of the *Praja* (Peoples) Socialist Party, offers the uncomplicated explanation that the fundamental common ground between the two countries is broad enough to bridge foreign policy divergences. In the final analysis, he says, it is the Jeffersonian ideal that unites India and the United States, and so it will be of crucial importance in their relations whether the United States in the years ahead goes the way of Jefferson or Hamilton.

Asoka Mehta. There is a resurgence of reciprocal interest in our two countries that is heartening. When I look at your country and when I look at mine, there are many things that strike me as dissimilar, but there are many that strike me as similar, surprisingly similar.

I remember that when I was a young boy studying at the university many, many years back, I did not know and I did not realize that the United States was the greatest industrial country in the world, because all the time we used to hear of goods imported from Great Britain, from Germany, and from Japan—very few goods came from your country because you manufactured goods mainly for your people. Today in a similar way, we are dedicating our energies to manufacturing goods mainly for our vast home market.

I think if you look at what is happening in your country and my country, if we are concerned with facts rather than fiction and with realities rather than myths, we will find that there are many things which are common. It is only when we come to the folklore that we find that we are poles apart. I am, of course, a Socialist. You have probably brought me here not so much to have a look at your country, but so that you may have a look at a representative of this somewhat fantastic philosophy, beard and all. But let me assure you that though my country has opted for socialism and you are, of course, the strong protagonists of free enterprise, in my country today there are between three to four times the private entrepreneurs that we had when the British left our shores.

We are Socialists and of course socialism is a word that is taboo in this country. But why are we Socialists? I remember sitting in a British prison, and I had all my schooling in the prison, I used to read about the Roosevelt revolution. It was in 1933 that in the first inaugural speech, President Roosevelt asked the money-changers to quit the temple of civilization. As a matter of fact, they had already fled before he asked them to flee. It was then that the people of the United States asked the government to move forward and do things for them. In the depression the people expected the govern-

ment to move forward and be the leader, their spokesman, the
architect of their new destiny.

Even today I find that when farmers are in difficulty, the government moves in to stabilize prices and in depressed rural areas to
plan industry. Whenever there is depression, the government moves
forward and free enterprise sits back. My ancient land, for two
hundred years, suffered from arrested development. We are in the
cradle of depression. We are stagnant. Is there anything surprising,
is it anything to be critical about if we opt for socialism, if we turn
to our government and say—if the Smiths of our country go to our
Washington, New Delhi—and say in Parliament, do this for us, or
undertake that?

In my country we cannot afford to follow the slow rhythm of
development that was possible for you in the past. We do not want
to adopt the methods of the Communists. But what we are trying
to do is to produce simultaneously both kinds of goods. The consumer goods that we need we expect the private sector to produce.
Side by side we want to produce capital goods also, and that responsibility we have to put to a considerable extent on the shoulders
of our government, mainly because the task is too big for our private
sector. It is in the fulfilling of that responsibility that we come to
you for your help and your cooperation—because we would like,
in a short time, to have both the consumer goods and capital goods.
And please remember, in expanding capital goods, we create the
ever-expanding superstructure of consumer goods, and these areas of
our economy are going to be occupied by the innovating entrepreneurs in Socialist India.

If we do not do this, if we do not have as a base to our economy
a Socialist attitude and a Socialist approach, the great fabric of our
dream will never be realized.

Sometimes, as I have said, I get puzzled and surprised. I have
been a great admirer of yours because of your gospel of production.
But what do I find: that the magnificent scroll of production is
there before you but the orchestra is so organized that very often
various instruments are muffled and the symphony is spoiled. The
soil bank—do not produce, do not produce food grains if you can.
I can understand that your soil needs some respite, but I am unable
to understand how your humanity can be given a holiday when
there are millions of hungry people in the world who ask not for a

morsel of food but to whom food would be an opportunity to work, to build a new future. How can we permit any productive capacity in this great country of yours to remain unutilized? When we come to you and say give us a little help, what are we asking for? Destiny has ordained that this great country of yours be the tool shop of the world.

May I in all humility say that in the last ten years of our efforts we have shown that we are at the end of the beginning of war against poverty. And, we are trying to create a bastion of democracy because we believe in democracy. Therefore I am very often surprised by the way the American people react to certain situations. I believe the Americans still have the psychology of the frontier. They are brave, they are improvising. But they are also prone to panic. Sometimes they feel that it is not enough to have faith in democracy. It is also necessary to work up steam against someone. Our institutions are strongly anchored in democracy and we therefore find it very difficult to work up steam against anyone.

The United States is proud, and rightly proud of the fact that its book of life is devoted to creation and construction. Only a few fugitive pages are given over to destruction. Is it not then surprising that the American people prize the friendship of those who engage in belligerent gestures and are cool toward those who have dedicated themselves to wholly constructive ends? These are things which I do not understand.

I have come here hoping that perhaps part of my puzzlement will disappear, that perhaps I shall be able to have better insight into the workings of the minds of the American people.

Two or three days back, Lady Jackson told me that in the last six years she has often come to America and has been quite anguished, but this time she looks forward very hopefully because she sees, rising across the horizon, a resurgence of the Jeffersonian ideal. If there is going to be that kind of renaissance in this great country you and I will be able to meet together because it is the Jeffersonian ideal that we know and cherish in our country.

III / THE DOLLAR GAP

At the beginning of 1960 the United States had loaned or given India more than $2 billion (see table, page 65) in varied forms of economic assistance for her First and Second Five Year Plans. This is an impressive contribution, and yet in the light of India's seemingly bottomless need it is a relatively small contribution which is likely to be multiplied many times in the Third and Fourth and Fifth Five Year Plans. A breakdown of this $2 billion total shows, moreover, that the biggest single item of the United States aid program in India has been surplus food disposal under Public Law 480. This necessary program provides assurance of adequate grain stocks and weakens, accordingly, the position of speculators in India who would otherwise force food prices upward. But it is no secret, least of all to informed Indian opinion, that Americans do not know what to do with mounting agricultural surpluses and are glad to minimize storage costs through disposal abroad. Aid in the form of food is relatively painless and does not carry the psychological impact of capital assistance, representing as this does money out of the taxpayers' pockets. Thus the test, as it were, of a disinterested United States aid program comes down to increased dollar loans in support of India's foreign exchange position. This is in any case the central factor in the arithmetic of Indian planning for development.

Newscaster Edward P. Morgan calls the disparity between foreign exchange needs and foreign exchange reserves India's "dollar gap"—which may turn out to be "even more important in the long-run contest with the Soviet Union and China than the missile gap." He was speaking of the United States contest with the Communist states, but India is in the eyes of many who support massive aid waging a special contest of her own with Peking. This is the rivalry between an open and a closed society, between a free or a statist economic and political model for the developing continents. Senator *John F. Kennedy's* discussion of this contest serves as a prelude to the review of Indian development efforts by Ambassador *B. K. Nehru,* Commissioner General for Economic Affairs in Washington. This leads, in turn, to an examination of a wide range of emerging issues concerning Indian development plans and United States aid programs.

John F. Kennedy.   No struggle in the world today deserves more of our thought and attention than the struggle between India and China for leadership of the East, for the respect of all Asia, for the opportunity to demonstrate whose way of life is the better. The battle may be more subtle than loud—it may not even be admitted by either side—but it is a very real battle nonetheless. For it is these two countries which offer a potential route of transition from economic stagnation to economic growth. India follows a route in keeping with human dignity and individual freedom, with only haphazard assistance from this country. Red China represents the route of regimented controls and ruthless denial of human rights, with considerable aid from the U.S.S.R.

It should be obvious that the outcome of this competition will vitally affect the security and standing of this nation. But do we fully realize how it is coming out? Both China and India began their development efforts at about the same time—1950. They started with similar economic structures, similar standards of living, and similar problems of skilled labor and natural resources. Actually India had certain advantages as in the case of transportation and trained personnel.

But the harsh facts of the matter are that in the last decade China has surged ahead of India in most sectors of its economy. Its gross national output has expanded about three times as fast. In terms of industrial capacity, investment, education, and even household consumption China has slowly pulled up and now moved ahead. Its food production has nearly doubled, while India's has increased by less than 50 per cent.

In steel production, China has moved from a position of inferiority to marked superiority. In 1950 China produced as much steel as Great Britain did in 1880. By 1958 China had moved to a point of productive superiority in steel, surpassing Great Britain today, and is making equal growth in coal and other major ingredients of national strength.

Since 1952 China has tripled the number of engineers and technicians in its industries and added four million workers to its skilled labor force.

In 1958, China's rate of economic growth was at least three times as high as India's. Perhaps the official figures which claim to have doubled both agricultural and steel production may be discounted. Still, the fact remains that they are based on a hard record of fact compared to the sagging performance in India, and this is the record which has such great appeal to those nations uncertain of which route to follow.

India's population represents 40 per cent of the uncommitted world. It is larger than the total populations of the continents of Africa and South America combined. Unless India is able to demonstrate an ability at least equal to that of China to make the transition from economic stagnation to growth, so that it can get ahead of its exploding population, the entire Free World will suffer a serious reverse. India herself will be gripped by frustration and political instability—its role as a counter to the Red Chinese will be lost— and communism will have won its greatest bloodless victory.

So let there be no mistake about the nature of the crisis—both the danger and the opportunity. And let there be no mistake about the urgency of our participation in this struggle.

B. K. Nehru.   Planned economic development has now been under way in India for nine years. The First Five Year Plan which began its course in 1951 has already been completed and the Second Plan is now nearing an end. Preparations are in progress for the Third Plan which will start in 1961. Let us examine the progress that has been achieved and the problems that have arisen in the implementation of the plans so far.

In keeping with the basic needs of the people, the First Plan gave the highest priority to the development of the irrigation and power potential of the country and to the improvement of a transport system which had deteriorated considerably during the war and in the early postwar years. Targets for investment and for increases in production and productive capacity envisaged during the First Plan were of a modest character. In restrospect, however, it would appear that this modest beginning in the First Plan was wisely conceived. Taking the First Plan period as a whole, national income increased by 18 per cent in real terms, which meant, concretely, an improvement of 10 per cent in the average standard of living of the people. For the first time in many a decade there was visible improvement in the meager lot of the Indian peasant and the artisan,

UNITED STATES AID TO INDIA (AS OF JUNE 30, 1960)

(In Millions of Dollars)

Fiscal Year	Mutual Security Program						Public Law 480 (Agricultural Surpluses)				Export-Import Bank	Total
	Technical Assistance	Development Assistance	Special Assistance	Asian Economic Development Fund	Development Loan Fund	Wheat Loan	Title I	Title II	Title III	Other		
1951	—	4.5	—	—	—	189.7		—	—	—	—	194.2
1952	—	52.8	—	—	—	—		—	0.4	—	—	53.2
1953	—	44.3	—	—	—	—		—	0.8	—	—	45.1
1954	27.0	60.2	—	—	—	—		—	1.7	—	—	88.9
1955	13.1	72.5	—	—	—	—		—	27.9	—	—	113.5
1956	12.8	47.2	—	—	—	—		3.5	29.3	—	—	92.8
1957	3.8	61.5	—	—	—	—	354.5	1.2	17.8	—	—	438.8
1958	6.2	(—.1)[a]	8.7	20.0	65.0	—	55.8	—	17.6	4.0	151.9	328.5
1959	7.4	(—.6)[a]	10.2	—	120.0	—	259.8	—	19.4	—	—	416.2
1960	7.7	—	15.5	—	153.3	—	616.8[d]	—	8.9	2.5	13.7	818.4
TOTAL	78.0	342.3[b]	34.4	20.0	338.3	189.7[c]	1286.3	4.7	123.8[e]	6.5[f]	165.6	2589.6

[a] Prior year funds deobligated and not reallotted.

[b] Includes $5.0 million for emergency flood and famine relief and $0.5 million ocean freight for PL 480 Title II commodities.

[c] The first $5 million of interest repaid by India established a fund for education assistance to India, of which $4.1 million has been obligated as of June 30, 1959.

[d] Includes $319 million for the first year of the four-year agreement of $1.276 billion signed on May 4, 1960.

[e] Includes market value of commodities and freight paid by International Cooperation Administration.

[f] Represents sales for rupees of commodities purchased in third countries with U.S.-owned local currency proceeds of PL 480 sales.

and this improvement, however modest, strengthened the faith of the people in their own future as well as in the future of the democratic institutions which they had just acquired.

What was perhaps as important as the increase in production and levels of living was the environment of financial and economic stability in which this progress was achieved. Nothing destroys social harmony and the atmosphere of honest endeavor in a poor country as effectively as inflation and, thanks to their wartime experience, the Indian people are fully conscious of this danger. That is why it is significant that over the First Plan period, the general level of prices in India actually declined. What is equally significant, the higher level of investment was financed almost entirely by an increase in the voluntary savings of the Indian people. As much as 93 per cent of the investment undertaken in the First Plan came from domestic sources with only 7 per cent financed by foreign aid.

While the First Plan was thus remarkably successful in creating confidence among the people and the government, it also brought to light certain basic weaknesses in the Indian economy. For one thing, the additional employment created by the plan fell far short of the increase in the labor force, so that there was actually an increase in unemployment. At the same time even the modest increase in production and in irrigation, power, and other facilities led to acute shortages in the supply of basic materials such as steel and cement and fertilizers. It was therefore felt that if these shortages were not to lead to a continuous and sharp increase in imports with a consequent dislocation in balance of payments, it would be necessary to give a high priority in the years to come to an increase in the production of these basic commodities.

Accordingly, in the Second Five Year Plan, which came into operation in 1956, a somewhat greater emphasis was placed on the development of basic industries. The Second Plan also envisaged a total investment roughly twice as large as in the First Plan and an increase in total national product at the rate of 5 per cent per annum as against the increase of about 3½ per cent per annum which was achieved during the First Plan. It was realized from the outset that a larger investment effort with a greater emphasis on the development of basic industries would put a considerable strain on the balance of payments and that this would require the flow of external capital on a substantially larger scale than during the First Plan period. But it was felt that a larger effort to mobilize domestic savings as well as foreign loans and grants was inevitable if India meant to take a decisive step forward in economic development.

During the last three years the level of investment in the Indian economy has in consequence been stepped up steadily and this, in turn, has led to a considerable strain on India's balance of payments. By and large, the internal price situation has remained satisfactory, and there has been a significant increase in the total domestic resources set apart for investment. But the emergence of balance of payments difficulties from the very start of the Second Plan has necessitated a cutback in the original targets. Generally speaking, it would appear that in the Second Plan we shall achieve no more than 80 per cent of our goals. It is, however, significant that even this partial success has become possible only as a result of substantially greater external assistance than was envisaged initially. As a proportion of the total investment effort, the contribution of external assistance during the Second Plan is likely to be of the order of 20 per cent as against the comparable contribution during the First Plan of just about 7 per cent. By far the largest proportion of the foreign aid we have received has come from the United States. For this, no less than for the manner in which it has been given, the government and the people of India are truly appreciative and grateful.

Now we are approaching the critical Third Plan. Looking back, while the Indian experiment in planning within a democratic framework has been modestly successful, with total national product increasing at the rate of somewhat under 4 per cent per annum and a modest but perceptible improvement evident in levels of living, the stresses and strains of this development are already being felt. Moreover, such increases in productive capacity as have been made in recent years have become possible only as a result of very sharp increases in taxation at home and a much greater flow of grants and loans from abroad.

The question, therefore, arises: "What is the course that India must follow in the years to come?" I think there can be hardly any doubt that despite the difficulties that have been experienced in recent years, the only course open to the Indian people is not only to maintain but to accelerate the tempo of development that has already been built up. To falter now would be to destroy the very foundations of self-confidence which have been so assiduously built up over the past ten years. If we are to continue to develop at the rate maintained so far, it will take us thirty-five years to give to ourselves a per capita income of just over two dollars a week. This rate of development is far too slow in the modern world.

It is too slow first, because the techniques of production have advanced so much that such low levels of living as are symbolized by an income of two or three dollars per week have lost all justification. It is too slow because we have before us the example of societies applying these techniques for development at a much faster rate. The fact that techniques of production have developed so much that poverty and misery can be eradicated in a very short period of time, and the fact that this is being done in countries which have no inherent advantages over us, lead to impatience and discontent with an admittedly just but incredibly slow process; and both impatience and discontent are capable of weakening, if not wholly destroying, the social fabric. It is essential, therefore, that if India is to continue to be a stable and contented democracy, the rate of her economic progress must be substantially increased.

This involves the increase of investment greatly beyond what we have been able to achieve so far. It is clear that we have to be prepared to tax ourselves to the hilt and to limit our consumption so as to increase the investible surplus to the very maximum point which the people will bear. But at present levels of living in the country the total resources available internally which can be mobilized within a democratic framework of society are insufficient for the task. And it is in this context that the flow of large amounts of external capital into India assumes importance, whether that flow is through governmental or private channels.

THE PACE OF DEVELOPMENT

Ambassador Nehru's statement that India has no choice but "to accelerate the tempo of development" is addressed pointedly to those Western financiers and economists who contend that the New Delhi government has attempted to go too far, too fast. Not only in the United States, but in important capital centers of Western Europe to which India must also look for sympathetic support, the 1958 balance of payments crisis was greeted in some quarters as the come-uppance of an economically overextended régime. The stern tone of West German reaction was apparent in a book authored at the time by editor J. M.

Hunck of the influential trade journal *Handelsblatt* of Düsseldorf. "Slackening the pace of economic construction hurts nobody and should not disappoint the masses," writes Hunck in *India's Silent Revolution: A Survey of Indo-German Cooperation.* "India is continually burdening itself with credits and postponing the day of reckoning. . . ."

In effect Mr. Nehru dismisses go-slow economics with a frankly political pronouncement that any slack in growth would indeed lead to dangerous mass disappointment. He speaks of national self-confidence rather than the national balance sheet. But he would be the last to suggest that there is not also a long-term economic answer to short-term doubt. "Technical momentum" is the phrase used by Professor *Wilfred Malenbaum* of the University of Pennsylvania to sum up his defense of the Second Plan targets and of the "Big Plan" school of thought in the present Indian debate on how fast to push development in the new Third Plan.

Wilfred Malenbaum. We know that the Second Plan, which set up targets of a 5 per cent annual growth of national product, has been encountering large resource problems; it must therefore now visualize somewhat lower targets. And there have actually been lesser accomplishments. This has given rise to a considerable discussion as to whether the Plan was not too ambitious. In the light of the short fall of resources, would not it have been more appropriate for India to establish a less ambitious goal—perhaps a 3 per cent, or a 3½ per cent rate of annual increase? It seems to me that in the India of 1955 and 1956, with a First Five Year Plan which achieved an average rate of national income growth of 3½, almost 4 per cent, technical momentum, to say nothing of psychological effect, would have been lost if a target below 5 per cent had been set. Given the fact that India's population is growing at an increasing rate, the 5 per cent rate, adjusted for such a population growth, certainly does not constitute an ambitious target. And it is important to stress, in this time of mobilization and preparation for a Third Plan, that something which builds further to a 6 or 7 per cent rate of growth is not at all an unrealistic point of departure for a country with India's resources of leadership and its significance in the world.

I think that we should simply accept these high targets as realistic, and then proceed to look at the resource side. Creating a 5 or 6 per cent rate of increase is primarily a technical problem. In economics we speak of it as the problem of the level of the capital coefficient, or the capital-output ratio. For various reasons the Second Five Year Plan envisaged an investment input of $12 or $13 billion. This, it seems to me, was optimistic, so optimistic as to be unrealistic. Investment requirements—the hard requirement, technically determined for achievement of a realistic 5 per cent target—should rather have been of an order of magnitude of $15 or $16 billion. At any rate, they should have been fixed above the $12 or $13 billion. In considerable measure, India's present inability to achieve the targets set arises from this technical proposition. The optimistic estimates on the investment inputs spilled over into requests for assistance from abroad which were less than they might have been if the input target had been formulated at what I would consider a more realistic level.

Some measure of the conservativeness of the Indian assessment is found in the very fact that the targets—for foreign aid, foreign loans, and other kinds of imports that would not be financed out of India's current production—were set at something like $2 to $2½ billion in the Second Plan. This target significantly understated the scope of possible foreign assistance. The technical requirements were for larger investment. This is simply a realistic consequence of the growth process. It is within this notion of a bigger program—not bigger targets, but an appreciation of bigger requirements to arrive at the necessary targets—that we should approach the resources problem for the Third Plan, and for the remainder of our association with India in its effort of economic growth.

Noted economist *Gardiner C. Means*, a former consultant to the Committee for Economic Development, author of *The Structure of the American Economy* and co-author (with A. A. Berle, Jr.) of *The Modern Corporation and Private Property*, believes that the Second Plan targets proved to be too high only in the sense that the United States failed to provide a proper level of aid. Offering his own estimate of the three major priorities in Indian planning, he praises the Indians for realism on most counts and foresees eventual dividends in the Second Plan's emphasis on heavy industry.

Gardiner C. Means. When the Indian Second Plan was being developed and was published in preliminary form, I read it very carefully and was intensely interested. I spent about a month in India —traveling around and having talks with the chief author of the

Plan, Dr. P. C. Mahalanobis, and the other economists associated with it.

I reached the conclusion that it was an outstandingly good job and that the chances of its success were high. I saw one major weakness in the plan—the heavy reliance on external capital and foreign exchange. If they could get the external capital, then I thought the plan could be met in its essentials. Also, if they could not get the needed foreign exchange by that method but had unusually good harvests, there would be some room for export of grain, rice, and so forth, which could bring in some exchange and make up for less external capital; but that was only if they had unusually good weather conditions. The third possibility was that neither of those could develop and the plan would have to be slowed down. Well, the third of these has turned out to be the case, but I think personally it is our own fault as a country that they did not get as much capital as the plan required.

Now, three priorities struck me very strongly in the plan. One was the high emphasis on heavy industry. Was this justified? Dr. Mahalanobis' position was that the level of living in countries throughout the world could be correlated to a high degree with the amount of steel they produced and, therefore, economic progress depended on having a rapidly growing steel industry. Statistically, he was correct, but I do not believe that lack of a high output of steel would mean that a country could not greatly increase its level of living. On the other hand, I fully agreed with him insofar as India was concerned. India has an outstandingly good supply of high-grade iron ore and coking coal lying close together and steel is a natural product for India. Also, progress in an economy depends very much on developing skill in the making of machines. Building up the steel industry and the machine tool industry—the heavy industries—would give a solid base even though it meant using a great deal of capital without immediate results. It was one of those cases where postponing the production of goods wanted immediately would pay terrific dividends in the future potential of the country. Maybe the Mahalanobis statistics and my theoretical analysis here are really saying the same thing. We both reached the same conclusion—that India's major drive on the heavy goods industries is appropriate.

The second priority that struck me is really an antipriority. India being a country in which capital expansion is a major problem due to the limited supply of savings, the problem of housing becomes crucial. In order to get a better house now you have to pay *now* for the housing which is still useful thirty or forty years from now. If you produce an extra billion dollars' worth of food and clothing a year, the level of living can immediately go up a billion dollars' worth. But a billion dollars' worth of housing will increase the current level of living by only a thirtieth or a fortieth of that amount in any one year. India's problem was to avoid new housing just as much as this was possible. So the antipriority here was to develop industry in a way that did not require relocation of population to any greater extent than was necessary. India has carried this to a very interesting extent in the case of bicycles, which are a major method of local transport. They have broken up the production of bicycle parts, having one village, one community, producing one part and another community producing another part. They farm out the production of the various parts and then bring them together for assembly—just the way the Swiss make watches, or many producers combine to make automobiles here.

This method has the great advantage of using the housing facilities that are already there and postpones or perhaps eliminates the necessity of absorbing capital in relocating people.

That brings me to my third priority, which has puzzled a great many people. The Second Plan called for a very considerable expansion in cotton cloth production. More than two-thirds of that expansion was to be through hand weaving. Now to an American textile expert that sounds just plain shocking. Well, I happen to be somewhat of a textile expert myself. I know a lot about both power and hand weaving. My wife and I took a trip around the world and in each country we visited I examined both hand-weaving and power-weaving mills with the idea of trying to establish the dividing line at which it becomes cheaper to weave by hand than by power. If you pay ten cents a week wages for a hand weaver and the same wages to the power weaver, it is quite obvious that it is cheaper to weave by hand than by power. Likewise, if you pay twenty dollars a week to each weaver, it is obvious that it is cheaper to weave by power. Somewhere between there is a break-even point.

After examining both power and hand weaving in Japan, Thailand, Burma, Indonesia, and India I came to the conclusion that somewhere around two dollars a week wages was the break-even point with the looms that were generally in use in India, and that the Indians could probably increase the efficiency on the hand looms they had by 50 to 75 per cent and raise the break-even point to maybe three dollars. Since the prevailing incomes of weavers in much of India were at or below two dollars a week, the emphasis that the Second Plan placed on hand weaving makes sense to me.

On the other hand, the emphasis they put on hand spinning did not make sense. Power spinning is many times more efficient than hand spinning. As you know, Mahatma Gandhi placed great emphasis on hand spinning, and so hand spinning has important psychological meaning for the Indian leaders. Because a hand spinner with a single spindle is very slow, they have tried to develop a hand spinning machine with four spindles—the *ambar charka*. I went down to Poona where they had one of these machines and they operated it for me. But even quadruple output from hand spinning is very inefficient. The Indians, with great realism, have already cut the plans for hand-spun yarn in half and I suspect they will cut it further. Power spinning is likely to take the place of hand spinning quite soon, while hand weaving continues to be economical for some little time.

Hand weaving has a further advantage when capital is scarce and labor is in surplus. Hand looms can be made locally with little capital expense. Power looms would usually have to be imported. Also, from the broad social viewpoint, there is real value in continuing the hand weaving when there is a great surplus of labor. If India can postpone the transfer from hand weaving to power weaving for another eight or ten years, by that time they will be able to make their own looms. Instead of importing thousands of dollars' worth of machinery, they will build it themselves. This alone would give ample justification for the emphasis on hand weaving.

I emphasize these three priorities in the Second Plan in order to bring out some of the problems of planning and points at which I think the Indians have made some very wise decisions.

MOBILIZING DOMESTIC RESOURCES

Place four of India's ranking fiscal spokesmen around a table to assess what they have done—and should be doing—to mobilize domestic resources, and their discussion inevitably reflects the poles of disagreement found within the governments of most developing countries on the issue of deficit financing. *P. S. N. Prasad* is Assistant Director of Technical Operations in the World Bank; *B. N. Adarkar* serves as a Director of the International Monetary Fund, with *I. G. Patel* as his Alternate; and *H. V. R. Iengar*, one of India's senior civil servants (a former Secretary of the Home and Commerce Ministries), has been Governor of the Reserve Bank of India since 1955. Mr. Iengar's is perhaps the most explicit official recognition on record that there are significant taxable internal resources which India has been unable to mobilize for domestic political reasons.

P. S. N. Prasad.   During the First Five Year Plan the problem of the mobilization of resources was rather easy for two reasons. First, the dimension of the effort was small. In the First Five Year Plan the total investment over five years was just a little over 19 billion rupees, compared with about 45 in the Second Plan. At that time we were helped partly by the circumstance of the Korean War which improved India's terms of trade with the rest of the world. The prices of commodities such as jute and cotton shot up, owing to the demands of war, and an alert government was able to skim the excess profits resulting from this trade into its revenues in this period. We also changed the monetary policy of the Reserve Bank of India by an upward adjustment of the bank rate, thereby creating an atmosphere of monetary stringency which helped to prepare for the increased measure of investment that was to follow during the five-year period. For that reason, we closed the plan accounts fairly satisfactorily. Roughly, the amount of external assistance needed to carry out the First Plan was $450 million. Deficit financing was limited to just a little over 4 billions out of the total investment of over 19 billion rupees.

Then came the Second Plan with about 45 billion rupees over the five-year period. When we came to the Second Plan period we directed efforts both toward increasing the limit of taxation, the variety of taxes imposed on the community, as well as toward obtaining more savings through direct market loans, small and big.

Various new taxes have been imposed; the rates of duty on all taxes have been increased. In the earlier stages the states have been somewhat lax and were dragging their feet, but now latterly even they have started moving forward, so that the amount of money mobilized through taxation and borrowing has been increased substantially over this period. Looking at tax revenues, for example, compared with 7.5 billion rupees raised during the First Plan, nearly ten has been the contribution during the Second. And the market loans which amounted to a total of about 6 billion rupees for the First Plan are estimated to yield a little over 10 billions for the Second Plan period. In fiscal 1955-1956 we raised about 820 million rupees by way of market loans and about 666 million by way of small loans. That amount went up by fiscal 1958-1959 to about 2500 millions in market loans and about 750 millions in small loans. This mobilization has not substantially interfered yet with the rate of private investment, at least in the industrial sector, as evidenced by the fact that even while this mobilization was going on we also experienced a large boom in the private sector in the first two or three years of the Second Plan period. It is clear that we have not starved the private sector in order to feed the public sector, and that both have substantially stepped up their contribution compared to what it was in the First Plan period.

But having said that, of course, I would be giving a very wrong impression if I went on to suggest that the investment could all be met by domestic resources. Even at the end of the Plan period we started to realize that the short-fall of resources was increasing; that the amount of deficit finance was increasing; that the amount that was necessary to cover the external gap was increasing; and that our external reserves in the shape of sterling balances were disappearing very rapidly. That is to say, the total impact of the Second Plan on our resources, as reflected in all these ways, was much larger than had been anticipated in the early plan period. Although we have been able, in the case of the Second Plan period, to achieve a considerable stepping up of the resource mobilization effort, the stepping up has not anywhere been in proportion to the increase in the size of the investment. That ought not really to surprise anybody—though some of us were surprised when it came out that way—for the very simple reason that on a per capita income of a little over $55 or $56, the amount that you could mobilize is really not very large. Though we have been scraping down to the bottom of the barrel there simply is not much in the barrel to scrape.

The limit is soon reached and beyond that point the Plan must be carried out by rough deficit financing or assistance from external sources. Yet deficit financing as a means of development is, in the final analysis, a method of compulsion, imposing such compulsion in an indirect fashion as against the totalitarian compulsion of directly depriving people of what they otherwise would normally consume. The crux of the dilemma of democratic planning is that it lacks the means to compel people to consume less, as a totalitarian economy would, and therefore beyond a certain point compulsion in a democracy has to be indirect. The way it is imposed is through what is known as deficit financing. This is at best a crude method, at all times an unfair method, and *beyond a certain point* is bound to be a frustrating method, because through the inflation that it generates it destroys the very basis of progress that is sought to be achieved in the field of economic growth. Therefore, ultimately it comes to this—that if India's rate of progress is to be kept up at the rate at which it has to be kept up there is no alternative in the Third and the Fourth Five Year Plans but to seek the resources for development in a larger and larger measure from external sources.

B. N. Adarkar. Mr. Prasad has described deficit financing as a form of compulsion, as a frustrating and destructive method. I am not going to start on a theoretical defense of this very unorthodox method of financing which the Government of India has had to resort to during the first two Five Year plans. But I shall attempt to present some facts and figures as to what role deficit financing has actually played in India's Five Year Plans.

What is deficit financing? The term has been variously interpreted, but as a practical guide to policy it is best defined with reference at once to the consequences that we wish to avoid, and the purposes that we wish to achieve. Deficit financing is understood in India to denote the amount of finance which government obtains by way of borrowing from the Reserve Bank of India, and by way of drawing down its cash balances with the Reserve Bank of India. This particular definition of deficit financing underscores the possible inflationary impact which deficit financing could have because both these operations—borrowing from the Reserve Bank of India, and drawing down of government cash balances with the Reserve Bank—have one effect, namely, to add to the money supply that is available to the community. Whenever there is an increase in money supply there is the presumption of possible disequilibrium between money supply and the flow of goods leading to inflation. Another way of defining deficit financing is by taking into account the net indebtedness of the government to the bank system as a whole—that is to say, by taking into account not only what government borrows from the Reserve Bank of India, but also from the commercial banks.

Now one alternative to deficit financing is obviously to keep down the rate of investment, to do what would be possible from the resources available from other sources. The other alternative, of course, is to maintain the rate of investment, but to try to obtain the required resources from taxation and borrowing from the public. Both these alternatives have their limitations. Increased taxation would have had the undesirable consequence, beyond a certain point, of destroying incentives, as Mr. Prasad points out. A plan has to go ahead both in the public sector and in the private sector. The private sector has a very important role to play in the success of the plan. And for it to play that role, it is necessary to maintain incentives, to maintain the buoyancy of the economic system. If taxation comes to a halt at a certain point, it is because of the government's desire not to destroy this buoyancy of the private sector. Deficit financing, therefore, is a device by which the government seeks to raise the necessary resources without destroying the incentives which are necessary for all around economic progress.

It is said that deficit financing leads to an increase in money supply. It surely does. It is also said that deficit financing does not add to the real resources at your disposal. Both statements have an element of truth. But both cannot be regarded as decisive in coming to a judgment on this matter. The statement that deficit financing does not add to real resources is, in the last analysis, a cliché. It is only half true. To the extent that deficit financing helps to maintain incentives, and thereby facilitates the growth of production in the private sector, it does really add to real resources. It does not by itself do that. Deficit financing involves extension of credit by the banking system to government. But the banks also extend credit, indeed create credit, for the private sector. Insofar as credit creation for the private sector supplies genuine capital needs, it facilitates the functioning of the economy and the growth of output. And if that kind of credit creation facilitates the growth of output in the private sector, the same happens when credit is created to finance expansion of output in the public sector. It all depends on what use is made of the credit. Deficit financing does add to money supply in the same way that credit created for the private sector adds to the money supply. That, to be sure, might possibly bring about a lack of balance between money supply and output and to that extent generate inflationary pressures.

Let us look, however, at the facts of the Indian situation. So far as the First Plan was concerned, the Government of India had to resort to deficit financing to the extent of 4.2 billion rupees. What was the effect on the money supply? The money supply increased only by 2 billion rupees. Why did this happen? It happened because, while bank credit to the government sector was increasing, certain changes were taking place in the credit extended by the banking system to the private sector. Certain changes were also taking place in the external position of the country. Although deficit financing by government was 4.2 billion rupees, the actual credit from the banking system to the government was only 2.7 billion rupees.

Only .46 billion rupees was added to the money supply as a result of the extension of credit to the private sector. Simultaneously there was a decline in foreign exchange reserves of the country to the extent of 1.4 billion rupees, and this is a contractionary factor. As the result of these various offsetting elements—the decline in external reserves, the restriction of credit to the private sector—the actual increase in money supply was only 2 billion rupees, or only 10 per cent of the money supply at the beginning of the period. As against that, the real output increased by 18 per cent during the First Plan, and prices actually declined. Now the same sort of thing happened again in the Second Five Year Plan. As a result of the various counteracting factors—restriction of credit to the private sector, the decline in the external assets of the country (which bring in real resources and provide an anti-inflationary element)— money supply has been going up only 5 per cent a year, whereas the real output of the country is also increasing by 4 per cent a year. Consequently, there is not anything like a serious imbalance between the growth of money supply and the growth of real output, and prices have been kept well under control.

I. G. Patel. There is a certain general, classical way in which one thinks and says: "Here is credit creation; This leads to high prices, which makes exports less competitive and imports more attractive, so that we have a balance of payments deficit." That is the sense in which one hears it said so often, that balance of payments deficits are an indication of inflation. Now I suggest in all earnestness that this is not the essence of what has been happening during the last two or three years in India. There has been no significant internal price rise leading to exports being priced out. All that has happened essentially is that because of the large requirements of machinery imports for the projects in the public sector, the government has to obtain the required foreign exchange by external assistance or by the use of the foreign exchange reserves held by the Central Bank—the latter being done by giving government securities (the so-called deficit financing) to the Central Bank in return for the foreign exchange. Thus the budget deficit is directly translated into a balance of payments deficit without affecting the internal economy. This is not a case of inflationary pressures raising prices and raising demands with larger imports coming in and exports being shut out.

I am not suggesting that there is no balance of payment problem. But imagine for a moment that instead of what it has done— borrowing from the Reserve Bank to pay for the foreign exchange for importing machinery—the government had raised all this money to buy the exchange from the Central Bank by internal taxation. If taxation were much higher and the nature and size of the development program exactly the way it is, do you seriously believe that the balance of payments deficit would have been significantly smaller? That is exactly the point I was making when I said earlier that for achieving an independent economy, you need not only the equation of savings with investment but—and especially if you want this equation at a high enough level of savings and investment—you need also a broad-based economy which enables you to avoid bottlenecks leading to payments difficulties. And today, not having that broad-based economy, if we had a certain kind of program, we would experience balance of payment difficulties irrespective of the manner in which we tried to raise resources internally.

H. V. R. Iengar. It is curious how the subjective political factor comes into the assessment of purely economic problems. There are some people in our country today who very genuinely, honestly feel that the less we depend on foreign assistance, the better for the country. And from that they jump in their calculations to the conclusion that it is possible for us to do without a good deal of foreign assistance. Well, whatever some of the economists might think, so far as the Prime Minister himself and the members of the Cabinet are concerned, they are not subject to any political inhibitions on the size of the foreign assistance that might be required for the Third Five Year Plan. What they are concerned with primarily is to see that the Third Five Year Plan is a success. This means that we cannot make the same mistake that we made in the Second Five Year Plan in underestimating the total size of the Plan and underestimating the total size of the external assistance required.

Much is said about deficit financing. We have to deal with this as a practical proposition. We are basing our policy in India on the advice given to us by the International Monetary Fund Mission headed by Dr. Edward Bernstein, that to some extent deficit financing is necessary but that there are practical limitations to this, and the matter can be judged only as you go along. I see no reason for taking the view that Mr. Prasad did. To condemn deficit financing—I think he used the word "frustrating"—well, it's nothing of the sort. He would agree, I hope, that the only question is the practical one as to what are the safe limits. Up to now we have indulged in what the theoretical economists hitherto thought to be pretty dangerous limits, but I think we have gotten away with it. The behavior of the price level in India, both of the wholesale price index and the working-class cost of living has been astonishingly good. Rest assured that we are fully aware of the dangers of just printing currency notes for the purpose of financing development, that we are constantly aware of this problem, but that we have no dogmatic approach.

The critical and the real problem is this: If you have a plan of $20 billion dimensions, and if it is assumed that the foreign exchange component of this is, shall we say, 25 per cent, how are we going to raise the other 75 per cent? Fundamentally the job has got to be done by *us*. And it is quite impossible for us to contemplate the Third Plan without a tremendous internal effort in raising resources. A good part of the balance of the resources required will have to come from taxation, from savings and the rest, and only a small portion, a relatively small portion, from deficit financing.

Now here our main problem is really political. Even as you have your political difficulties, we are suffering from certain inhibitions which are a throwback from our political past. It was suggested to the Finance Minister some time ago that one of the ways by which taxation could be raised in the country would be by imposing a salt tax. This would be a universal tax. The incidence by head of population could be extremely small and would hardly be noticed, but we could get a fair amount of money out of this tax. He ruled it out in one sentence. He said, "Mahatma Gandhi was against this tax." Now he was perfectly right in this respect, that the idea of a salt tax raises in the minds of the public, and the minds of the Parliament, all kinds of political associations which would make such a tax really rather offensive. It was the symbol which Mahatma Gandhi used in his political fight against the British. He wanted to pick some symbol in order to rally the people 'round, and so he picked out the salt tax as a symbol because the British government in those days imposed a salt tax on everybody. Even poor people living on the seacoast could not make a few pounds of salt without having to pay a tax to the government. So he singled out that tax, and he fought for the abolition of the salt tax. And, in fact, in 1932, when I was a District Magistrate in one of the districts on the west coast of India, it was my unfortunate job to arrest one of the political leaders there for an offense against the salt tax. What he did was, he gave me notice—that was the way in which the fight was conducted against the British government, of which I was one of the limbs—he gave notice to say that he was going to defy the salt tax. And how was he going to do it? He was going to the coast. He was going to pick up some salt and say "I am going to use this in my house" and "I will not pay a tax to the government." That being an offense, I was supposed to have him arrested, and have him sent to the "jug" for a couple of years. But I went along with him because he was a very important leader in our district.

Well, he collected some rather dirty-looking muck from near the sea. Then I turned toward the police inspector and we had a discussion as to whether there was any salt in this mud. The police inspector said—he scratched his head—he said, "I don't really think so." Then the Congress leader said, "Let's march along another few yards and look at something a little more likely." So he picked up another little bit of mud and said, "What about this?" The inspector said, "Well, if you picked it up and said, 'I am going to use it in my house,' then I think I could arrest you." He said, "Right!" and picked it up, and he was arrested. And he was sent to the "jug" for two years. I mention this simply to show the political history and the emotional reactions that are associated with what should today be regarded as very practical fiscal problems. It will take us a little time to get over these emotional reactions.

Take land revenue. Everybody who owns land in the country has to pay a tax, whether he holds two acres or a hundred acres or even a tenth of an acre. Some of our peasants own as little as a tenth of an acre. A peasant may have to pay one rupee or two rupees, but he does have to pay a tax. There is no minimum limit. Now, this tax is now out of date in its incidence. The tax was initiated many, many years ago. Since then prices have risen, and there is every justification for increasing this tax. But the governors have not done it yet. They are afraid of doing it, for the simple reason that this also carries emotional political implications. The first great fight against the British government, even before the salt tax, was about the assessment of land revenue in a certain district in Bombay. Nevertheless, in recent discussions that have taken place in the Congress Party it has been explicitly stated that as one of the measures for increasing internal resources the government must seriously consider matters such as the increase of land revenue. I think it will take us some time before we get down to the salt tax, but I think this business of land revenue will be more quickly solved.

In connection with the necessity for certain tax increases there are also quite contemporary political problems. The Communists in the country have been watching the situation closely. They have no responsibility and they are free to criticize. Recently we began levying what we call a "betterment tax" in the Punjab. That is to say, when canal water is brought into a region the value of land goes up. There is, therefore, no justification why the farmer should not contribute some portion of the cost of bringing canal water into his region. But when the Punjab government started this betterment levy the Communists conducted a serious agitation against it only about two months ago. The general point I want to make is that it is possible for us, although extremely difficult politically, to raise more internal resources through a combination of direct taxes like land revenue, and indirect levies such as excises along with, say, increased railway fares. We just have to do it or the Third Plan will simply have to fold up. There is no alternative.

HOW MUCH FOREIGN ASSISTANCE?

Whether one settles for Mr. Prasad's assurance that there is little to scrape at the bottom of the barrel or joins with Governor Iengar in the belief that the bottom has yet to be reached, the crucial fact remains that a much greater influx of outside resources is a prerequisite for Indian development. Even if India should find political devices consistent with the politics of consent for increasing, let us say, agricultural taxation, the Iengar analysis still assumes that 25 per cent of the resources for development must come from abroad. And in any case, argues *Max F. Millikan*, Director of the Center for International Studies at the Massachusetts Institute of Technology and a former Deputy Director of the Central Intelligence Agency, India's increased mobilization of her own resources is not an unmixed blessing. Too much stringency can discourage domestic private investment. Adequate outside aid channeled in particular to the public sector—"$5 or $6, not $2 or $3 billion" for the Third Plan—offers the special virtue of assuring maximum application of domestic resources to the task of development.

Max F. Millikan. It all depends on the way you interpret the data. I should like to state two paradoxes about external assistance. These bear on the relation between the public and the private sector in the Indian economy.

The first proposition I would like to assert is that a larger volume of external assistance is necessary in order to make possible the full mobilization of Indian domestic resources. Normally we tend to think of setting a target for total capital, and we ask how can we divide this between domestically supplied capital and foreign capital; quite frequently, the way the computation is carried out is to say first what is the full output in India and then what proportion of this can we expect the Indians to save, with the balance being what we require for external assistance. I think this is an unreal way of performing the exercise. In fact, if you perform the exercise in this way you are likely to come up with an understatement of the requirements for foreign capital.

The second of my paradoxes is that extensive foreign support for the public sector is in India a necessary condition, indeed, for expanded foreign private investment.

To get at the reason for these two paradoxes let us look at the public-private sector problem without the usual reference to ideological considerations. This is essentially a technical problem. There are certain kinds of activity which the Indians have decided will be in the public sector. In my view they have made this decision correctly. I do not believe that the kinds of activity they are trying to promote in the public sector of the Indian economy would or could be effectively promoted by the private sector. This is a matter for dispute, but I want to set that up as an assumption to begin with. Now I believe that the kinds of activities that are being carried forward for the public sector under the Second Five Year Plan and proposed under the Third Plan, and the kinds of activity that it is hoped will be carried forward in the private sector are complementary and not competitive. It is my conviction that unless the public sector investment is maintained at a very substantial level—unless activity in both heavy industry and in public social overhead is maintained at an adequate level—the private sector is going to be depressed. This is so for two reasons—first, because it is going to be unable to secure the basic resources needed in the way of inputs of services, power, transport, and of essential raw materials; and, second, because of the interactions on the demand side of an adequate level of activity in the public sector resulting from an inadequate level of public purchasing power for private sector activities.

On the other hand, if attention is concentrated too exclusively on the public sector there are going to be similar difficulties. If attempts are made to mobilize from the private sector a very large volume of resources for public sector investment by taxation and other means, the incentives which are required for adequate levels of activity in the private sector are going to be very seriously endangered. And if there is not balance in these two sectors, then the economy will not move forward. We have seen some evidence of this recently in the agricultural economy in a very large development recently of large irrigation projects. There has been, according to Deputy Chairman V. T. Krishnamachari of the Planning Commission, some deficit in the volume of small-scale private investment in agriculture needed to make use of the water made available in these large-scale irrigation projects. Small channels have to be dug; the farmer has to put in an investment of his own resources in order to make effective use of the water that is made available by these large-scale public investments. The same sort of thing can be illustrated in area after area of the economy. Now, the final fact that has to be held in mind before we have demonstrated our paradoxes is that the required ratio of investment in the public sector is very much higher as a proportion of total investment than the ratio of total incomes that are generated in the public as against the private sector. When total national income is divided into publicly directed and privately directed activities the public sector accounts for only about 10 per cent of the Indian economy and the private sector accounts for about 90 per cent. In the Second Plan investment targets, on the other hand, the public sector investments were planned at about 61 per cent. As a matter of fact the private sector did substantially better, relatively speaking, than the public sector.

Looking forward to the Third Plan, what can be inferred from these public-private relationships? If you simply try to mobilize from Indian resources the capital necessary for Indian development, this will require major transfer of savings from the private to the public sector. Such a transfer of savings will require very heavy levels either of taxation or of deficit financing, thus producing inflation and cutting down consumption, or of levies of various kinds on private savings. Some calculations have been made by some Indian economists about the volume of external resources that would be required to finance the Third Plan on the assumption that the Plan is established at approximately a $20 billion level of investment. These calculations were made essentially on the assumption that there was no problem of transferring resources between public and private sectors. In other words, you could assume a total aggregate level of Indian investment out of Indian domestic product and you could assume that whatever proportion of this it was necessary to transfer from the private to the public sector could easily be transferred. And you could assume further that the only requirement for external resources was a requirement for specific kinds of goods that cannot be produced in India, goods that must, therefore, be purchased from abroad. On this basis, out of this $20 billion investment level, it was believed that the requirement for net foreign assistance over and above what could be purchased with exports would be at about $2 billion over the whole Second Plan.

Now this I believe to be a gross underestimate. I believe that if the effort is made to make this major transfer of domestic Indian resources from the private to the public sector the incentive effects are going to be such that aggregate Indian output is going to be reduced substantially below the sort of full-effort figure which was used in these basic calculations in the first place. Moreover, I believe that investment in the private sector is likely to be depressed to a point where the balance required between the kinds of activity pursued in the private sector and the kinds of activity pursued in the public sector would be destroyed. A larger volume of public services and of heavy industrial goods will be produced than will be absorbable by the balance of the economy unless the level of investment is maintained in the private sector at a high level.

This, I think, gives an explanation of my two paradoxes. I believe that a larger volume of foreign assistance will be required. My rough view is that at a minimum, for a $20 billion investment program, compared roughly with the $12 billion of the Second Plan, the correct figure for foreign assistance is very much closer to $5 or $6 billion of external capital to be supplied than to $2 or $3 billion. I believe that it will be necessary to have this volume of foreign capital coming in to reach the $20 billion level. I think, indeed, that a somewhat higher level of foreign capital assistance might permit an even higher level of domestic Indian capital formation.

If the public sector must be promoted at the levels indicated by the Indian government—and I would agree with them that it *does* need to be so promoted, for technical reasons—then I think it is clearly in the public sector that foreign capital is most urgently needed in order to maintain the buoyancy in the private sector, in order to avoid the kinds of measures for capturing private savings which would be required if the foreign sources of capital for the public sector were not available. My conclusion is, in short, that a liberal policy on the part of capital-supplying countries with respect to the public sector is likely to do more to promote the buoyancy of the private sector and is, in fact, likely to do more in the long run to promote foreign private investment in India than a policy of attempting to force foreign capital into the private sector from this side.

Throughout the Third Five Year Plan, *Geoffrey Wilson* reminds us, India will start off $380 million poorer each year than in the Second Plan.

In getting down to specifics on the scope of an adequate aid program, one must first take into account the gap left by the exhaustion, for all practical purposes, of the British-held sterling balances drawn during the Second Plan—and go on from there. Mr. Wilson is Deputy Director of the United Kingdom Treasury and Supply Delegation in Washington and Alternate Director for the United Kingdom of the World Bank.

Geoffrey Wilson. How has the foreign exchange part of the Second Plan been financed? It has been financed very largely by the running down of what we in the United Kingdom call the sterling balances, and what in India are commonly known as the sterling reserves. The United Kingdom emerged from the war owing India something in the region of $2 billion in payment for goods and services which the Indians had provided for allied forces in India during the war. That $2 billion was banked in London and was payable on demand. The limitations on the drawing down of the money at any excessive rate were partly that the Indians very wisely wanted to keep it for the development programs they saw ahead, and also that any sudden removal of $2 billion would have broken the bank. The result was that these balances were used modestly up to 1955. By the end of 1955 about $500 million had been drawn.

It was with the beginning of the Second Plan—from 1956 to the middle of 1958—that we began to repay our debts to India, and India began to use its reserves in London in a very big way. Fortunately at that time the United Kingdom was in a position to repay this amount of indebtedness. Now sterling balances were used not only for purchases in the United Kingdom, but also, at the option of the Indian government, for purchases in the United States, Germany, and Japan. From 1956 to the middle of 1958 the balances fell to something rather under $400 million and just about touched rock bottom. Over a period of two and a half to three years, that is to say, they fell by $1.1 billion or at the rate of $360 million a year. And it was in the middle of 1958, when the reserves had reached rock bottom, that the World Bank convened in Washington the meeting of the United States, Canada, Germany, Japan, and the United Kingdom, to see what steps could be taken to deal with the situation.

What we were confronted with then was the short-term question of how necessary imports for the remainder of the Second Plan period from mid-1958 to 1961 were to be financed. The scheme that was drawn up mainly took the form of credits to finance contracts which had already been placed, or were shortly to be placed in the future. As for the Third Plan and beyond, however, the fact that sticks out a mile from this recital is that the sterling balances, the Indian reserves, are no longer there to draw on for the purpose of financing development. Therefore, quite apart from any increase in foreign exchange expenditure in the Third Plan, the problem is how to fill the gap of $380 million a year which the Indians have hitherto financed from drawing on their balances.

Leon H. Keyserling speaks of a flow of $15 billion per year from the United States to the developing countries in public and private capital and *Hubert Humphrey* emphasizes that aid "is a continuing task which will not be finished next year or even the year after or the year after that."

Leon H. Keyserling.   I think it is true, as said frequently, that the free world is thus far losing ground in the Cold War, whether you define that Cold War—and this is partly a matter of semantics—as a struggle against poverty or a struggle against something else. And the basic reason why we are losing ground is, first and foremost, that the resources of the free world are not being adequately applied to the struggle; instead, we are applying only a level of effort which is beating the frail wings of inadequacy against the granite hardness and massive strength of the increasing totalitarian effort.

When we were in World War II, we didn't try to fight that war by recruiting our Olympic teams or a group of sharpshooters. We knew that, in addition to a good quality army, we needed to have a large enough army, a large enough complement of massive forces to do the job. And this is equally true of the peacetime struggle.

Taking private and public capital together, we have been exporting about $3 billion worth of capital a year during the last few years. Apportioned among the one billion people of whom we have been talking in the underdeveloped parts of the free world, this is about $3 a year per capita. If this were apportioned on the basis of 40 per cent to India, which is about 40 per cent of the free world, it would be only a little more than $1 billion a year, or about $2.50 a year per capita for the people of India. To be sure, this capital outlay could not be spread over the whole population; it would be concentrated in the development of capital equipment and related areas. Nonetheless, we in the United States are investing in producers' durable equipment alone about $150 per capita per year. And I am firmly convinced that $3 a year per capita, or $2 a year per capita, or $4 a year per capita, flowing from the free world to the underdeveloped areas, will not prevent the gradual —and I say this advisedly and maybe irrationally—the gradual development of a situation within our lifetimes when most of the world could be brought predominantly under the programs, under the ideology, if not under the flag, of the totalitarian states.

I would say, roughly speaking, that we ought to be moving toward a goal in the next few years of $15 billion a year of capital export from the United States to the underdeveloped parts of the world, divided approximately into a public flow two or three times what it has been recently, and the balance or larger amount in private capital flow.

In this connection I should refer briefly first to the question of the absorptive capacity of the free underdeveloped nations. I think it rather strange that we Americans, with our dynamic sense of what can be done, should wonder whether the underdeveloped portions of the world can absorb $3 worth of capital import per capita per year. I think that, if we conduct the program on a tentative basis, if we make others feel that they are merely the recipients of embarrassing surpluses which we temporarily have, if we make them feel that this aid is accompanied by other strings which should not be attached, then free and aspiring peoples will hope that they will quickly reach the stage where they will not need to "absorb" anything. But if we conduct these programs with practical magnanimity, and if we apply anywhere near the efforts which we applied to the fighting of a different kind of war, anywhere near the organizing skills, anywhere near the managerial abilities, then there are almost no limits to what can be absorbed usefully and for mutually beneficial purposes.

Another point, frequently raised, involves the capacity of our economy to stand the costs. And there I must take some very slight issue with the eloquence of Barbara Ward. Barbara Ward is more discerning than most economists, until she comes to reside for awhile among the economists in the United States. And then, beginning to imbibe some of their "wisdom," she begins to talk about whether we need to give up two packages of cigarettes a week in order to do what we need to do in the world. In fact, the fan-

tastic moral and economic challenge to the United States is not
that we have to ration scarcity in order to help other parts of the
free world and to work with them. We are faced, rather, by a
challenge of abundance. We are failing to do what we need to do
at home and abroad, not because we would have to sacrifice more
of our material enjoyments, but rather because we are committing
the abysmal economic default of not mobilizing our full material
strength.

Just to take a simple example. If, over the next six years, we were
to grow at the rate of which we are easily capable—according, for
example, to the Rockefeller Report—we would have about $400
billion more of national production for the period as a whole than
we are likely to have if we repeat the very low-growth experience
of the last few years. A $15 billion level of capital export, private
and public, from the United States to these underdeveloped areas
would come on a yearly basis to only a small fraction of the difference between the total productive output which we shall marshal
here in the United States, if we fully mobilize our economic
strength, and our total productive output if we do not.

Hence, the problem is not mainly one of economic capabilities.
It is rather a political problem, in the broad sense of a consensus of
opinion in the United States. I am sympathetic to some degree
with the popular leaders who feel that they should ask for a
quarter of a loaf because it would not be feasible to get more. But
I am not satisfied ultimately with this answer. This answer seems
to me like a euphemistic way of saying that the free world does not
have the political capacities to win a cold struggle; that we must
lose because we can mobilize only after the bombs begin to fall,
which would be far too late. And in the second place, I think that
if the American people were confronted with a program of the
magnitude required to do even the minimum essentials of the job,
they would at least have brought home to them what really needs
to be done and thereby might become more responsive than they
are today.

I think the greatest tragedy we have faced since World War II,
in short, is that we have not in any sense translated the instrumentalities which existed at that time for cooperative action, for
the unification of opinion, for the development of an integrated
program into the service of the immense tasks we face today, that
we have not built the United Nations or some other instrumentality,

or combination of instrumentalities, into a tool which would organize, deploy, and utilize, for the purposes of winning the peace, an amount which, if it were $15 billion from the United States annually, would still be only about one-third of what the United States alone has been mobilizing annually for the purposes of creating military weapons which become obsolete year by year.

We speak of India's Five Year Plan. But in war we never talked just about the British effort, the French effort, the American effort. We talked about the *total* effort. We talked about the fact that we were bound together in a blend of effort, with each putting forward the best within him to win and succeed in the job which needed to be done.

Hubert H. Humphrey. This Conference will go down, I think, in the history of our country as a significant one. It's a sort of people's Bretton Woods and Dumbarton Oaks Conference all at once for a specific purpose. This represents, and I hope the world will note it, people planning; people discussing their mutual problems, friends in honest frank discussion, debates, and then in the process of decision-making. This represents the tone and environment on which our foreign policy decisions should more often be made. What we need in this country more than anything else is not a change in program but a change of heart.

Too often it seems to me that our foreign aid programs have been sold to the American people on the basis of being against communism rather than being for people, and for people that need some help and that deserve it. Now don't misunderstand me. I fully recognize the evil forces of communism, but I'm also of the opinion that when you design programs and policies with a negative attitude of being merely opposed, that within that one action you lose some of the vitality and some of the inspiration of a program which is required. What we seek to do should come naturally out of our own revolutionary heritage, political and spiritual, and out of our own concepts of economic progress and political and social progress. President Truman stated almost eight or nine years ago that "the only kind of a war we seek is that good old-fashioned fight against man's ancient enemies, poverty, disease, hunger, and illiteracy!" I know that's a statement repeated often but it needs to be remembered and it needs to be the basis of action, because you see the real trouble is not so much what the Communists are attempting to do in this world but how much less we are doing than we can and we should do.

Let us recognize that the task of our cooperation with and helping other nations to help themselves is a continuing task which will not be finished next year or even the year after or the year after that. Our struggle against communism, against man's ancient enemies of disease and poverty, will last for generations. So let us prepare accordingly and let other people prepare accordingly on a long-range basis.

KEY ISSUES IN AID PLANNING

The record of United States aid to India to date (see table, page 65) is reviewed by *Hart Perry*, Deputy Director for Loan Operations of the Development Loan Fund. Formerly in private business and in the Bureau of the Budget, Mr. Perry was assigned to the Fund at its inception. His brief concluding statement of the case for long-term financing of the Fund inspires a dissent from *Arthur Smithies*, professor of economics at Harvard and a consultant in 1959 to the President's Committee to Study the Military Assistance Program, headed by Brig. Gen. William L. Draper, Jr.

Hart Perry. The first really great effort as far as the United States government was concerned in extending help to India took place in 1951 when the $190 million India Wheat Loan was adopted by our Congress. This was followed in 1952 and 1953 with the initiation of a program of direct development assistance coupled with a fairly large amount of technical assistance. The development aid in those years ran at about $50 million per year. At the end of 1953, as the plans were taking shape for the fiscal year 1954 program, the retiring administration decided upon a dramatic increase and the budget made provision for a step-up of the aid to a level of nearly $200 million. But the new administration did a complete redo of the budget from stem to stern, and as you know most governmental programs were cut back—the foreign aid program along with the others. This meant a fairly drastic cut in the amount intended for India. The amount was further reduced because the Congress dealt rather harshly with the aid program. The amount of development aid for India came out at $65 million.

Beginning in the fiscal years 1958 and 1959 new elements were added to the program with the entry of the Development Loan

Fund and the Export-Import Bank into the financing picture. The decision was made in the United States government that henceforth development assistance would be financed on a loan basis through the Export-Import Bank and the Development Loan Fund, and that India was to be one of the major recipients. The Ex-Im selected those projects in which it made sense for the procurement to be in the United States, projects for coal-mining equipment, power, and various kinds of manufacturing equipment and transportation. All the projects financed by Ex-Im and the D.L.F. are in the so-called core of the Second Five Year Plan and largely financed either in capital goods or components of capital goods. The D.L.F. is collaborating with the World Bank in the field of transportation.

All loans that the D.L.F. has so far made are repayable in local currency. The interest varies from 3½ to nearly 6 per cent, depending on the type of project. The maturities vary also with the type of project. These are all government-to-government loans which make available to the Government of India foreign exchange which is then made available for capital goods imports.

Our concern will continue to be, until the completion of the Second Plan, helping the Government of India finance projects that fall within the core. However, we are beginning to handle, or at least examine, transitional projects. These are projects which are being started under this Plan, but will be completed under the next.

In the future we are hopeful that we will be able to change somewhat the basis of our operations in India. Rather than continue to finance exchange for annual periods which is then allocated for various capital goods imports, we would prefer to finance whole projects, the completion of which might very well extend over a period of years. The projects, of course, will be part of their comprehensive development program. For example, we might finance a dam project, or perhaps a large industrial complex, the completion of which would take several years. We would also like to make some loans directly to private businesses in India.

We are delighted to have the opportunity of working with the Government of India in the prosecution of their development programs. We know that to the extent that we have resources they will be one of our major borrowers. But I must point out that we are in the difficult position now of not being able to plan very far ahead because we are on a year-to-year basis with our capital. Intermittently we have been completely out of money. With this great uncertainty as to the amount of resources which will be available to us, it is difficult to be able to indicate even in a general way the extent of our assistance that we will be able to offer in the form of loans in the near future, or over an extended period.

We hope that sometime soon we will be able to get on the long-range basis suggested by the President in his May, 1958, press conference when he agreed to the need for long-range commitments. Perhaps new legislation will increase the resources available to us. This would permit us to engage in better longer-range discussions with the Government of India on the resources which might be made available to them. This in turn would permit them to engage in even more orderly planning than they have so far been able to accomplish.

Arthur Smithies. Somehow it is getting to be an article of faith that long-term financing is necessary for this program. No one would be more delighted than I if a bill to provide a million and a half for the Development Loan Fund on long-term financing went through. I think, however, that there is some peril in nailing our flag too firmly to that particular mast because there is some danger that such a bill will not go through. I do not think one should thereby get the idea that the foreign aid program is inevitably doomed. After all, the Marshall Plan was financed on the basis of annual appropriations. We did have a general declaration of Congress at the beginning that it was a five-year program contemplating a certain amount, but every year the annual process of authorization and appropriation was gone through. This took up a lot of time on the part of everyone, but the program worked, and the program was not doomed by reason of the annual process. It is far more important to have general political support for the program than to have any particular kind of financing. If you do have firm and general support for the program, the kind of financing doesn't matter too much. If you do not have it, no attempts to get long-term financing are likely to do much good.

Perhaps, too, and speaking now as one who has seen something of bureaucracies at work, a little uncertainty is not always a bad thing.

Max F. Millikan.   I certainly agree that we should not pin our flag so firmly to the mast of some particular form of long-term financing that if we find we cannot get it, we abandon the goal altogether. On the other hand, Mr. Smithies' argument that some uncertainty may be a good thing reminds me a little bit of the attitude of my father toward four-wheel brakes when they were first suggested for automobiles back in 1923 or 1924. I have a little the same feeling about long-term financing. He was very much against them because he felt the driver would come to rely on them, and then what would happen if they failed to work? I cannot really feel that it is all that beneficial for us to be that uncertain from year to year.

Long-term financing of economic aid was rejected by Congress in the 1959 defeat of the Senate Foreign Relations Committee proposal for a five-year, $5 billion Development Loan Fund. The effort to give the D.L.F. greater year-to-year assurance of funds continues, and so do annual D.L.F. appropriations ($550 million in 1959 and $550 million in 1960.) Debate on the form United States aid should take raises many complex technical questions. For example, *I. G. Patel* points out that for all the importance of development capital there are other vital areas of the United States aid program with room for improvement and expansion.

I. G. Patel.   Very often the kind of aid that is provided does not take into account the need of countries like India for aid in the form of commodities and materials. There is a tendency to think that since development requires capital and since capital is in short supply, whatever aid or credit is given should only be for financing the purchase of capital goods or machines and equipment. Such an approach creates many difficulties. What a country like India essentially needs is resources to supplement her own resources. I do not say that the present programs entirely rule out assistance for purchasing materials and commodities. Public Law 480 program is a commodity program. We get assistance in the form of commodities from Canada also—not only wheat in their case, but also other commodities such as nickel and some other metals. But aid should be given with as wide a commodity coverage as possible so that it can really begin to operate quickly and effectively at all crucial points in the economy.

Mr. Patel is careful to emphasize, however, that a massive influx of United States commodity assistance, including the present surplus food

and fiber program (P.L. 480), presupposes sensitive Indian fiscal management. The consequences could be inflationary.

I. G. Patel. Far too often undue attention is devoted to the
mobilization of existing resources rather than to the ways and means
of augmenting these resources. Whenever one talks of resources
for the private sector, for example, the first thing that comes to
mind is some finance or refinance corporation. These are necessary
and have a useful role. But they take over, so to speak, only when
the beginning has been made—that is, once the resources are there
and people have saved and are willing to invest. Then, of course,
somebody has to come forward to put these savings together and
try to distribute them in the right channels. But without the basic
savings, all these corporations can be a source of inflation. The
resources of the Industrial Finance Corporation of India come
mainly from the government. It transfers to the private sector the
resources that the government has already raised; but it doesn't
create a resource in itself. The Industrial Credit and Investment
Corporation of India has had at its disposal real resources which it
has obtained from agencies outside India; but in part it also acts
as an agency which transfers to the private sector the resources
already raised by the public sector.

The Refinance Corporation is even more likely to mislead one
into thinking that all the resources it puts at the disposal of the
private sector come out of additional savings. The resources of the
Refinance Corporation, to the extent that they come from P.L. 480
funds, do not really add anything to the resources of the country;
they only put into circulation the local currency already collected
and, so to speak, lying idle. No doubt the initial injection of food
or cotton or what-have-you is an addition of a resource, vital resource, which makes it possible for us to develop further and to
provide additional employment without any inflationary consequences. But when the wheat is sold and the rupees are collected
and then given to the Refinance Corporation, or a similar agency,
you have potentially an act of credit creation. It may be that the
credit creation is justified and that it stimulates production and
employment. It is still credit creation and one must be careful as
to how much credit one creates out of all these different pockets
and to whom one grants the power of credit creation.

Even the banks, to the extent of their participation with the Refinance Corporation, do not necessarily create real resources. They are able to do so only to the extent that there is a safe margin for this kind of credit creation in an expanding economy. Clearly, while there is genuine need for financial or credit institutions, we should not fall into the error of recommending a mere multiplication of institutions without equal emphasis on how exactly these institutions are going to find the resources. Too much preoccupation with institutions might lead us to neglect the basic aspects of the problem of resources.

The debate over the form of aid turns on capital versus commodity aid and then, in the case of development capital, on annual or long-term financing—which reflects, in turn, significant differences concerning the relative merits of over-all ("balance of payments" or "resources gap") aid as against assistance earmarked for designated development projects. The Development Loan Fund was established on the premise that the "project" approach, allowing no doubt as to where aid monies were going, gave the greatest promise of businesslike aid management.

Geoffrey Wilson.   In England, as you know, during Marshall Plan days, American aid was on a balance of payments basis and not on a project basis. But for highly commendable publicity purposes in this country there are great virtues in a project basis. You can take photographs of a project and you cannot take photographs of a balance of payment. We were under constant pressure, perfectly understandable, during the whole of the Marshall Plan, to see if we could not find some projects in the United Kingdom. This comes back to what Mr. Patel has said. We took our Marshall aid almost entirely in the form of commodities, because commodities were the great bulk of our imports from the dollar area. And the difficulty was that as soon as the commodities we got from North America arrived at a port, they were mixed in with other commodities that had arrived from other parts of the world. It became not only difficult, but impossible, to take a picture of them at that stage, so they had to be photographed arriving at the docks. I think it depends on the type of economy whether the project basis is the right one; whether the requirement is for commodities, as it was in the United Kingdom, or whether there are a special number of projects with a sufficiently large foreign aid content in them to do a thing on a project basis. In any case, I would like very much to reinforce Mr. Patel's argument about the importance of financing commodities quite distinct from financing capital goods.

Arthur Smithies. I think the alternatives to the project approach, either a balance of payments approach or a resources gap approach, both have the weakness, which we discovered in the Marshall Plan, that they furnish strong disincentives to the countries concerned. If you underwrite a country's balance of payments, it will not have much or any incentive to get its balance of payments into shape. This has been found also in some underdeveloped countries of East Asia. Similarly, if we provide the capital requirements in addition to what the country raises for itself (the so-called resources gap approach), here, too, perhaps, the country loses the incentive to raise the maximum amount for itself. This is a serious weakness and my own judgment is that one has to place a good deal of reliance on the project approach for the underdeveloped countries.

In contrast to the Marshall Plan case a good deal of imported capital equipment will be needed. The rationale for commodity aid under the Marshall Plan often was that the recipient countries themselves could most economically produce their own capital equipment while we provided food and other materials. This is by no means true in the case of the underdeveloped countries.

Max F. Millikan. I should like to make a plug for a program approach at least in the planning phases. I think that it is exceedingly important that the underdeveloped countries receive our encouragement—not so much in the case of India, which is doing it already—to develop and plan long-term programs. With respect to each project, we should ask not only, "is this a sensible project in and of itself, and in terms of the availability of raw materials to go into it, and the market to supply the thing," but "how does this fit into your scale of priorities for an over-all development program?" I think this is important not only for economic reasons but for political reasons. The governments of the underdeveloped countries ought to be encouraged to do just what India has been doing, which is to try to work out a systematic fitting together of all of the various elements in their proposed development effort.

HELP FOR INDIA'S SMALL BUSINESSMAN

The internal social and political consequences of one form of aid as against another do not necessarily conform to simple economic ratios in which more aid, affecting more people, automatically means more significant consequences. One almost unknown facet of the United States aid program destined to have a democratizing social, which is to say political, influence out of all proportion to the $2.5 million budget so far involved is the surplus machine tool program quietly approved by Congress in 1959. This program for the transfer of leftover Defense Department holdings of World War II machine tools was enacted at the urging of the small business advisor to the Air Force, *Kennard Weddell,* who visited India in 1958 as a Ford Foundation adviser to the Government of India in the development of its much praised program for the promotion of small-scale industries.

The importance of the Indian government program of aid to the small businessman can be appreciated only in the light of the enormous power wielded by the relatively small group of industrial entrepreneurs who got a head start during British rule. Great names such as G. D. Birla in cement and jute (burlap) symbolize in Indian eyes the preponderant economic power of certain entrenched social groups; Birla is a leading figure in the so-called Marwari community. The fact that these groups are making a rapid transition to modern attitudes of progressive business management does not alter the popular image of rapacious moneylenders and profiteers. Nor does it alter the actual fact of disproportionate economic power, and the consequent antagonism of would-be entrepreneurial rivals from other social groups which is such a deep subsurface political fact of India today. The Economic Minister of the Indian Embassy in Washington, *Govindan Nair,* who organized the small industries program as a Secretary in the Commerce Ministry in New Delhi, is frank to say that Indian "socialism" is in this and other fields inspired in part by a desire to head off further concentration of industrial power. Economist *Eugene Staley* of the Stanford Research Institute emphasizes the importance of the findings by *James J. Berna, S.J.,* that the base of small industrial entrepreneurship in India is in fact widening.

Govindan Nair. There have been two major motivations underlying our small industries program in the First and Second Five Year Plans, and these motivations stem directly from the larger problems of economic development. First, one of the very real problems that we have is the problem of resources. Our problem is not merely that there is a scarcity of resources in India. There is also the problem of organizing even the scarce resources available. We do not have a money market of the type that exists in the Western countries. Most of the savings will be found with small people, tucked away here and there, farmers, peasants, small householders, artisans, and the like. And it is not a very easy task to tap these savings. This, I think, is one of the primary economic justifications for the small industries program.

Then a second factor lies in what we call "the socialistic approach" in our Second Plan. One of our problems is, of course, that when we increase production through our plans we would like at the same time to prevent too great a concentration of wealth in the hands of those who might already hold it, or those who would be able to mobilize sufficient resources to increase their wealth. And one of the reasons we placed this emphasis on small-scale industries was, we wanted to see a greater distribution of economic opportunities. We wanted to encourage as many small entrepreneurs as possible.

Eugene Staley. I should like to ask Father Berna to tell us something about the small industrialists that he interviewed in Madras and Coimbatore. They were in the light engineering industries. Where did they come from? What social origins, technical training, and so on, did they have? This is a very important point. It bears on the question that Mr. Nair spoke about initially—the question of resources. Not only capital resources, but also skill resources, and especially entrepreneurial ability, are very important in developing a country's industries.

James J. Berna, S.J. When I began this study a great many people told me it would be useless. They said, "Oh, we know that. All these men are merchants. They're the only ones with capital in this country, and anyone who's got a little factory employing fifty people comes from the merchant group." I was told also, "You will find that they have not grown from small-scale industries employing less than fifty. You will find that they were established as larger units by men with capital."

Well, I did not find that. I made a very careful study, as careful as I could, in the vicinity of Madras and around Coimbatore, of fifty-two firms in the engineering industry—that is, producing some kind of a metal or plastic product with use of machinery. Some were making electrical products such as insulators and switches; others textile machinery and spare parts. There were several rolling mills, making steel and brass sheets and circles, foundries turning out rough and finished castings; some were building truck bodies, bus bodies for local bus lines; eleven were in consumer goods industries, manufacturing household utensils, radio receiving sets, plastic buttons, automobile accessories, fountain pens, and bicycles.

This is what I found out about the background of the entrepreneurs. Of the fifty-two, I found that five were formerly rural artisans. They were small rural blacksmiths servicing implements in rural areas. Ten were domestic merchants—that is, merchants engaged in internal trade, not importing—and five more were importers, so that makes fifteen merchants in the whole group. Thus a little less than one third of the whole group is from the merchant class, which was a big surprise to me after what I had been told. More surprising still, I found that there were six ex-factory workmen, that is, men who had begun as village boys in local factories and foundries, spent ten or fifteen years in such work, some of them eventually reaching the rank of foreman, then left to establish a small workshop of their own, often in partnership with another workman. These places typically began as small repair shops, gradually grew by plowing back earnings, borrowed further, and eventually became manufacturing enterprises.

Another surprise was finding among the fifty-two entrepreneurs twelve men with graduate engineering degrees. These were young men who had gone to an engineering college, five or six of them outside India; one or two in the United States, several in Great Britain. Most, however, had received their engineering training in India. There they had gone into industry for themselves, and were running very fine efficient little enterprises. Then I found that four entrepreneurs were former manufacturers in some line other than engineering. Four or five others had originally been landlords engaged in cultivation and sale of farm products. The remaining entrepreneurs, about six, came from very varied backgrounds. Some were white-collar workers, one or two were former teachers who had one way or another gotten into industry—one was the operator of a small bus line. My main conclusion was that entrepreneurs come from a surprisingly wide range of occupational groups. Not all by any means are from the merchant class. And it is important for us to remember that this experience also conforms to what we now know of the early Industrial Revolution in Europe. In the eighteenth and early nineteenth centuries some very reliable studies have shown that in the early stages of industrialization small entrepreneurs were coming from all kinds of groups—landlords, ironmasters, merchants, traders, and so forth. The iron industry of South Wales is a case in point. Probably this will change, and probably is already changing in India. As industry gets better established, the initial size of plant being established tends to rise, people with more capital are attracted to industry, and it gets more difficult for the little man to get established and compete.

Mr. *Staley*, author of *The Future of the Underdeveloped Countries*, has conducted a comparative study of the role of small industry in the economic development of the newly industrializing countries. India, he reports, "has one of the very most important and well-thought-out programs in the world for aiding the small private industrial enterprise." The nature of this uniquely promising program is discussed by *Mr. Nair, Father Berna, James T. McCrory*, author of case studies of small industry in a suburb of Delhi, and *Mr. Weddell*, who points to the peculiarly important role that United States surplus machine tool stocks can play in the Indian effort.

Govindan Nair.   There are two aspects to our program of assistance. One, which I will call for want of a better word, the negative aspect, is embodied in a form of protection applied particularly to the traditionally hand industries of which the hand weaving industry is the biggest and the most important. On the positive side is the fact that we have tried to provide what you might call an Industrial Extension Service to small industries. We took the view that the large-scale organized industry possesses sufficient resources to effect improvements in technology; to organize its marketing, and to secure credit. Either it has its own resources, or if it wants it can call in assistance from a business consultant. Now the small industries do not possess these. And at least for a certain interim period the government said we would have to provide these services free to the small entrepreneur.

The Industrial Extension Service, under a Small-Scale-Industries Board, was more or less adapted from the idea of the agricultural extension service which you have in this country. This Extension Service falls broadly into three categories. There is first the Extension Service to improve techniques—techniques of production and of marketing. For this purpose we established one in every state. That is about fifteen Small Industries Service Institutes. Then we established a number of Extension centers, about fifty-two already working. The Institutes are staffed by a number of technical and economic experts in an economic section. The economic and technical section goes out and conducts certain investigations, finds out what it is that a small industry needs, both on the marketing, the economic, and the credit side, as well as on the side of improvement of technical efficiency, and this is put before the Institute. They send out field officers who go and actually help the small industry to do this. They provide schools and classes there for business management. They provide at present, I think, about forty-eight mobile vans which tour the country—and we hope to increase this number—demonstrating to the small entrepreneur the advantages of using improved equipment and modern tools.

James J. Berna, S.J. I was very much impressed by those mobile vans. They are something like buses, equipped with machine tools and other equipment which can be demonstrated to the small industrialists, and they travel into the areas where these small industrialists are. Very often they are located on the perimeters of cities and may be out ten or fifteen miles. These men are running their own factories, and are very much tied up in managing them with the result that they do not have time to come into the city for extended stays to visit demonstration centers that may be set up there.

Kennard Weddell. I also watched those vans in operation. They are very well conceived and operated. My only concern is this. These vans come into the villages, maybe at the time of what we would call a county fair, and these entrepreneurs see what can be done by some mechanization of their processes. They become interested—and it is a hard job to get them interested. You have to get this man who's been making holes in wood by running a bow across a string to see that he can do it better and in shorter time with a drill press. So, he wants the drill press. And he cannot get it! The Government of India has so far been able to supply only an extremely small fraction of the demand which they have been able to create. That has got to be taken care of. I am very hopeful that we can do something about that from the huge stocks of surplus machine tools and factory equipment that we have in this country, government-owned, completely surplus to our needs.

Govindan Nair. This is precisely the problem. Connected with our Extension Service, of course, we have to provide the means of meeting certain demands. There is a commercial side to our organization, designed to help in providing machinery and selling it on easy terms. There is a Small Industries Corporation to supply machinery to the small entrepreneur. Now according to the latest reports they have got, I think, on hand applications for about $8 million worth of machinery. They have been able to supply only $4 to $5 millions worth.

Kennard Weddell. And there would be a great deal larger demand than that $8 million if any of these firms who had applied for it two years ago had been able to get them. On my last trip I sensed a discouragement, a reluctance now on the part of the small entrepreneur to apply for machine tools when he realizes that there's one chance in fifty that he will get them in time to do him any good.

Industrial estates are also a very important part of the Government of India's program to aid small industry. You can train apprentices through Service Institutes, and through Extension Institutes, and through engineering colleges; you can provide all kinds of management training and theoretical training, but if there isn't any place where a person who has gained that knowledge can apply it—if there's no place for him to go, except to decide, "I'm going up for a higher degree," and finally you run out of the degrees that you can get—you really haven't accomplished anything except having a lot of frustrated, highly trained, highly educated people on your hands. There has got to be a factory, or a place that they can go to and apply this training and knowledge and increase it by practical experience. I am happy to say that I know of no country that is seeking to increase its industrialization that comes any place near India in its recognition that any program has got to be a comprehensive one. Along with the training of the apprentices, and the training of the managers, and the financial assistance to supplement or to augment the capital that a small entrepreneur might have—along with that the government has recognized that there must be a place for them to put their best licks in after they have learned.

In India one approach to this problem has been the building of Industrial Estates, a pattern adapted from experience in Great Britain, and particularly in Scotland, shortly after World War II,

which the Government of India has carried to really effective
fruition. State governments, using central government funds, have
built large compounds of about anything from thirty to sixty small
factories in each—modern buildings, well ventilated, good sanitary
conditions—in other words, good working conditions for the em-
ployees. The floor space runs from 3000 square feet to 5000 feet—
really small-scale industries. When these are built, and with the
necessary electric power and water resources available, and put in
there, they lease these buildings to private industries—not only
existing private industry which might want to move out from some
desperate working shop conditions, but also to new companies. And
the Government of India has taken care to diversify the industries
in any one of these compounds, better known as industrial estates.
They lease them on very favorable terms—approximately 50 per
cent of what it would take to amortize those properties in a reasonable period of time. There are now 100 of these estates in operation
scattered around through the countryside, embracing over 3000
small, modern-type factories, employing about 50,000 people.

Govindan Nair.   Many of these small industries need certain common services which they cannot afford on their own. For instance,
you find in North India a very wide-spread system of light engineering industries in the Punjab, which make bicycles and bicycle
parts and sewing machines and sewing machine parts. Well, these
require certain processes like heat treatment and electroplating and
things like that which cannot be done efficiently by the small man
himself. Now the whole concept of the Industrial Estate is to
bring all these services together.

Another great feature is—and perhaps I should not confess to
this—that it saves the small industrialist a tremendous amount of
red tape. I mean, if he has to do all this himself, he probably has
to spend two years getting the necessary power and water connections and the license from the municipality, and conforming to
building regulations, and this, that, and the other.

James T. McCrory.   In America there is a tendency to view India
as a country which is sort of exotic, and has only rather backward
people. This may be quantitatively true, but if you have two or
three million people who are already semiskilled, who are already
protoentrepreneurs, who are already able to work with their hands

and use machinery, that's an awful lot of people. And I think the assumption of this whole program is proving out magnificently. If you put in electrical connections, if you'll put up roofs, if you'll make services available, you've got an awful lot of people.

Eugene Staley. There's a lot more entrepreneurship there than. . . .

James T. McCrory. There really is! Who will just appear from all kinds of places and show up and plug into the electrical connections and go into business—they're waiting for it.

Eugene Staley. By way of summary, it seems to me that one of the most important points that has come out of this whole discussion is the revelation of the intense interest in India on the part of the government, and on the part of industry—both large and small industry—in the development of the small independent industrial entrepreneur. Secondly, we have brought out some of the purposes which the planners of India's development have in mind in encouraging small industry. One is to tap resources of their country which could not otherwise be effectively tapped. Much of the capital which does go into a small individual or family firm would not be invested in bonds, or in the stock market. Resources of entrepreneurship are being tapped. These small firms become seedbeds of talent out of which some enterprisers rise into the medium category and perhaps in future even into large-scale manufacturing. Parenthetically, it seems to me that insofar as this happens it will make it easier for India to control industry in the social interest without so much need for government intervention. The more competition there is from the rise of new, aggressive little firms the less you have to fear from the monopoly of a few large firms.

With respect to India's policies on small industry matters, we noted that there is a double line of policy. One stresses the protective or negative approach, in some cases even handicapping large industry, like textile mills, in order to favor small-scale and particularly village and handicraft or hand enterprises such as the hand looms. This is, in the thinking of the government leaders, a transitional policy. The second aspect of the government's program, very encouraging from the point of view of long-range industrial development, is the effort to upgrade the small establishments. The Government of India has set up quite a comprehensive program revolving around the Small Industries Service Institutes. We have learned of the Industrial Estates—a very important program which helps the small industrialist to get better, cleaner premises, better provided with utilities and to avoid red tape.

Father Berna's report on the origins of entrepreneurs in one industry in South India supports the conclusion that also comes from much other evidence, namely that things are changing in India. Graduate engineers and other educated people in the old days—you know how often we have heard this about India and other countries—did not want to get their hands dirty. Now they are entering industry. The general outlook for the upgrading and improvement and expansion of small industry in India is encouraging.

Kennard Weddell has made it a personal mission to marry the United States machine tool surplus and the Indian need. It was his appearance before the Senate Foreign Relations Committee on May 22, 1959, which resulted in Congressional approval of the machine tool program now in operation. After reviewing India's efforts to promote the growth of small industries, he spelled out why the United States is peculiarly situated to be of help.

Kennard Weddell. You should understand that there is only the bare beginning of a machine tool industry in India, and the government is very short of foreign exchange, whether sterling or dollars. To the extent that any foreign exchange could be made available for this purpose, it would be two years or more after an order was placed before it could be filled under the Indian government's small industries program and the applicant would lose interest.

As I ran more and more into this situation, I recalled the huge stocks of used machine tools, government-owned, which the Air Force alone had piled up at its storage sites in the United States, many of which were of World War II vintage, of relatively little use in the highly competitive economy of this country, but which would be a godsend to Indian industrialists.

On my return from India in 1956, I informed Mr. Dudley Sharp, Assistant Secretary of the Air Force, of the situation, and arrangements were worked out whereby certain selected machine tools which were surplus to the needs of the military departments were turned over without charge to the International Cooperation Administration for shipment either to the Railway Board or to the National Small Industries Corporation of India, the shipping and crating charges to be paid by the Government of India.

In late 1957, I had a request to serve for six months as a consultant to the Government of Burma on a leave of absence granted by the Air Force, and while there, in early 1958, was asked by the Government of India to make a short two-week tour of that country and appraise the progress that had been made.

I wish the members of this committee could have been with me, just a year ago this month, when I stood in a small model workshop a few miles outside of New Delhi and watched two Indian mechanics setting up an American-made double-spindle boring machine, and there, painted on the front, was the Air Force number. They showed the machine with pride, the expression on their faces was good to see, and again my thoughts went back to that ever-mounting stack of surplus machine tools lying idle in our storage sites.

I knew they were being disposed of, through periodic sales, gradually, and in very small and deliberately limited quantities so as not to have too harsh an effect on the machine-tool industry in this country. On the better machines we realize about 15 per cent of acquisition cost; the older ones are sold for their scrap value. And all the time storage costs are going on.

I also believe that the machine-tool industry in the United States will not for some time, if ever, have a market for its product in India. That country must and will develop its own machine-tool industry, which will take many years.

India already has progressed to the point where it could put to productive use some 5000 machine tools and items of factory equipment suitable for small plants. Our government would take out of its surplus stocks approximately that number of tools and equipments which the Government of India says would be immediately useful, and would deliver them on the docks of Bombay, Madras, and Calcutta without cost to the Government of India. The cost of this crating and transportation is estimated at $2.5 million.

On its part, that government, India, would set up workshops at selected centers, for apprenticeship training in the inspection, overhaul, and repair of light machine tools. The machines delivered to India would be put through those workshops, and this would serve a double purpose. Inspection and overhaul in India could be accomplished at a fraction of the cost that would be involved if done here and, of major importance, it would provide practical training for Indian nationals.

In closing, I would make this point. The United States is in a unique position to do what is here proposed. Only in this country is there a huge stock of idle machine tools, on hand, ready to ship. And only in India is there the present capability of putting a sizable number of these tools to work in a program to raise the standard of living in the pattern of true democracies.

However it is done, the thing that sticks in my mind—and it hurts—is that here is a tremendous need and immediate use for these over in that part of the globe, and over here are our warehouses bulging at the seams with unused tools, and it seems to me we ought to work out something.

All that Congress was asked to authorize in the 1959 Mutual Security Act was the expenditure of $2.5 million to cover packing and delivery costs which would otherwise have been one more item aggravating India's foreign exchange difficulties. But the 5000 machine tools to be covered by this authorization would have an estimated value near $30 million if purchased at auction through Defense Department surplus disposal channels. With some 10,000 machine tools and industrial equipment items still left over from World War II and Korea; with India's domestic machine tool industry still in its infancy, and with the proliferating expansion of India's small industries, the possibilities of an extension of the 1959 authorization are now under study.

"These tools can make a spectacular contribution to economic development in underdeveloped countries," said the Foreign Relations Committee in reporting out this new provision of the Act on June 22, 1959, "particularly when they can be placed in the hands of small business concerns. The encouragement of small business in these countries will have the further benefit of shaping the nature of economic development toward a free, competitive society rather than one dominated by a few giant firms."

THE POLITICS OF FOREIGN AID

The experts can come to certain conclusions as to desirable forms of aid and the priorities to be given each, but it is one thing for the experts to decide and quite another for the political sponsors of adequate aid to translate decisions into legislative results. *Frederick Holborn* of the Harvard Government Department has served as Senator John F. Kennedy's special assistant on foreign aid policy since 1957.

Frederick Holborn. What are the prospects for an improvement in our foreign aid program?

I cannot suggest to you any particular chemical compound by which we can gather a new surge of progress within the Congress. But I might describe what I think are the major barriers at the moment and then two or three openings that might be exploited. The most serious barriers at the moment, of course, are first that within Congress as a whole, and I am speaking in particular of the House, but I think to some degree it is true of the Senate as well, there has been relatively little replenishment of leadership in the foreign aid field during the past few years. This is due in part to the shift in attitudes which has taken place both on foreign trade and on foreign aid in the South, many of whose spokesmen have seniority on the responsible committees, especially on Appropriations. It is due in part, perhaps even more so, to the fact that there have really been no new programs in foreign aid which would help to elicit new leadership. During the past three years the foreign aid battles have largely been a recycling each year of an old task rather than the projection of a fresh idea. And in such a situation the established and consolidated leadership along the lines of the lowest common denominator has tended to predominate.

In this atmosphere we have come into a somewhat unnatural situation in which a kind of strategy of mutual terror exists between Congress and the State Department. The Senators and Congressmen who might want to put forth new ideas are hesitant to do so for fear that the fires would quickly be extinguished in the Department of State. At the same time, the Department of State argues that in many cases it is unable to present such and such a program because there is not sufficient playback in the Congress. Each complains that it does not have playback, one from the other. To some degree there is obviously an element of truth in these complaints. But to some degree this has all been a game of bluff which serves the need of each side.

Perhaps the present rather unnatural fluid situation is caused by the fact that those people who *are* interested in making some progress in the foreign aid field have at the present time no real sense of unity as to how they should proceed. In the House, for example, there has been a feeling that the most important thing is to devise a new and more satisfactory set of laws governing private investment. Yet useful as this is, the private investment problem, taken in the large, does not bear particularly on the larger problem in India. There are others, both in the House and in the Senate, who feel that the most vital and important thing is to revise and to expand Public Law 480, making more effective use of the local currency counterpart funds which are built up. This again is no substitute for an adequate program of development assistance. Both within the Administration and in Congress there has at least been a small but I think significant group which has emphasized what was originally known as the Monroney Plan—the new International Development Association. While the I.D.A. has a place, I think it has been, at this stage, something of a diversion. Our difficulty is that with such a scattering of effort the central task of enacting legislation so the Development Loan Fund may find adequate, long-term financing has not received the concerted, unified support which it merits and the majority support which is, I think, latent in the present mood of critical restlessness.

Senator *Kennedy* was a co-sponsor with Foreign Relations Committee Chairman J. W. Fulbright of the unsuccessful effort in 1959 to give the Development Loan Fund assured financing for five years. However, his special contribution to political leadership in the aid field has rested in a persistent emphasis on the participation of other Western governments in concerted aid efforts.

John F. Kennedy. On August 25, 1958, the World Bank convened in Washington a conference of economic officials from the United States, Great Britain, Canada, West Germany, and Japan. This meeting, which considered the establishment of a consortium to channel assistance to India, suffered from the handicaps that are inevitable for a conference of civil servants rather than of political leaders; but it marked the first recognition of the need for a broader effort to mobilize Western resources in support of the legitimate goals of the Indian plan. As a result of this meeting, and successive Bank-sponsored meetings, there have been encouraging signs in India itself of a new appraisal of the means and methods, both public and private, by which the plan might succeed.

The United States answer to the challenge in Asia today lies in part in Congressional support of an adequate Development Loan Fund with long-term financing. But the job should not and cannot be done by the United States alone. We need—as we needed ten years ago—another historic effort in international collaboration among the capital exporting nations in the world, and India herself, comparable to the experience of the Marshall Plan.

That is why Senator Cooper and I have recommended and why the Senate unanimously supported the creation of an international joint mission to India to work out with the Indians an accurate appraisal of their needs over the life of the Third Plan, to weave together the various aid programs of the Western nations, and to give both assurance and incentive not only to the Indians but to democratic leaders throughout the underdeveloped world. The moment is ripe for giving new meaning to the Atlantic Community and relating its peaceful enterprises to the aspirations of the uncommitted world. If the President and Congress give new momentum to our foreign assistance program, then we can expect with reason that the nations of the Common Market and the Commonwealth will also give realization to a larger effort of their own. Both the Secretary-General of NATO, Paul-Henri Spaak, and the world spokesman of the Common Market, Jean Monnet, have underscored in recent months that the great issues facing the member nations lie outside Europe and preeminently in the underdeveloped areas.

The creditor states of Europe are deeply involved in India's future, as are Japan and other potential members of this common enterprise. Our task now is to harness all of the resources of these nations more effectively, and to work out with the Indian government the most effective method of participating in their developmental plans.

Wilfred Malenbaum. Senator Kennedy's proposal and others like it have in mind some sort of international machinery for joint and cooperative study of the requirements as a basis for Indian-United States, and other participation in the total development effort. But let us examine more closely the parallels mentioned between this program of 1960 and the situation a decade ago in Europe. There are aspects of the Marshall Plan experience which I think are not so well remembered today. The Marshall Plan might not have materialized—might not have achieved more, for example, than the Kennedy-Cooper resolution has yet achieved—had two things not occurred in 1947 and 1948. First, a man named Ernest Bevin, then the Foreign Minister of Great Britain, immediately responded to

Marshall's challenge. There was immediately organized the machinery and the cooperative mechanism for formulating a Marshall Plan Program into which American effort and aid could fit. Secondly, that organization, the Committee for European Economic Cooperation (CEEC), now the Organization for European Economic Cooperation (OEEC), constituted a screening, studying, cooperative mechanism. If there is to be a parallel today, there must also be a parallel in the response and in the machinery that would launch this cooperative effort.

The Kennedy accent on a joint Western program reflects in part a politician's sensitivity to the Why-Be-Uncle-Sap mood which began to gain strength in Congress as early as 1957. Many longtime aid supporters had become uneasily aware that West German businessmen—to take a conspicuous example—were benefiting from recipient countries' capital goods spending under United States aid programs at the same time that the Bonn Government was declining to extend significant government-to-government aid credits comparable to the Development Loan Fund program. This, at a moment when German gold and dollar reserves had reached $4.5 billion and the United States, which had helped Bonn amass these reserves, recorded an unprecedented balance of payments deficit.

It was both equitable and a political necessity in Congress to couple United States aid initiatives with a broader effort toward joint Western aid. The Kennedy-Cooper resolution adopted unanimously by the Senate on September 10, 1959, called on the Executive to "explore with other free and democratic nations and appropriate international organizations the advisability of establishing an international mission that would consult with governments in the area of South Asia on their needs . . . and . . . recommend methods by which the participating countries could jointly assist these South Asian governments in the fulfillment of their economic plans."

The idea was that the recommendations of such a mission would strengthen the case for an adequate Development Loan Fund which would be the United States counterpart to new companion national or multinational Western instruments. Senator Kennedy explicitly appealed to the widespread sentiment that Western Europe should bear more of the aid responsibility when he declared, in reporting out the resolution in behalf of the Foreign Relations Committee, that "the sponsors . . . do not seek to involve the United States in another assistance program, but to encourage other prosperous nations to take a greater and more active interest in the problems of South Asia and to make the most effective use of existing United States agencies." The resolution and Kennedy's subsequent pressure prompted the negotiations between Undersecretary of State C. Douglas Dillon and World Bank President Eugene Black which resulted in Black's convening of a three-member international commission to assess South Asian economic needs (Britain's Sir Oliver Franks, Hermann Abs of West Germany, and Allan Sproul as the United States member).

In its deepest sense the growing realization that the United States should not expect to do the aid job alone signifies also a new awareness of the overwhelming enormity of the task of development. The much publicized "population explosion" becomes in the anti-aid lexicon an effective argument for the widespread view that development is in fact a futile task. This new sense of the futility of aid is one of the reasons why some such as *Max F. Millikan* and *Eugene Staley* suggest that the time has come to invite—or shame—the participation of the Soviet Union in large-scale economic aid. Perhaps the only attack on the Why-Be-Uncle-Sap mood is indeed the ultimate attack of a fully international development effort. But at the moment the fact that the Indian government accepts Soviet aid at all is a danger signal to political opponents of United States aid to New Delhi. *I. G. Patel* presents the characteristic Indian reply.

I. G. Patel. The reason we accept aid from Russia is simply that, as a nation, we still believe in living on the best possible terms with everybody. And if somebody comes forward and says 'we will help you' I personally feel there is no reason at all to spurn them. There has been talk from time to time of America and Russia putting their money together in some sort of a development fund with the rest of the world, and if it so happens that we are on good terms with Russia, to the extent that we can get some technical or other type of assistance, I for one see no reason why the Americans should feel bitter about it. Look at it, if you will, as one way of sharing Russian wealth.

Many Americans feel this is likely to lead at some time to interference in our internal policies. To this I would say that so long as the Government of India is as it is, there is no reason why, because, say, a hundred million dollars comes from Russia over a period of five years, this is going to make any difference whatever. Now you are quite right that one has to see, whether it is Russian help or any other help, whether it is going to influence our policies unduly. If at any stage the Russians try to suggest, as they did in

Yugoslavia, that "we will cut off this aid unless you do XYZ," we would have to react accordingly.

Max F. Millikan. Quite a lot of us are saying from public platforms exactly what you are saying.

Eugene Staley. Further on Russia and the Communist countries and assistance, it seems to me we might even go so far as to ask the question whether it would not be a good policy for the United States to encourage more of it. My analysis of the national interest of the United States, in the problems of world development, is that we would gain by genuine progress in India and other underdeveloped countries so far as these countries can progress independently and in line with the present ideals of the Indian leadership. If they can be helped by getting assistance from the Soviet Union without political connotation—that is, to the Indians—it seems to me that more of it would be to our advantage.

Why should not the United States take the initiative on this matter and why should not the President of the United States send a letter to Mr. Khrushchev—this time *we* should initiate the correspondence. It would run something like this: We're very much in favor of building up the economies of the underdeveloped countries; we've been contributing quite a lot to do this, and there's a little danger that when we do it bilaterally we get charged with being imperialists, which we don't intend to be and we don't want to be. We would like to put more of our aid through international agencies but if we put as much aid through the UN agencies as we are now giving bilaterally it would swamp the UN, which would no longer be an international agency but rather 90 per cent American. For our part we would get a wider spread of larger contributions in the UN and similar multilateral agencies and we are prepared to recommend this to our Congress. Will you come along with us?

Suppose that you get a negative answer from the Soviet Union. Well this, I suppose, would help us in the Cold War. Suppose you get a positive answer. This would help us in winning the peace and might even be an entering wedge by which we could get some common things on which the East and West could cooperate, farfetched as this might seem at first glance.

Why, the critics ask, should aid be given with "no strings attached" to a neutralist government? *Arthur Smithies,* who is not so sure it should be, finds some support from veteran journalist *Harold Isaacs,* author of *Scratches on Our Minds: American Images of India and China.* But the provocative Indian commentator A. D. *Gorwala* warns against attempting to influence Indian economic policy in favor of a Western-style private enterprise system. This is of special interest in view of Gorwala's role as a vocal pro-American in India.

Arthur Smithies. I am not sure that there might not be some case for redressing the balance slightly in favor of the Biblical injunction that it is more blessed to give than to receive. At the moment the world tends to operate on the basis that it is more blessed to receive than to give and this creates a frightfully complicated situation. One cannot altogether approach this subject on the basis of a mutuality of interest, when one nation or set of nations provides the resources and the other receives them. I can think of no really clear-cut and definitive way to view this problem. One school of thought suggests that one should give countries what they want with no conditions on aid—if countries want to build stadiums, one should help them to build stadiums. The Russians have derived a certain amount of success from this kind of operation. They have won short-run friends at any rate. But I think there is a substantial amount of difference between the Russian position and our own. The Russians are not, presumably, interested in the success of these countries in the free world context. They are basically interested in the *failure* of development. For our part, we cannot remain uninterested in the outcome of our aid program. And that means, I think, that the question of conditions must come up.

We do want these countries to develop in a free world context. We also feel, I think, that we do know something about this type of development. In the case of India there are some singularly difficult questions. First of all, there is the population question. Now what is our attitude to be about that? Are we to try to persuade the Indians to do something drastic or something substantial about population control? It seems to me, quite frankly, that not enough is being done in this area at the moment. Quite a different scale of valuation seems to apply when we are deciding to build a dam or to limit the birthrate. There seem to be profound ·political difficulties, which I can well understand, in the way of governments taking positive action.

Senator Kennedy has discussed a joint Western approach to development. In my view the time has indeed come for mutual effort on the part of all the Western countries. This is directly related to the question of conditions: it is much easier for a group of countries to talk about conditions than for a single country. A group of countries has been able to talk to India in its recent crisis. In this way the World Bank has achieved greater success in raising for discussion the general financial policy of the country than when talking solely about specific projects. An international body or group of countries does not seem to suffer from the same political embarrassment when it is raising the question of conditions.

A. D. Gorwala.   Sir, what is shocking about these conditions? What conditions would you wish to impose? It is all very well to talk about the free world context, but the great difficulty arises from the fact that in America there seems to be what might almost be termed a Chamber of Commerce determinism. Private enterprise is considered to be the only way here. Now a country like mine, while it has a use for private enterprise, does not necessarily believe that this is the *only* way. There are other ways, and in our circumstances it is very necessary that those other ways be used. Those other ways do not necessarily mean a departure from democracy or freedom and there is no particular reason why aid should not be given to a country that uses them. But if, as has been stressed again and again by successive directors of your Development Loan Fund, for example, by Dempster McIntosh on his visit to India in 1958— America is to insist that development must be done very largely through private enterprise, well, then the question of conditions becomes very difficult. In that case what you are trying to do is really to impose a system and a philosophy which has worked well, perhaps, in your conditions, on a country where it is quite obvious that it does not and would not work.

Arthur Smithies.   I would attach absolutely no conditions on ideological grounds. I feel that what India calls socialism is a system for preserving the values that I value in the American system. On the question of private enterprise, I am very, very much of an amateur on the specifics of the Indian situation. But I do have the impression, from such study as I have given it, that India has possibly been overprejudiced against the economic efficiency of private enterprise, in some areas. For instance, in the matter of contracting, it might be more efficient for the Indian government to contract with a private enterprise, either in the United States or Western Europe or in India itself, than to try to construct projects itself. I think it might be perfectly reasonable for the aid-providing country to ask the Government of India to explore the possibility of using private enterprise in this manner more extensively.

A. D. Gorwala. Really, that depends upon the circumstances in each case. If you put in some such condition, you almost invariably bring in the suggestion that you want to get business for your people, your own firms, and that the aid is really given and used very much for the interests of your country rather than ours.

Arthur Smithies. Well, I very carefully suggested that the contracting should be done with *Indian* private enterprise and I think in many cases this is the most desirable form of contracting because I imagine Indian private enterprise has a clearer conception of relative scarcities of capital and labor in industry than American private enterprise.

Hart Perry. It is quite true that when the Director of the Loan Fund was in India he made several speeches encouraging greater use of private investment and private enterprise in development. Many of us, particularly those who have had the opportunity of working both in government and out of government, in private industry, are very much impressed by the dynamism of private enterprise and the possibility of greater efficiency—the absence of general accounting offices and auditors and the tremendous bookkeeping approach that so often tends to hamstring us all in the operation of government. He was suggesting that within the appropriate sphere, free rein be given to private enterprise, and that we would be delighted in our lending activity in India, where appropriate, to make loans directly to private firms.

I. G. Patel. Whatever is done to assist India to find the external resources she needs will have to meet a twofold test. It will have to be related to India's own ideas as to how it wants to develop. The assistance will have to fit an Indian pattern, an Indian plan. At the same time, I agree that if the other countries are going to assist they will have to find some way of judging and seeing for themselves whether the program they are asked to support makes sense or not. In any enterprise where people are going to work together, you have got to meet such a twofold test.

This then is the problem: that a way will have to be found for getting more than one country and agency to look together at India's problems, and to cooperate in meeting India's needs, and that this has to be done in a manner which fits into India's own plans and policies, giving at the same time the assisting countries the feeling and the assurance that they are helping to push forward a program which is soundly conceived. How do we do it? I think we are fortunate in the case of India in that we have adopted a democratic process of planning. This is a process in which the preparation of plans takes time, as much as two years or two and a half years during which plans are drawn up and revised. There is thus a fairly long period with occasion and opportunity given to everybody to comment on the plan, whether he comes from India or abroad, from an international agency or from elsewhere—anybody at all. In this process of planning, the process of thinking about it, assessing it, reassessing it, modifying it, changing it, reacting back and forth, there is ample scope for considering all relevant points of view.

Harold R. Isaacs. Recently at a conference in South America, Fidel Castro and other speakers told us very bluntly of their desire for large annual capital grants with no questions asked. We have had experiences like this in the Middle East. I have a notion that this gives a good many Americans the feeling of being taken for suckers. It is the fate of American "imperialism," if that is what it is, to come to its fruition when it has to pay for everything instead of collecting from everybody else the way all the others did.

We have heard how the British operated in their time. But very little is said about what the British got back for all these outlays, including their investments in the United States. Now we have the peculiar and unique task of finding ways of sharing our resources rather than adding to them in the classical manner of the relationship of the great to the small or the strong to the weak. This is something new and we must see it very clearly. Our problem is, to stop seeing this as a form of philanthropy and to begin to see it as the use of our resources to help create the kind of world we want. It is this that leads us to the question: What strings on foreign aid?

Some years ago, when this issue first arose, an official of the Indian Ministry of Finance came to this country. He addressed a large luncheon in New York and declared that India would brook no strings attached to any aid. I asked him whether or not, as an example, an examination of the Indian tax structure and India's marshaling of its own resources as part of the whole program of extending aid would be regarded as a string. He said, "Why, of course, we are quite satisfied with our tax structure." I pointed out that *we* have to revise our tax structures in this country in order to carry out programs such as aid, and I wondered whether or not revisions of the way in which Indian internal resources were mobilized was not a subject to be considered in this connection. Now perhaps in order to achieve this we must, as Professor Smithies has suggested, get into large and multilateral operations. We have to get the stink of power out of it and the stink of militarism out of it and if we can do this by finding larger international instruments for carrying out our aid programs—fine. But let us be clear that, if we want to go into a massive program over the next generation to help reconstruct the social economies of the world, we want social economies that are changing in the direction of the values which we hold to. We are not doing it for its own sweet sake.

IV / THE FOOD GAP

India's demographic point of no return might be a short few years away—1966.

This is the startling projection which has emerged in a World Bank-supported study conducted by the Princeton Office of Population Research. The book is *Population Growth and Economic Development in Low-Income Countries: A Case Study of India's Prospects*. The authors, demographer Ansley J. Coale and Economist Edgar M. Hoover, project three alternative possibilities. In all cases it is taken for granted that public health programs will bring a decline in the death rate of at least 40 per cent by 1986. The first projection assumes no reduction in India's present rate of population growth and a consequent population of 775 million by 1986. Increases in living standards would thenceforth be progressively canceled out by population growth. The second projection, based on a downward trend in the birth rate initiated after 1966 and progressing to a 50 per cent drop by 1981, places the 1986 population at 634 million and does not wholly rule out gains in living standards. Only the third projection of a downward trend initiated *immediately* and progressing to a 50 per cent drop by 1981—that is, a population of 589 million in 1986 —holds out reasonable hope for an economic breakthrough.

POPULATION AND THE FOOD CRISIS

The Coale-Hoover projections have an obvious relevance for all of India's economic—and political—planning, but they come to their sharpest and most searching focus on the food problem. Population pressure is a pressure, above all, on limited food resources which must somehow be increased at a rate far beyond what has so far been achieved by a variety of government efforts—notably the "Community Development" program initiated with private and public United States technical and financial assistance. *Ansley J. Coale* sets forth the nature of the population problem in its broad general perspective and *Sherman E. Johnson*, Chief Economist of the United States Department of Agriculture Research Service, points specifically to its urgent import against the backdrop of insufficient food production. Mr. Johnson headed the 1959 Ford Foundation mission to India which made the controversial report, *India's Food Crisis and Steps to Meet It.* He and his mission anticipate a gap between annual supply and need in food grains nearing 28 million tons as of 1966—the same all too imminent year of decision encircled on the Coale-Hoover calendar. They have aroused great interest with their emergency approach to increasing food production, their warning that, if a 28 million ton food gap does materialize, "no conceivable program of imports or rationing could meet a crisis of this magnitude."

Ansley J. Coale.   What are the facts about the population of India? There are today some 400 million Indians; and the rate of growth is authoritatively estimated at very nearly 2 per cent, some seven to eight million additional persons each year. Now this increase of nearly 2 per cent a year follows a period of some thirty years—that is between 1921 and 1951—in which the growth rate was pretty close to 1 per cent, and those thirty years in turn follow several decades in Indian history in which there was almost no growth, from 1890 to 1920. The question is, why has there been this acceleration from no growth to 1 per cent and within the past decade to nearly 2 per cent? It is not a rise in the birth rate that has accounted for this accelerated growth. There is every evidence that the birth rate in India has been remarkably stable for the past fifty years and probably on back into the remote past. But the death rate is another matter. In the thirty years prior to 1951 there were no major famines or epidemics of the dimensions of the flu epidemic in the terminal years of World War I. In addition, India has begun to exploit the possibilities of low-cost modern public health. Within the last decade the death rate in India has dropped from an estimated level of perhaps 30 per thousand (that is, 30 per thousand of the population dying each year) to a level of 20 per thousand. A similar development took many decades in the history of European countries.

In neighboring Ceylon, during the same decade, the death rate has declined from 20 per thousand (where it is today in India) to 10 per thousand. It's not at all impossible that a continued decrease at the pace that Ceylon has experienced will be observed in India within the next ten or fifteen years. And since during the past decade there is no evidence whatsoever of any substantial decline in fertility, the result is a population growth that is now nearly 2 per cent a year and may within a decade or two reach 3 per cent a year, as it has in many countries in Latin America. In the next decade it is almost certain that India will add more to her numbers than the now current population of England and France combined. If these health developments continue, as they almost certainly will, and if the birth rate does not decline, the population will probably double in thirty years, reaching some 800 million.

The question is, can the economy keep up with such a growth rate? There is a rather surprising answer. Even if there were no decline in the birth rate, and if the health conditions continue to improve and the population were to double in thirty years, it is quite likely that India would be able at least to double its national output during this period. In fact, a colleague of mine has, after a survey of the evidence, come to the conclusion that the food output, probably the slowest growing sector in the economy, would double. It is not at all impossible even if the population were to double that the Indian standard of living could advance during the next thirty years. On the other hand, it is quite clear that no conceivable means of advancing living standards and increasing output could keep up in the long run with a population growth of 2 to 3 per cent a year.

A lower birth rate would have a direct positive effect on India's economic development. The reasons for this have to do with the choice of allocating resources to current consumption on the one hand and allocating them to investment on the other. A large number of young children, the result of a high birth rate, is a large number of consumers for the next fifteen years or so who are not going to contribute in a productive way to the economy. A reduction in the birth rate will not for a period of fifteen or twenty years have a sizable influence on the labor force available, but will in the meantime reduce the demand on current output for consumption. In other words, if India were to feed a reduced number of children, it would be possible to use more resources for capital investment. We have estimated that if there were a 50 per cent reduction in Indian fertility, which would bring the Indian rate into the same general neighborhood as what we consider the high birth rate in the United States today, the total national product would be some 10 to 20 per cent bigger, as an accumulated result of having more capital to invest. More capital yields you a higher national product, which in turn results in still more capital.

Clearly, part of the plan for the economic development of India must be an effort to bring its population problem under control. No one can afford on humanitarian or other grounds to suggest a slowing up of the introduction of all the medical advances that India can absorb. The only possible and acceptable solution to this problem of population is some way of reducing the birth rate in India in the not distant future. The Indian government was aware of this problem at the outset of the First Five Year Plan, and that awareness is growing more acute and more widespread. Perhaps the most encouraging feature is that the Indian government, to my knowledge the only government in the world that has taken a positive position, has achieved an actual overt recognition of the necessity of intervening in this population question.

This is the sort of policy decision that has to be made within the Government of India and by the people of India themselves. The American attitude on this issue has to be one of recognizing the problem and sympathizing with the efforts that are made by India in trying to solve it, while perhaps offering a limited amount of technical assistance and expert advice on some of the technical problems involved.

Sherman Johnson.   Here is the basis for the impending gap in food production. In the next seven years, India's population will increase about 80 million, to a total of 480 million people—the population projection that the Indian people are working with in developing their Third Five Year Plan.

That tremendous population explosion is the primary reason for the food crisis. There has been a continuing increase in food production in India since independence, an average rate of increase of 2.3 per cent a year in food grain production since 1949–1950. That is pretty good, but not enough to provide food for the added millions, for what would be pretty close to another nation the size of Japan in the next seven years. If food production increases no faster than at the present rate, the gap by the end of the Third Five Year Plan in 1965–1966 will be 28 million tons of food grains, equivalent to something like a billion bushels of wheat. No conceivable program of imports or other measures can meet a crisis of that magnitude. Now certainly the United States is not in a position to supply that kind of an import program, and even in concert with other nations I doubt that we would do it. Thus it is really important that food grain production in India be stepped up, and that brings to the fore the need for a high priority for agriculture in India's Third Five Year Plan. Food production must be regarded as a real emergency if the impending crisis is to be met.

As steps that might be taken to meet the food crisis, first of all, we suggested the need for stabilization of farm prices, not at high prices and not in terms of transfer payments from the rest of the population because the urban population is, after all, only 20 per cent of the total. About 80 per cent of the people live in the farm villages. Seventy per cent are directly dependent upon agriculture. We therefore suggested price assurance in terms not of transfer payments but of a guarantee to the cultivators—letting them know in advance of planting time the minimum price that they would get.

Second, we suggested a public works program in rural areas to put the village unemployed to work to produce more food. That involves a lot of things, but you have to understand that of the 50 million families directly dependent upon agriculture in India, 20 million of those families have little or no land. About half of those 20 million are completely landless and there is terrific unemployment and hardship among that group of people as well as among the small farmers. There is much work that can be done largely by hand labor, such as building bunds, fixing up the irrigation tanks, and building masonry wells.

Third, there has got to be a lot more chemical fertilizer provided to Indian farmers. At the present time, farmers would buy about three times more chemical fertilizer if it were available to them, despite very high market prices for fertilizer in India. More fertilizer must have a top priority and, of course, that means immediate competition with the industrial sector because it involves scarce foreign exchange. Here, of course, an over-all program of financial aid could help a great deal.

Often the need for irrigation and drainage is stressed. Our emphasis was on the smaller irrigation structures such as tube wells and Persian wheel masonry wells, powered by bullocks or camels, which can be built very largely with hand labor. This is no criticism of the big irrigation projects. They will help to increase production, but time and scarce capital is needed to construct them. More important perhaps than new irrigation is better use of available water.

They also have serious drainage problems in some of the irrigated areas.

Then we suggested selecting for intensive effort areas where a combination of improved practices can be applied—including more fertilizer, better use of water, and improved seed.

Land tenure is an extremely important problem. There is a lot of discussion about land ceilings at the present time, and other tenure problems are still unsettled. Getting the land ceiling question settled as quickly as possible and giving farmers security of tenure would provide incentives to increase production.

A very real need exists for the expansion of cooperative credit. At the present time, about 85 per cent of the credit used by Indian farmers is supplied by individuals and professional moneylenders. The rates are extremely high, ranging all the way from 27 per cent to 75 per cent a year.

In general I should like to stress the need for a coordinating authority that would approach the problem of increasing food production on a crash "wartime" footing. Food production will have to be tackled as an emergency if the vision of a new India is to go forward. It is inseparable from the other aspects of the Third Five Year Plan and the other visions of a new India.

PROGRESS IN THE VILLAGES

"Community development" is the name given to the much publicized program for progress in rural areas which has been since 1952 the official Indian answer to the problem of increasing food production. The program has a special significance for Americans because it was the American architect and town planner, Albert Mayer, who developed the experimental project, at Etawah in north India, which was to become the model for an all-India program; an American Ambassador, Chester Bowles, who brought United States technical assistance funds (and moral support) to bear in the crucial early stages when the program was under discussion in New Delhi; and an American rural sociologist, Douglas Ensminger, who skillfully directed Ford Foundation-supported training of the Indian personnel for the new "Community Projects." The program is analyzed by *Albert Mayer*; *Arthur Mosher*, a pioneer in Indian rural development work at the Allahabad Agricultural Institute; *Richard L. Park*, collaborator with Mayer in the editing of *Pilot Project, India,* a documentary record of the Etawah experience; and *Jack Gray,* former director of United States technical assistance to Community Projects in the state of West Bengal.

Albert Mayer. To achieve an agreed, systematic definition of "What Is Community Development?" would take a full, closely-reasoned discussion in itself. I will simply therefore state some permeating characteristics which are, I think, generally agreed on. It is a question of improving land and improving people who live with the land so that reciprocally the physical and the social and the individual can step up on and with each other and get to some higher levels, whatever they may be: to improve the land to improve rural productivity, whether from land or from local industry, to enhance production and the quality of living. Second, it is to improve people's alertness and their sense of personal validity, their sense that they can accomplish something on their own, that nature isn't quite the inexorable force that it is generally supposed to be, and that the individual himself as against other forces that he deals with has more validity than he may have thought. It is a question, too, of improving the demand for continuing and cumulative information and research. Now research is a high-grade word to apply to this thing. But the people are not going to get all the answers from us, from the community developers, for always, and the objective is to get them into the habit of mind of demanding answers progressively and demanding services that hitherto they didn't know they were entitled to. And in so doing to improve the quality of life in the village which is by and large a dull place for all of the many vestiges of interesting things and traditions, to revivify the village so that people aren't leaving for noneconomic reasons as well as economic reasons.

Arthur Mosher. Community development is a vague term with several meanings. There are, in general, four different types of programs, all of which are indiscriminately called extension or community development, depending upon the speaker and the country with which he has had experience.

The first of these is the type found in the United States Agricultural Extension Service, namely an educational program dealing with a single body of subject matter (agriculture) that goes to rural people where they live, and operates dominantly through the techniques of farm visits, meetings, method demonstrations, result demonstrations, tours, exhibits, and fairs.

The second type is what might be called multi-subject matter extension. The methods here are the same, but the subject matter dealt with is broader. Instead of dealing only with agriculture, it deals with health; it deals with sanitation; it deals with village facilities. It may also deal with village organization. It deals with many of the interests of rural people, not just agriculture alone.

The third type of community development program uses quite a different method: the local self-help project. This method is to go to a group of people and find out what they think their needs are, what they would like to do. Out of these needs they are encouraged to select one that they can meet largely through their own efforts. They are helped to organize themselves to meet this need. Maybe it's to build a bridge. Maybe it's to build a school building. Perhaps it is to dig a drain through the village. In any case, a group of local people organize themselves to do a particular job together. And when this is completed the process is repeated.

The fourth type of community development is where people say, in effect, that existing social organizations are those of a static society, not capable of undertaking the tasks of change. In order to have a dynamic society, new forms of social organization are necessary. Therefore, we will set up cooperative societies. We will set up farmers' organizations. We will organize 4-H clubs. We will organize women's institutes. And once these social organizations have been created in the village they will become the channels through which the village people will tackle a variety of problems.

Now note the difference between the third and the fourth types. In the third type you first choose a particular job to be done. You organize to get that particular job done. You let the organization evaporate. You've done that job. You discuss again. You organize again. In the fourth type, you put the first emphasis on social organization. You create new organizations. Then subsequently, after you have an organization, you give this organization one job after another to do.

The fifth type, which is also sometimes called community development, is like TVA in the United States or the Damodar Valley Authority in India. This is the process of an integrated program to meet the total problem of a whole region.

In practice, I know of no single program that fits exclusively under any one of these definitions. What is called community development in India is basically a combination of multi-subject matter extension (Type 2) with reliance on the method of the local self-help group project (Type 3). By contrast, the program in the Philippines is primarily of the fourth type. It set out first to develop village development councils, the theory being that after the councils are developed these councils will become the organizations through which general rural development will take place. India attempts this also through the revitalization of the village *panchayats* (councils).

The one type of community development one does not find in India is single-subject matter agricultural extension. Why not? Anyone who worked in the early years of extension in the United States knows that there was plenty of inertia in the United States, and there are still large pockets in the United States where there is plenty of inertia against change. But in the places where single-subject matter agricultural extension has been relatively successful in the United States, and in parts of Peru, Colombia, Brazil, and Japan there was a relatively large number of commercial farms the operators of which were farmers already looking abroad for innovations—abroad meaning outside of their villages—and eager to take this information if they could get it. By contrast, in India, practically all of India, community development faced a task of persuading farmers that a change was possible, that they could make changes, that the results of research were at least semidependable.

The great virtue of multi-subject matter extension over single-subject matter extension in circumstances like those of India is that it makes it possible to build on whatever interest on the part of village people already exists. If a person is interested in health, then start with health. If he is interested in recreation, let's start with recreation. It isn't so important what the nature of the first success is. What is important is that there be success in the individual changing of a traditional pattern.

Please note that I do not use the term multi*purpose*. This idea that the village worker in India is a multipurpose worker is, I think, an error. He is a single-purpose worker, but a multi-subject matter person.

Albert Mayer. One facet of community development is central to all the rest.

What is a village-level worker? He was created because of two things that came together. One was that there simply wasn't enough in the way of money resources to have as many workers in a village or in a group of villages as would normally be needed if you visualized them as specialists in the United States extension system. So that what had happened was that the Public Health Department had maybe one little worker in heaven knows how many hundred villages, who very rarely, if ever, turned up, and was not known, was not relied upon, had no rapport with the situation. In the Agriculture Department they had another underpaid worker who was mainly keeping records in some remote place that could be filed in the state capitol, and he rarely got around. And the result was you had a number of people who didn't add up to much actually because separately they couldn't be afforded in sufficient numbers. There was not a small enough group of villages so that the village people recognized a *friend and adviser*, readily recognizable, available, and approachable: somebody who was their kind of person.

The coming together of all this led to the creation of what was called the multipurpose village-level worker.

When we created this man originally, we made an analysis, with the man himself, of how much he could be called upon to do. Of course, this consultation is not loss of discipline. It's the way of creating more discipline and more moral commitment, rather than just handing him down schedules that he has no voice in working out. And we, at that time, arrived at a four-village to a five-village orbit for this generalist who was to make no claim really to knowing much beyond the day-to-day situation. He was to be backed up by specialists, or what we call in America, subject-matter men.

Now this village level worker was later debauched, so to speak; in other words, they kept on piling on more functions, more villages, so that now he strangely begins to look like his predecessors, who didn't get around at all.

Richard L. Park. It is instructive, I think, to examine one of the recent experimental pilot projects on which has been based the vast community development effort building in India since 1952.

There were, of course, many older development experiments carried on by Gandhian constructive workers, by missionary societies (for example, the Wisers' establishment out of Lucknow), by a group with which Dr. Mosher was associated, the Allahabad Agricultural Institute, and by government itself. Information made available by these groups should have "trickled down" to the peasantry. But, as a matter of fact, this data did not trickle down very often to those who could use it best. The skills of the peasants were not harnessed to the best knowledge of science.

In the period following independence, it had become clear to leaders in the Government of India that something special—something dramatic—needed to be done as far as the rural population was concerned. A happy set of circumstances brought a number of able minds together on this rural problem, involving, among others, Albert Mayer.

Instead of embarking upon a vast new rural program without evidence of probable successes, a pilot project was proposed. This pilot project has become known as the Etawah project. It was started initially in 1948 after a good deal of exploration in the state of Uttar Pradesh, a populous and important north central state of India. The center of the project was Mahewa in the Etawah district; and initially the pilot project started with a group of sixty-four villages. To give some of the statistical symbols of development, the pilot project started with 1948's initial experimental area of sixty-four villages, expanded to five separate pilot project areas within the one state of Uttar Pradesh in 1951, covering three hundred villages; in 1952 a big expansion began under the Government of India's Community Development Program with Community Development Projects and National Extension Service efforts. In 1959 one finds close to half of the villages of India touched by one of the phases of rural development planning.

What is the Etawah project? Very briefly, one can say that the Etawah pilot project is a continuing experiment, started in 1948, in the attempt to enrich the lives of India's rural people by means of a multipronged, but integrated approach to the problems of Indian rural life. It is a test of what might be accomplished on an all-India scale. Differing from many of the other experiments that have been carried out by thoughtful district officers in the past, and in other experimental areas in India, one of the ingredients in the Etawah scheme that gave it support from the State of Uttar Pradesh was the essential constructive and productive element, namely, economic advancement. Etawah's planners knew that it would not be enough to add only social welfare benefits to village life, or physical improvement to the village—the improvement of village lanes, preventive medicine, etc. Underneath there must be the productive element, especially the improvement of agricultural production through improved techniques of agriculture, including the use of improved seeds, improved fertilizers, and the like. One of the things that was dramatic about Etawah was the substantial improvement in agricultural production over the first few years of the project's work.

I would like to put some emphasis on this economic factor at the outset because it seems that people discussing community development in India talk about every other element. But there were, of course, other efforts that were carried out. Improvement of nutrition and the diversification of crops—both interrelated; bringing education to the village if it did not exist before, and improving education if it had been started; social welfare; cottage industries; curative and preventive medicine; cattle breeding methods; prevention of cattle diseases; better seeds, etc.

More than that, new methods of social relations within the village were developed, usually based on already existing social patterns that were understood, but building upon these traditions—one might say expanding upon tradition—using the traditional, local elements to the extent that they were constructive and productive. The technique was to involve local people with things that were familiar, and at the same time introduce methods and objectives that were new. This method of involvement was enormously difficult, and I believe it is one of those tasks that remains difficult to carry out in India today. Many anthropologists who have observed Indian village life over the past ten or twelve years maintain that the single least effective element in much of current village work—whether at Etawah or elsewhere—has been the failure to understand *local* culture (as opposed to the great cultural tradition of all-India).

Let me now turn to certain problems of administration that have affected Community Development Projects and National Extension Service projects in India today. One problem lies in the district administrative system in India—a hard-boiled system which is the strong long-arm of the state and the central governments in the districts of the country. It is utilized to execute state and central legislation at local levels, supported by an administrative hierarchy going right down to the village level and upward to the state governments. It is a hierarchy that has a lot of experience behind it, but the frame is rigid. In the attempt to put community development into the middle of this rather hard-boiled structure of administration, errors were made in developing the right kind of sophisticated practice. A delicately balanced community development had to operate under the strong hand of the district collector and his immediate subordinates. Here difficulties arose. For example, the collectors and their immediate subordinates are excellent men in *general* administration, but most of them are not technically competent in the specialized fields of agriculture, agricultural engineering, or irrigation. So they have limited capacities to advise, to control, or even to encourage the specialized development that is central to community development.

There is also in this established hierarchy a relatively rapid shifting of personnel. A good general administrator has been looked upon as a person to be shifted from one place to another. With Etawah, and later with community development, there seemed to be the necessity of building what has been called "inner administrative democracy," that is, a sense of *all* participating: the low man having his say; the high man having his say; the people talking together and trying to come to adequate decisions on a mutually agreeable basis. There is need for a long-term commitment by upper administrators for this kind of work, and long-term commitment cannot take place with men of power like collectors in districts unless they are in one place for a considerable length of time and feel a sense of *historical* development in what is happening. In the ten or twelve years since independence, there has been a great shifting of personnel at the collector's level. This has been necessary because there were so many demands being made on the total government of India that it was impossible not to pull up into important posts at higher levels those men who were essentially very able people at the district level. But community development has suffered because of high-level needs for top administrators.

Jack Gray.   One of the few things that I can be dogmatic about in reviewing the West Bengal program is that the limitation on progress there certainly was not because of the lack of response of the village people to our proposals for change. About a month before I left India I visited one of these villages in this particular project and talked with a village leader. I asked him what he thought of the community development program. It had been operating there for three years at the time. He listed a number of accomplishments that had been made there. Among the accomplishments were a very good road with concrete culverts and brick topping—and a good school. And he also went into the fact that agricultural extension work had been very successful there and that they (the community development workers) had introduced the use of mixed fertilizer and a number of other things. I think he also mentioned that they'd made some progress in irrigation with a gasoline engine-driven centrifugal irrigation pump.

But he said he felt that the most significant thing that had happened in his village was that his people now felt a responsibility for what happened in the village, and felt that they could control it. They had some control over their own destiny, their own welfare. I felt that this gentleman had put his finger on the real aim of our community development program.

Now I can honestly say that this is not an isolated case. This happened all over West Bengal in eleven different projects that I was fairly closely associated with. It is interesting, however, that in my conversation with this village leader I gathered that he was surprised that the people had responded to proposals for change as well as they had. This, I believe, has been a pretty universal feeling; that the villagers in India, and maybe in other countries in Asia and Latin America, are too conservative to change. They're tradition-bound. And they're illiterate. And a number of other explanations are given for why they haven't changed.

In my view the program in West Bengal very clearly demonstrated that this is not so. To be sure, one of the first qualifications one must make with this statement is that they'll change when the benefits of a proposed change are very clearly demonstrated to them, before their eyes or in some other effective way so that they are really convinced that the change will help them—or that it will pay them.

Also, the other qualification, especially in West Bengal as compared to maybe some other parts of India, is that any proposal for change certainly has to be within the realm of the villager's financial capacity. This is very definitely a limit on their capacity to change, on their ability to take up improved practices.

Specifically, in West Bengal you might divide the activities or the work that the multi-subject matter worker attempted to do into two broad general categories. These are: the promotion of improved practices of an individual nature such as green manuring, the use of fertilizer, the use of a sanitary latrine, and secondly, the promotion of community improvement projects such as a school, a village road, or a small irrigation project. In the project I have mentioned, I found that in the case of almost every one of these practices, once some of the villagers implemented them, there would be a waiting list for the materials to implement these practices, three to four times the number of the first group of villagers.

Arthur Mosher. Jack Gray and Clifford Taylor have stressed that Indian farmers are not conservative, that tradition is not against change, that they do change when they see some reason for it. Now this is true. But this was not true twenty years ago and my conclusion, looking back on what happened prior to 1947 and what's happened since 1947, is this. That it was the political struggle for independence which opened up the traditions in the Indian village sufficiently that when community development came along, it caught on. When you took these same proposals to Indian farmers in 1933 and 1938 and 1942, you could demonstrate this just as well as you can today, the economic advantage, you could get an intellectual assent that this should be done but inevitably the end of the conversation was—we don't do it this way, this is not our custom. But what the political struggle for independence did was to undercut the fatalism of the Indian people. I mention that because when we begin to compare what happens in other countries with what is happening in India we see that the old conservatism and traditionalism is just as strong in some other countries today as it was in India twenty-five years ago.

QUANTITY VERSUS QUALITY

If the Indian peasant's traditional fatalism is a bar to development, the disappearance of the "old conservatism" also creates problems. Prompted by new popular expectations—by "higher political considerations," as Albert Mayer puts it in *Pilot Project, India*—the Indian government has attempted to duplicate the successful Etawah experience in thousands of new Etawahs "bedeviled by the need for overspeedy tangible, immediate annual showing in terms of miles of roads, numbers of new buildings, thousands of yards of paved drains." "We are exceeding a realistic rate,"

Mayer concluded sadly in a 1955 letter to Tarlok Singh, secretary of the Indian Planning Commission. There is a "serious deterioration. . . . It is relatively easy to multiply the mechanics of the early prototypes, but not so easy to multiply and reproduce their inner content." The frank comments of sociologist *Carl Taylor*, who has had continuing contact with the "Community Projects" as a Ford Foundation consultant, reflect widespread anxiety among many of those closest to the program. They provoke, in turn, comments from *Arthur Mosher, Albert Mayer, Asoka Mehta*, Chairman of the Praja Socialist Party, and *George F. Gant*, Director of the Overseas Development Program for South and Southeast Asia of the Ford Foundation. Mr. Mehta and Mr. Gant see the weaknesses of the "Community Development" program as essentially administrative and political in character.

Carl Taylor. By way of preface I wish to say that everything which sounds critical, I can put quotation marks on because Indians have said these things to me. So this is not merely a fellow from outside who comes in and says, "This is what happened."

I saw this program first before village level workers were in the field, but when the training schools were in operation. I then returned fourteen months later when the program was rolling, this time for seven months. I was then away three months, and went back and watched the program in its third and fourth years of operation, when it was rolling at a terrific tide. And then about a year and a half ago, I became aware of the fact, from reading reports that came out of India, reading the *Times of India* every day as if I were in Delhi, that a great deal of self-criticism of the community development program was taking place.

My question to the people with whom I visited on my last trip to India was, "What has happened to a program that was so splendidly designed, successfully launched, and now you Indian people are putting it through a terrific examination?"

I have no hesitancy in saying, as a sociologist and as a person who has had an opportunity to study this sort of program in many countries, that if I were to sit down and try to put together conceptually the things that have been called community development, I couldn't conceive a program, the elements of what was to be done and how to do it, more perfect than the model which India set up for herself.

The first basic element in their program is the village level worker. He was himself to be a villager who had, if possible, a high school education, who, if possible, was the son of a cultivator, who would be capable of being trained for the different jobs to be done, and better trained in agriculture because that was the big job to do.

They said this village level worker should be a friend and counsellor of the villager, that he should be a multiple-purpose technical assister, and that he should be the person who would mobilize and help to organize effectively the local people to render the great assistance which they could render to the improvement of their own community and to the building of India.

Back of the village level worker they set up a block, with a technician in each of the particular fields—agriculture, animal husbandry, health, sanitation, public works, engineering, cooperatives, Panchayats. These people represented the various ministries or the technical services of the nation or state, and through them were to be channeled all types of technical assistance down to the village-level worker and the villager. At the head of this block was a BDO—a Block Development Officer—who was the captain of a team of these technical persons, each a specialist in his own field, and from ten to twenty village-level workers.

The idea was that as people developed confidence and competence they would do what might have to be done in the form of nongovernmental groups in the beginning; that these groups would develop into local institutions. Right from the very beginning there was the idea that in some way or other there would be rebuilt the ancient and honored *panchayat,* or something like it.

So the whole machinery was set up with each block, on the average, handling 100 villages. In due time, the whole country would be blanketed, and there would be something like 5000 of these blocks to cover some 558,000 villages in India. Now what happened to the process when the whole thing was thrown into big administration and began to expand?

I think the answer is that when targets were handed down from the top rather than worked out in the block, as was the case at Etawah, they were accepted by the people who were administering the program as assignments to be carried out. Each level of administration, and this is the way an administration works hierarchically, handed the target down to the next level of administration. And the programs and plans to be carried out and the money to help carry them out were handed down. No matter what the people who planned and set the targets intended should happen by way of social processes and people's processes, in doing things this is what happened. In this, the Etawah processes of target-making and planning got terribly diluted. The fundamental first step in this process, discussion among villagers, just didn't take place in very many places.

To be sure, for every one of these things about which I draw broad generalizations one can cite block development officers and chief project officers who have done an almost perfect job.

In the block, the staff was supposed to be a team, yet I have sat in fortnightly meetings of the block staff, and the village-level workers say nothing. And yet, that is the place where the fellow higher up, who never lived down at the bottom or worked there, can learn what is at the bottom and what the task there is. In these staff meetings, others should listen to the village-level worker; they just don't do this very often.

What has happened to the whole genius of the community development extension method? I'm quoting Indians now, top people who were right in the middle of this thing and on the firing line, not in Delhi. Here are the quotes. "It became an administrators' program," one of them said. Another said, "It became a construction program. It was so much easier to mobilize the people to build roads, and clinics, and schools, and things of that sort, than it was to carry on the extension programs." "It became an amenities program," one of them said, "they got to putting a lot of emphasis upon consumption and forgetting the thing that is fundamental, to get increased production."

Perhaps the important fact is that the Indian leaders are putting their whole program through a very critical examination and they are recognizing the defects in practice which I have mentioned. They are now launching what they call the Second Front. They have learned out of their own experience the things which I have recited in my critical appraisal of the program and are now launching activities which they think will be correctives to the weak spots in the program. When they ask me what can be done by way of correctives, my answer is clear—just do what you started out to do in the beginning and do it by the community development method. Indians wouldn't use my terms, but my terms are, "I don't know how to make Christians out of administrators."

Albert Mayer. I would like to recount a breakfast meeting which preceded this discussion. One of the objectives was to decide on the ethics, as it were, of treating these issues. If you internally feel criticisms that are rather strong, do you express them to a group that isn't a group of technicians, of "insiders," and will they lose confidence in the thing, will they throw out the baby with the dirty bath water? What is the effect on a mixed group of people, of telling them what you fully think? One of the expressions we used was: "Shall we unleash Carl?" I want to say this, that we thought the best thing to do was to have each person present honestly what he thought. We feel that we all are mature enough and understanding enough to draw the right conclusions—namely that we must recognize defects, must help to identify them and correct them, not to sugar-coat and to fail to present realities. The conclusion then is that we must help more, not stop helping. And we were the freer to decide on unleashing, because it turned out that Arthur Mosher has a somewhat more optimistic estimate of the situation and this therefore shows what people equally qualified, equally sincere, and all of them friends of India and of the underdeveloped countries, are thinking.

Carl Taylor. Make no mistake about it. I still have faith in the Indian program. I think it was a perfect program as designed, and I think the Indians are making good criticism of their program and will introduce the corrections.

Albert Mayer. I think you have retracted too much. I think there are definite defects which are worth discussing for enlightened consideration.

Arthur Mosher. Well, as for how perfect the Indian program was to begin with, I think there were certain flaws from the beginning. The first was that far too much confidence was placed on preservice training of village workers and there wasn't nearly enough provision made for *in-service* training. It would have been better if the preservice training had been reduced and much greater provision made for frequent conferences and in-service training of the village workers themselves, continued year after year.

Second, there was not nearly enough in-built, continuing experimentation. Etawah is still an experimental project, but India needs a hundred or two hundred experimental projects, free from all of the directives and the procedures of the standardized national program, each allowed to develop as it wants to internally, just to see what happens and to measure the results.

In general I was terribly concerned when Albert Mayer showed up in India because it looked as though all the eggs were going to be put in his basket, and if this failed, if Etawah did not succeed, it seemed to me that the whole cause of rural development in India would be set back immeasurably. Fortunately, that didn't happen. It turned out to be a good basket. Again, when the Etawah process was then repeated *rapidly* all over the country, this "impatience," I thought, was a mistake. I've changed my mind. I think it is well that the program has taken the course it has. Why? Because you now have scattered all over India, through all of these development blocks, village workers, block workers, district workers, who have learned an enormous amount about this process of community development. You have within the program at the present time the seeds for the correctives that Dr. Taylor was talking about in the fact of the experience of the people who have been working at it in many parts of India, at many different phases of the problem.

Asoka Mehta. Dr. Taylor has stressed the importance of the village panchayats in connection with the mobilizing of the effective participation of the people. But, a defect which was brought home to me three or four years back, when I was working on the Land Reform Panels is that a village panchayat is too small a unit to stand up against the massive administration at the other end.

Here is a central government with all its vast resources and expertise, Indian and foreign, this whole galaxy of people coming to advise them, guide them, challenge them; next the state administration, again with great resources, and finally the poor little panchayat or village council, on the other end. The whole thing is completely out of balance. What is needed is an effective amount of counterweights and we came to the conclusion that the local panchayat could never be an instrument for mobilizing real participation unless two things are done.

One, that the community block as a whole is made a block of government, that it becomes an elective unit, that the block panchayat becomes the lowest unit of elected administration in place of the village panchayat, which is simply too isolated, too small, too weak, too incapable of standing up against this mighty man coming from Delhi, Bombay, or Calcutta, whatever is the state capital. Well, as a result of some of the suggestions made by the Land Reform Panels, a committee was set up and it has produced a very interesting report in which this line of thought has been accepted. But acceptance of an idea at the committee level is very easy. What happens when there is a block panchayat? What would happen when hundreds of villages form a panchayat and become completely self-governing?

I have been told that when the Tennessee Valley Authority was developed, the administration tried to enter into contractual agreements with the small local town councils, the village bodies, and there was no effort to impose anything from above. In the absence of some such procedure the little man gets frightened and does not feel that he counts. However, the moment that you suggest some kind of a block panchayat embracing a hundred villages or two hundred villages or whatever it is, the state politician then feels, what remains of *his* power? As matters stand, power in the state capital is limited to a small group of ministers. For the two hundred or three hundred members of the legislature, their strength ultimately lies in being the sole and only cock of the walk so far as the constituency of each is concerned. If he ceases to be the cock of the walk, well, who is going to look up to him?

George F. Gant. The great impression that the Indian Five Year Plans give is one of size and of urgency. The problems are great in terms of the numbers of people involved, and in terms of the amount of money required, and the impression given is that results must be achieved every year. I would like to suggest that this emphasis upon quantity is inclined to divert attention from the quality of development programs in India, and also to postpone adequate attention to participation of a much larger proportion of the Indian population in this process of growth. India has done an amazing job in creating a community development program. The objective is by the end of the Third Five Year Plan to cover India with a community development program. This calls for about 100,000 village workers—that is, approximately one village-level worker for each five villages. Already India has upwards of 20,000 village-level workers, which compares in size to the total number of extension workers in the United States of ten thousand. This rapid growth in the bureaucracy is in itself a remarkable achievement. However, these village-level workers, upon whom India is depending so heavily, are graduates of junior high schools or high schools who have had an additional twelve to eighteen months of training. They were put into the field before adequate supervision was available for them, and their jobs assumed the availability of competent technical help from other departments such as agriculture, health, education, and industry. And yet that help has not been forthcoming in adequate quality or volume. This is the result of the demand for speed and haste which provides a framework for growth, but which for the time being, as has already been shown, is producing disappointing results.

One of the outstanding problems of India is in my view the adjustment of the bureaucracy to meet the challenge of the Five Year Plans. By and large the administrative and governmental procedures of India have not changed in the past twelve years to suit the new development programs. India has made great progress, in my opinion, in increasing the size of the bureaucracies, in setting up new agencies, and in getting these agencies staffed. But these agencies are compressed within the old outdated, outmoded methods of administration, so that the very good people who are staffing these agencies are actually not free to discharge their functions.

V / NEW PATTERNS OF
PRIVATE INVESTMENT IN INDIA

"Only a few years ago," observed H. V. R. Iengar, Governor of the Reserve Bank of India, addressing a distinguished audience of United States business leaders, "there was considerable resistance in many countries to the very conception of India manufacturing items such as machinery, machine tools, and the more complicated chemicals. This resistance arose from a disinclination to lose a market and to part with know-how to a country which, it was felt, might use it eventually to compete with its teachers in the world markets. This view was clearly misconceived and is no longer held by any responsible corporation in the world. It has come to be recognized that in a competitive world, India will have no difficulty in acquiring know-how from some country or other and indeed it has been recognized too that the setting up of production in India with a relatively low wage structure might be of advantage to the foreign corporations in exporting to certain regions. The difficulty is now fundamentally that of capital."

"Considerable resistance" understates, perhaps, the psychological barrier which has impeded the entrance of United States private investment to India on a significant scale. The barrier lies not only in the stereotype of the have-not countries as markets which should be kept as markets but in a fear of risk-taking on far-off shores while unexploited investment opportunity still remains on the more familiar political and social terrain of Canada, Latin America, Western Europe, and the United States itself. With the passage of time and increasing mutual familiarity between India and the United States, some, but only some, of the hesitation among United States investors has given way to a new quickening of interest. Even before the President's visit to New Delhi in 1959 the Government of India had begun to stress its desire for more American private investment in the Third Five Year Plan. Much may still have to be done, notably in the form of tax concessions by the Indian and United States governments, if any substantial increase is to be expected. Although the Indo-United States double taxation treaty of 1959 was a step forward, most experts and businessmen maintain, neither government made enough concessions from its respective orthodoxy. But whatever the pace of expansion, few doubt the long-range trend to a heavy United States private investment commitment in India. Already United States capital invested in India has increased from $110 million in 1957 to $260 million at the start of 1960. This trend, as Vice-President *Richard M. Nixon* stresses, has many incidental foreign policy advantages and should be officially promoted in our future relations with India.

Richard M. Nixon. When we consider the importance of India and its relationship to the security and freedom of the free world, I think that perhaps we can best put this in context by pointing out one of the great crises which confronts us today and measuring the problems of India against that crisis. To take one example, I would not underestimate the importance of the Berlin crisis; but I will say that in my own mind what happens to India, insofar as its economic progress is concerned in the next few years, could be as important, or could be even more important in the long run, than what happens in the negotiations with regard to Berlin.

Now having made this statement, let me indicate why I believe that is the case. As we know, in the great struggle which is going on in the world today, primary emphasis at the present time is on the nonmilitary aspect of the struggle—in Asia, in Africa, in the Near East, and in parts of Latin America. And the whole world—not only the Asian world, but the American world, this hemisphere—is watching that struggle in Asia. There are two great peoples in Asia. The peoples who live under the Communist government of China, and the people of India. These are the two greatest population centers of the world, and of course the two greatest in Asia. One of these peoples is attempting to achieve economic progress without freedom. The other, the people of India, are attempting to achieve economic progress *with* freedom. They are very different in many respects, but they are alike in this respect. They both need —they both *want*—economic progress, and so the question which will be answered in the next five years—the next ten years—will be this: Can a people who need economic progress to satisfy the wants of their greatly increasing populations, achieve it in a climate of freedom, or must they pay for progress by giving up freedom? Thus what happens in India will have a tremendous impact on the decisions made in other countries in Asia, in the Near East, in Africa, and even in the Americas. So this indicates the tremendous stake that the free world has in the economic problems of India.

Now, a second point that I would make is with regard to the attitude of the Government of the United States—the attitude that our government and our people should have insofar as it affects any aid we are able to provide for the economic development of India, or any other country in a similar status. I have often heard it said, during debates on this subject, that there are times when countries which we have been able to assist through loans or other programs should not receive such consideration in the future because their leaders do not always agree with our leaders in the United Nations, or in other world councils. And my answer is always this: The purpose of United States aid has been, is, and must always be, not to make any country dependent upon us, but to allow all countries to be independent of us or of any other foreign domination. Now—how can we justify, my friends in the Congress might ask then, the allocation of government funds when we agree at the outset that those funds may not, in some instances, obtain complete agreement with the policies of the United States. My answer is this: Our stake, the free world's stake, in India and all the other countries which are in this category, is that they are able to get the economic stability which will enable them in turn to have political independence. How does this serve us? It serves us because international communism and national independence are completely incompatible.

Now, a third point that I would make is this. We agree that India needs economic progress. There is, of course, considerable disagreement as to how other nations may assist and work with the people and Government of India in attaining that progress. The easy answer would be, as far as the United States is concerned, to suggest that we best could assist by expanding what government does, and I would certainly say here today that our technical assistance programs, the programs of loans through the Export-Import Bank and the Development Loan Fund, and other governmental programs, certainly should be approved in the minimum amounts which have been requested by the Administration. But I would be less than realistic if I were not to point out that if you were to place exclusive or even primary reliance on government assistance from the United States in order to attain this economic progress, we would be most unrealistic. We should consider always how private capital may also be attracted to this area of the world. And I would mention just three advantages that private capital has over government capital, recognizing at the outset that both are necessary, and both have their place.

First: Private capital is expansible, almost to an unlimited extent, whereas government capital, insofar as our country, the United States, is concerned, is limited—limited by our own budget and by the considerations which always come up when budget problems are before a country.

The second point is that where private capital is concerned there is and can be no question of any political influence going with it, and on occasions there is, of course, a question where government capital is concerned that there might be political implications involved.

Thirdly, private capital brings with it the skilled technical assistance which is needed, and without which capital might be wasted. There are these three advantages, but the greatest advantage of private capital is that it is expansible, whereas government capital is definitely limited.

And now if I could go to one last point. It is related to my first—the importance of India in relation to the security and freedom of the free world. Speaking now as an official of the American government, and as an American citizen, I do not think the case for government assistance, the case for the interest of the American people in our friends in India, should rest simply on the negative defensive issue of helping India in order to save the United States from communism. I think the case can better be presented in terms of—not the defeat of communism, in which of course we are interested because we realize that freedom can live only where dictators are defeated—but our primary interest must be the victory of plenty over want, of health over disease, of freedom over tyranny of any type, wherever it exists in the world. As far as our friends in India are concerned, we should assure those in that great land so far away, in which we have always had such a warm and friendly interest, that we welcome the opportunity to work with them in economic development so that it may be proved to all the world that it is possible to have progress with freedom.

That is our aim, and we know also that it is theirs.

A PARTNERSHIP APPROACH

If United States private investment is, in fact, to increase on a substantial scale, the investor will have to act on an awareness of the new national economic objectives of an independent India. This view is expressed in similar terms by Washington lawyer *Matthew J. Kust,* former legal counsel (1951–1954) to United States embassies in South Asia and a specialist in international investment and tax problems; and by Columbia Professor *Wolfgang Friedmann,* author of *Joint International Business Ventures in India.* Both emphasize the same emerging new pattern of doing business in India—Mr. Kust's "technical collaboration agreement" and Professor Friedmann's "joint venture." Mr. Kust presents a definitive analysis of the Indian legal and administrative structure as it helps and hinders the foreign private investor.

Matthew J. Kust. An American lawyer approaching the countries of South Asia for the first time finds that very little business can be done without government sanction; industrial undertakings appear to be unduly regulated and highly taxed. He is apt to conclude without probing further that these countries are unfriendly to private business, particularly foreign enterprise. Nothing could be further from the truth. All these countries espouse the philosophy of a mixed economy in which the private sector is allotted a primary role. But private business is required to conform to the objectives of the countries' social and economic policies. Within the framework of these objectives it is not only welcome but encouraged.

Shortly after independence on April 6, 1949, the Prime Minister of India made a policy statement on foreign enterprise in which he assured and admonished foreign investors that:

(1) there would be no discrimination in the treatment of domestic and foreign enterprise;

(2) foreign enterprise would be permitted to earn profits subject only to regulations common to all;

(3) there would be no restriction on the remittance of profits or repatriation of capital except that remittance facilities would naturally depend on foreign exchange considerations;

(4) if and when foreign enterprises are compulsorily acquired, compensation will be paid on a fair and equitable basis;

(5) the major interest is ownership and effective control of an industrial undertaking and it should, as a rule, be in Indian hands, and;

(6) training and employment of Indians for higher posts should proceed in the quickest possible manner.

This policy statement remains unchanged and has been faithfully honored since that time.

The regulation of industry in India is governed by the Industrial Policy Resolution of April 20, 1956, which sets forth the development of a socialist pattern of society as the objective of social and economic policy in India. This has frightened many Americans, perhaps more than Europeans, but it means very little more than the achievement of a welfare state. The socialist pattern of society means primarily rapidly increased production and more equitable distribution of the increased wealth.

The increased production is to be achieved by a division of responsibility between the public and private sectors. Three categories of industries are established for this purpose. Those listed in Schedule A, such as, arms, ammunition, atomic energy, railways, air transport, iron and steel, mining, etc., are reserved exclusively for the State. Those listed in Schedule B, such as, machine tools, chemicals, fertilizers, road transport, sea transport, etc., are to be developed jointly by public and private enterprise with the State ultimately responsible for their development. Those industries not listed, which are many, are left to private enterprise. The Resolution adds that these categories are not watertight compartments and private enterprise will be permitted to undertake even Schedule A industries where it is able and willing to do so. The license granted the Tatas to expand their steel capacity by 1 million tons demonstrates that this is more than mere words.

While the Five Year Plans provide specifically for projects in the public sector, they merely establish objectives and priorities for the private sector. There is no legal compulsion of private enterprise to undertake certain projects. Yet it is obvious that if there is to be sound economic planning surveillance over private enterprise must be exercised to assure that its capital and skills are used to attain national objectives. Limited indigenous capital and skills and a shortage of foreign exchange make this imperative.

India resorts to several legislative and administrative mechanisms for this purpose foremost of which is the Industries (Development and Regulation) Act of 1951. As amended this Act requires the registration of existing and the licensing of new enterprises in forty-two categories of industries. The Act provides for a Licensing Committee, consisting of representatives from the Ministries of Commerce and Industry, Finance, Railways, Production, and the Planning Commission to examine license applications.

The efficacy of this legal and administrative mechanism for coordinating the public and private sectors under the Plans remains to be seen. Foreign enterprise generally views the Act as an undue obstacle to private investment. Indian business accepts it as a necessary mechanism of economic planning. There is considerable complaint of administrative delay and impediment. But it is a matter of record that in 1956 the Licensing Committee reviewed over 1000 applications and granted some 850 licenses for new undertakings and expansion of existing enterprises.

The Capital Issues (Continuation of Control) Act, 1957 provides the government with additional control over new and existing enterprises. This was a war measure extended twice by Parliament. Its stated purpose is to secure a balanced development of the country's resources by directing available capital into the right channels. This Act requires a prior approval of the government for capital issues in India by any domestic or foreign company. The Controller of Capital Issues possesses the power not only to pass upon the amount and type of capital issue, but can establish the price of issue. A certain amount of ineptitude in exercising the latter power a few years ago caused widespread criticism in the Indian capital markets. Moreover since the enactment of the Industries (Development and Regulation) Act the regulation of capital issues for the purpose of channeling capital into desirable investment appears somewhat superfluous.

The new Companies Act of 1956 not only dominates the field of business organization in India but contains many restrictive provisions which conform to the pattern delineated earlier.

Two types of corporate forms of business organization are permitted in India—the private company and the public company. A private company is a company which by its articles of incorporation (a) restricts the right to transfer its shares, if any, (b) limits the number of shareholders to not more than fifty, and (c) prohibits any invitation to the public to subscribe to any of its shares or debentures. A public company is a company which does not include such restrictions and limitations in its articles of incorporation.

The new Act permits only two kinds of share capital, namely, equity share capital and preference share capital. Every holder of equity share capital must have the right to vote in proportion to his share of paid-up equity capital in the company. Preference shares may be issued with preferential rights with respect to both dividends and liquidation. An Indian company may also issue debentures, but cannot grant the holders any voting rights. It may, however, make the debentures perpetual and convertible to equity shares.

The new Companies Act contains elaborate and detailed provisions on the management and administration of companies in India, with restrictions on compensation.

A unique and controversial form of business organization in India is the managing agency. A managing agent is a company or firm which under a long-term contract for a fee or percentage of profits manages another company's business and provides it with a wide range of financial and technical services. Some of the large managing agents control fifty or more companies. The bulk of the engineering, coal, jute, tea, paper, flour, and rice industries are managed this way.

The managing agency system served and still serves a useful function in the development of industries in India. In a country where there is a shortage of capital and managerial and technical skills, the managing agency system provides an organization form which makes these limited factors of production available to a greater number of individual enterprises. On the other hand, the system has lent itself to abuse by creating monopolies and permitting unconscionable profit-making.

The Government of India, however, decided to retain the managing agency system in the face of strong opposition but, at the same time, to restrict its use so as to make its abuse less likely. The two most important restrictions found in the Indian Companies Act, 1956, in this connection are (1) the number of managed companies is limited to not more than ten, and (2) profit participation in the managed company is restricted to a maximum of 10 per cent of net profits. The central government is also empowered to designate specific classes of industry and business which shall not employ managing agents.

A foreign company which establishes a place of business within India is required to deliver to the Registrar for registration (a) a certified copy of its charter, (b) the address of its principal office, (*c*) a list of the directors and secretary of the company, (*d*) the name and address of a person or persons resident in India authorized to accept service of process and other notices on behalf of the company, and (*e*) the address of its office in India. Each calendar year thereafter it is required to deliver to the Registrar three copies of a balance sheet and profit and loss statement as prescribed by the Act for Indian companies.

Side by side with the restrictive legislation in the Indian legal system exist many concessionary measures for promoting private investment. These are found primarily in the tax and tariff laws.

The Indian Income Tax Act of 1922, as amended, provides first for a Development Rebate of 25 per cent of the cost of new investment. This permits depreciation of 125 per cent of original cost and is in effect an investment subsidy of about 11.25 per cent. It permits, next, extremely liberal and accelerated depreciation which allows a new enterprise to write off 85 per cent of its investment during the first three years. Finally, if there are any profits of the new enterprise still subject to tax they are exempt from the income and supertax for a period of five years, to the extent of 6 per cent per annum on the capital employed in the new industrial undertaking. In addition, the tax law permits a carry-over of business losses for eight years and favorable treatment of expenditures on research. The net effect is to permit a new enterprise to operate free of Indian income tax for the first five years unless its profits exceed 25 per cent by the end of the period.

Dividends received by a foreign or domestic corporation from an Indian company engaged in any of twenty categories of industries are wholly exempt from supertax under Section 56A. The twenty industries are of the type generally referred to as capital or producers goods industries such as iron and steel, chemicals, heavy machinery, pumps, motors, etc. Thus a foreign company investing in an Indian subsidiary engaged in any of these industries pays an Indian income tax of only 20 per cent on its dividends from such company.

All of the foregoing tax concessions are available to foreign enterprise with a few added specifically for foreigners. Interest payable on a foreign loan or credit for the purchase of capital plant and machinery abroad by an industrial undertaking in India, which is approved by general or special order for this purpose by the central government, is exempt from Indian income tax. Salaries of foreign technicians are also exempt from Indian income tax for one year without and two pears with prior government approval of the contract of service.

At the same time there are a number of deterrents to private enterprise. The income tax rates are pitched high. Indian companies pay 45 per cent. Foreign companies pay 63 per cent. Indian tax authorities do not consider this discrimination against foreign corporations, claiming the differential is designed to equalize the burden since shareholders of foreign corporations are not subject to Indian income tax. This argument hardly satisfies an American company unable to charge the Indian tax off fully against the United States income tax under the foreign tax credit. Personal income tax rates are equally high averaging about 30–50 per cent more than United States rates on salaries of managerial and technical personnel.

The doctrine of business connection under which India taxes extraterritorial income further than most countries is highly disturbing to American business. While this doctrine affects exporters more than investors it could under the holding of the Remington case impose Indian income and supertax on sales of raw materials or components made outside India to an Indian subsidiary, or Indian company with which there is a licensing and technical assistance agreement, even though the dividends from such subsidiary are free of supertax under Section 56A. Contradictions and anomalies of this kind of which there are a number, ought to be purged from the Indian tax system for effective inducement of foreign investment.

Another anomaly is the absence of any tax concession for royalties and technical services. Although technology is as important as capital there is no concession for its transmission to India. Royalties and fees for technical assistance are taxed at 63 per cent. Moreover until recently the Indian government refused to approve foreign licensing agreements which asked for more than 5 per cent royalty. This left the foreign licensor 1.85 per cent in royalties which can hardly be calculated to attract the latest technology to India.

The Indian income tax does not permit a depletion allowance for the mining industry. This may no longer be important, however, since mineral development is now allotted to the State under the Industrial Policy Resolution of 1956.

The Finance Act of 1956 imposed a special supertax on dividends of Indian companies in excess of 6 per cent of paid up capital. It is a graduated tax of 10 per cent on the dividends in excess of 6 per cent but not in excess of 10 per cent, 20 per cent on dividends between 10–18 per cent and 30 per cent on dividends in excess of 18 per cent. Although the dividends tax is imposed without discrimination it hits hardest the British owned export industries such as tea, jute, and others which traditionally pay handsome dividends. This tax was subsequently repealed by the Finance Act of 1959.

The tax measure which disturbed foreign and domestic enterprise most, perhaps, was the compulsory deposit of accumulated and current profits with the government unless used for government approved reinvestment in the business, enacted in 1956. I shall refrain from going into the details of this unique measure, which was obviously designed to channel corporate profits into desirable productive investment, since the Indian government appears to have retreated from it. It was repealed by the Finance Act of 1959.

Equally disturbing are the wealth and expenditure taxes enacted in 1957. The former applied to companies but this has since been repealed. Wealth outside India of foreigners was also exempted by Parliament. The expenditure tax does not apply to companies but will affect foreign managerial and technical personnel when it comes into full force in a few years. Perhaps India will make some allowance for such personnel before that time.

What is the future of foreign enterprise in India in the light of this maze of postindependence legislation, regulation, and policy? It is becoming apparent that the old patterns of doing business are dead or of limited duration. The day of the enterprise wholly owned and controlled by foreigners, whether in the old export industries or the new industrial undertakings, is past. By the same token the days of the pure export market are numbered.

The people wish to build their own industries. For this they need, welcome, and encourage the import of capital goods and technical knowledge from abroad. This calls for a new business relationship between governments and private enterprise in these countries and foreign enterprise. Such a new pattern of doing business is now emerging and is known as the Technical Collaboration Agreement.

The Technical Collaboration Agreement is a genuine business partnership between domestic and foreign enterprise in which each provides the productive factors appropriate to its role. The local partner usually provides and finances everything except the capital goods and technology required from abroad. Foreign enterprise supplies the patents, technicians, machinery, and equipment and the components or raw materials required from abroad. It may do this with or without capital investment in the enterprise. Today all of these countries are short of foreign exchange so that outside financing is required. This can be done by the foreign collaborator or a financial institution abroad.

The Technical Collaboration Agreement has many advantages. The job of complying with the multiplicity of laws, regulations, and policies can be left to the domestic partner who is better able and possesses the necessary mental attitude to cope with it. When the Agreement is sanctioned by the government great advantages ensue which sometimes assure a virtual monopoly, though perhaps limited in time, in the local market for licensing, technical services, and components or raw materials.

Europeans are conforming to this new pattern of doing business in South Asia more readily than Americans. American companies, however, appear to be growing increasingly more interested. It is probably safe to predict that sooner or later the Technical Collaboration Agreement will be the dominant method of American business in South Asia.

Wolfgang Friedmann. A few years ago I attended a United Nations conference in Southeast Asia on the subject of public industrial enterprises. There it became apparent that the Southeast Asian States, and in particular India and Burma, were increasingly interested in joint enterprises. Like other newly independent but undeveloped countries, they came to see that they could not do without foreign participation. Yet they did not wish to abandon control over their basic economic plans.

On the other hand, the Western industrial countries have had to understand, and to an extent they still have to realize, that if they wish to maintain and increase their share in the industrial development of the undeveloped countries, they will have to abandon many established practices and ideas and experiment with new forms of association.

What does "joint venture" mean? In a strict sense, it means

equity participation. When you consider equity participation, the major problem is whether you insist on a majority or accept a minority share. As you know, there are a number of industries for which national legislation, including that of India, prescribes minimum shares to be held by nationals. But that is not, I think, a problem in most of the industries here in question.

The majority of United States enterprises still tend to insist on majority control although, I think, an increasing number do not regard this as absolutely essential. There are also those which, like General Motors, will not contemplate anything but a wholly-owned subsidiary, and I will venture the opinion that this attitude will become increasingly less feasible and practicable as we go on. It is also to be borne in mind that quite often a minority share is quite sufficient to establish control over the enterprise, either because the other shareholders are scattered or, more importantly, because the essential know-how will have to be supplied from the American side for many years to come.

Now joint ventures are more feasible and more frequent in the case of the pharmaceutical industry or other producers of mass-manufactured products than they are in individual engineering ventures. For example, the three steel mills at present under construction by the Russians, Germans, and British respectively, are all owned by the Indian government. In all these cases the foreign entrepreneur provides a long-term loan which is used for the supply of equipment plus technical assistance but not equity participation. (In the German project a 10 per cent equity participation was originally contemplated.) This is generally the form in which joint ventures in heavy industry are likely to proceed. All, however, require some partnership—not in the equity sense, but partnership in the sense of long-term collaboration with all the problems it involves, such as the choice of the top managerial and technical personnel as well as problems of personnel collaboration and remission of profits.

There are a multitude of special investment laws and regulations. India, as you know, has not enacted investment laws; instead the government proclaims investment policy statements from time to time, usually in budget speeches, which are modified in accordance with current requirements. I do not think the difference is very great because when you have a predominant party like the Congress

Party, an investment law can in any case be altered fairly easily. But investment policy statements give at least tentative indications as to what principles are being followed in regard to foreign investment.

When you move among lawyers, as I do, you are struck with their fantastic preoccupation with the problem of nationalization and confiscation. I think that this is due largely to the preeminence among Wall Street lawyers of oil companies, which, to be sure, have been concerned with this problem, especially in the Middle East. But we should see this matter in proportion. We should not regard the problem of nationalization, and certainly of confiscation, as the number one problem in foreign investment. It is an extreme pathological occurrence in case of major revolutions. And if a major revolution occurs, then the most elaborate legal safeguards would be of no use whatsoever. In the case of a country like India, it is clear from the record and inherent in the situation with which India is faced that she will not nationalize or confiscate unless she is prepared to cut off her ties with the West, with the World Bank, and other sources of finance.

An example of what can be done lies in the agreements made in 1953 with three oil companies for the construction of refineries in India. The Indian government gave a promise of nonexpropriation for twenty-five years and of reasonable compensation at any time thereafter. Now that is published as a solemn statement and although there are no sanctions behind it, this is only because in international law we do not have sanctions in the sense that we can send the bailiff. The point to be remembered is that when a government has gone on record with a promise to abstain from nationalization for twenty-five years—short of major revolutions, such as a Communist conquest, in which case these considerations will go overboard with many others—this is as much as a foreign investor can expect. In the great majority of cases he is, of course, not concerned with extreme cases of expropriation but with a multitude of daily problems such as licenses, taxation, remission of capital and profit, import quotas, and other matters which are usually not suitably incorporated in a general investment code (of the kind the Germans are at this time particularly interested in). This is usually a matter of negotiations with the government and other agencies concerned.

Matthew J. Kust. Up to the last few years, at least, many Americans have felt that they had to have 100 per cent control—if not 100 per cent control, at least 51 per cent control. I think we should bear in mind that the essence of a technical collaboration agreement is that control remain in Indian hands, that Indians be trained to run the enterprise, but that the foreign collaborator supply those essential ingredients which are usually the technology and the capital goods which have to come from outside.

American enterprise has been rather reluctant, in the past, to conform to this new pattern of doing business and some of the Europeans have done it faster. European countries are more dependent on foreign markets and have to conform to the new patterns if they are to survive. The Germans were among the earliest to conform to this pattern of taking a minority interest or sometimes no interest at all—but simply going in on the technical and managerial job and with the supply of components, while the phase program of manufacturing was going on. The figures on the redistribution of trade are worth noting. In 1952, the United Kingdom had 67.2 per cent of the market in India in heavy machinery and this dropped to 42.5 per cent by 1957; Germany had 13.4 per cent of the market and it went up to 36.3 per cent in 1957, and the United States remained rather constant at 19.4 per cent in 1952 and 21.2 per cent in 1957. I do not want to leave the impression that the only reason the Germans got much of the market is because they were able readily to enter into these technical collaboration agreements with the lucrative supply of components. There was also the element of the attractive price of German capital goods so that even on open bidding they would get a great deal of the bids, but, nevertheless, I think that a large part of the explanation for their increased share of the Indian market was that they conformed readily, much more readily than did the Americans and the British, to help establish these new manufacturing enterprises in which they had both a technical and a component selling stake.

FIVE CASE HISTORIES

C. B. *Marshall*, Vice-President of the Standard-Vacuum Oil Company, J. *Delano Hitch*, *Jr.*, Chairman of the Dorr-Oliver Corporation, and *Michael Webster*, Assistant to the President of Johnson and Johnson International, describe case histories of private investment which grew out of a measure of preindependence contact with India. Distinguishing the problems he has encountered from the Johnson and Johnson experience, another pharmaceutical manufacturer, *Antonie Knoppers*, representing Merck, Sharp and Dohme, narrates a record which may be more typical of the shape of things to come. The Merck-Tata joint venture exemplifies the new pattern of investment previously described by Mr. Kust and Professor Friedmann.

C. B. Marshall. During the wartime period, and I guess we can talk about it now, it so happened that one of the things the United States government wanted to do was to see whether a refinery in India would be a good thing. It was thought strategic to have a refinery there. We were asked to look into it. A great many plans were made, but unfortunately they had to be scrapped. After the war, it was but natural that the Government of India should ask that these plans be revised, reviewed, and brought up to date.

The first survey, at that time, indicated that probably a refinery could not be an economic proposition. Subsequently, in 1951, I had the pleasure of going out to India, as head of the group to negotiate with the Government of India the terms under which we would build the refinery.

When we got to India, the Government of India made available to us five or six of its top people with whom to negotiate the refinery agreement. We settled our differences of opinion in a very short space of time. I don't know whether they now think quite as well of the agreement as they did at the time it was made. I hear that they don't. I'm sorry if this is so. I must say in all fairness, however, that I've never sat down with five or six tougher, keener, more able negotiators than we did in that particular instance.

In light of these negotiations, it is significant that we have been talking in some other countries for a period of two and three and even four years about refineries, simply because a lack of organization, among other things, makes it impossible to come to a meeting of the minds. Meanwhile our refinery in Bombay has been operating for a good number of years. We presently have invested in that refinery some $40 million.

In 1953 I had the pleasure of going back to India as a member of another team. This time we were seeking exploration and producing rights. We feel that there is some oil in India. We hope there is. This time we again talked to a group of very fine, able men.

We soon came to an agreement. We are spending a lot of money there now, looking for oil.

Over the years we have had confidence in India. If we hadn't, we wouldn't have gone ahead and invested as we have.

I think also, in my private capacity, I can occasionally be critical. I do wish, sometimes, that they would make up their minds exactly what taxation they're going to have so that we would know whether our next nickel is going to be worth one cent, or four cents. I do wish that when a policy is dictated that it would be carried through. This is not always the case. The will is there, but sometimes the people who are to carry out the policy detailed by their lawmakers are unwilling to accept it.

There is a favorable climate for private investment in India. You have only to have something they want and need, and be able to sell it to them. They will provide terms necessary to make it possible for you to invest. I sometimes think, however, and this is being critical, that the honeymoon is over very shortly afterward. Naturally, you get into all of the difficulties of running a business there. But we haven't run a business in India for seventy years just to be willing to sell out tomorrow morning to somebody who feels we should be nationalized; that our distribution system should be nationalized, or that necessarily we should take in a disproportionate amount of local capital. Those are the things upon which opinions differ.

J. Delano Hitch, Jr.   We are an engineering company. We design various and sundry plants. We supply large-scale process equipment— the largest is 375 feet in diameter and it requires the needs of considerable industries to make it worth while to try to go out and sell our services and equipment.

These designed plants are for basic industries, such as sugar, alumina, chemicals, and fertilizers. Our equipment is used in cement, many chemicals, ore dressing, sewage treatment, and water treatment. The latter comes under public health and is a very major concern in India. All metallurgical plants use our equipment as well as pulp and paper plants.

Our first contact with India was in 1912 when we first sold one of our machines to Tata Iron and Steel. It is actually still in operation. Since 1912 and, you might say, up to 1947, all the work we did in India was through our own engineers who travel from one or the other of our companies. We are an American company with six wholly owned subsidiaries in Europe, one in Australia, and one in Canada.

And then in 1947 it became obvious that this was not a suitable method of operating in India. We had a very considerable faith in the growing future of India, particularly of its industry, and had in fact back in 1942 employed an outstanding Indian student from M.I.T. to train him for the purpose of going out to India. In 1947 we sent this Indian and an American to India to make a study of how we might operate to our mutual benefit. We found it a confusing era with laws and practices in a state of flux. Deliberately, as a matter of a stopgap arrangement, we formed another subsidiary, an American subsidiary, with a branch office in Bombay and we continued for the next few years through that branch office to supply our services and sell our equipment from our various sources. We also designed various and sundry plants.

All of the equipment came from one or the other of our companies around the world. Then when the exchange crisis arose in India, it became quite obvious that it would be impossible for India, with its shortage of exchange, to proceed with the building up of industries as they had previously been doing by importing. Therefore, we discussed the possibilities of indigenous manufacture in considerable detail with the authorities in New Delhi and received a considerable amount of encouragement and support, and our enthusiasm increased as we went at it. After some six months of study, we picked out three or four local shops, some of them not too close to Bombay. These shops we found could very satisfactorily manufacture, depending on the machine, anywhere from 60 per cent of a given machine to, say 99 per cent, where only a very small component part would have to be imported.

We immediately started manufacturing in these different shops and even though these shops had not had experience in this sort of manufacture, they did have the machine tools and good trained workmen. After a considerable number of difficulties, we were able to produce our machines in these various shops. Because our staff engineers also covered the general area of Southeast Asia we did sell equipment for export from India. It has been the practice of all our other companies in other countries to encourage and increase the exports from those countries. We have received considerable encouragement in the exporting of equipment from India to create foreign exchange.

In order to get into this more complicated manufacturing type of work, rather than just selling and importing, it became necessary for us to build our engineering staff. We started four years ago with about three; we now have forty-two people, about half of them engineers, and all but one being Indian engineers for whom we have considerable respect. The only limitation that I can see on the business that a company such as ours does is the amount of steel that can be made available and the facilities—manufacturing facilities—that can be made available.

There is a very great need for the equipment that we have because it all goes into the basic industries the Indians need for their progress. We have had very great encouragement and assistance in the way of licenses and help in importing small components to complete large machines. The percentage of imported components is very definitely decreasing, for which we are glad and I believe the exchange people are, too.

Recently we have decided, after considerable study and also conferences with very helpful officials in New Delhi, that what we would like to do would be to convert the corporate operations there from a branch office of an American company to an Indian company with Indian participation. We have been told by people whom we consider important that the reason we have had such an excellent reception on this proposal is that instead of hoping, thinking, and planning, we actually went into this work and did it. And instead of importing $2 or $3 million worth a year to India, we have been manufacturing about the same amount there and have been exporting a percentage of that. I have every confidence that our work there will continue to increase at a satisfactory rate.

Michael Webster. Our company had traded in India for many years on an export basis when it was decided, shortly after India's independence in 1947, to make a more determined penetration of the market and to gain a greater intimacy with it. The following six or seven years were a valuable period of preparation for us. The nucleus of our future management was trained and acclimatized. Local manufacturing and distribution arrangements were pioneered and market potentials and customs were assessed.

In 1955 we decided we wanted to invest in full-scale manufacturing and selling activities in India and we put a proposal before the authorities in Delhi. This was approved in 1956 and today we have established a very fine plant just outside Bombay which is now in production.

There are probably many representatives of companies who have reviewed the Indian market and have decided against investment there or who are as yet undecided. It will probably be of interest therefore for me to recount some of our experiences and our feelings about India as a climate for investment.

First of all, let me discuss the political situation as the businessman might look at it. The attitude of the government and the political parties is one which, in India of all places, the potential investor must study and understand. This is because of the intimate way in which the economic activities are associated with the political life of the country and are subject to central planning by the government. Let us understand, however, that the often-stated principle that India intends to establish a socialistic society does not mean that India's aim is the achievement of a Marxist society. What is intended is that the individual elements of society be harnessed to make their most effective contribution to the welfare of society as a whole.

To the businessman, this means that the private sector of the economy, in which he will operate, is subject to certain broad strictures which are intended to ensure that its principles conform to the over-all plan. This philosophy should not cause the potential investor a disproportionate amount of alarm. Baldly stated, it may sound like a considerable deterrent to him. But if he has founded a business which contributes to the economic growth of India (and he will not obtain the necessary industrial license unless it does), I think he will find that in practice his operation will be subject to a very minimum of interference. Furthermore, because these principles have been established, and by and large are maintained, the investor can take comfort in the fact that they afford a considerable degree of stability and permanence.

Nationalization of private enterprise is another topic which through the years has received wide publicity abroad. In the first flush of independence, as a result of the tendency to identify capitalism with foreign domination, there is no doubt that nationalization had a considerable appeal. However, as early as 1948 Mr. Nehru pointed out that nationalization, apart from a few basic areas of the economy, was something India simply could not afford, even if she wanted it. Demands on the financial resources of the country were so great that the government could not provide the amounts of compensation necessary to nationalize private concerns. In the whole twelve years since independence there have been only a few isolated cases.

Today I think the political enthusiasm for nationalization of industry has greatly diminished, reflecting in part the subsidence of interest in it in England and in Europe in general. Certainly in our own corporate thinking nationalization is not a factor to be feared in the foreseeable future.

Because India's is an economy subject to centralized planning, business activity is undoubtedly exposed to a considerable degree to government controls. These are first encountered in negotiating one's original proposal to gain government support. Any really major change or expansion of the business will require similar authorization. However, apart from the controls exercised on imports, and these are to be met with in virtually every country, government interference in day to day operations does not seem to be any greater than one would meet in the majority of other countries. I think, in fact, the practice turns out to be far easier than the theory.

In surveying India as a place for investment, I think an American businessman would find a considerable number of attractive features. In the first place, the business language, at least in a majority of circles in which you will have contact, is English. The legal and accounting systems are ones which he will find, for the most part, familiar. Patent, copyright, and trade-mark law is well developed. There is a mature financial system. In addition, there are some specific advantages to consider. Counterpart funds under P.L. 480 are now available to the American investor. A guarantee of convertibility of rupees into dollars can be obtained from the International Cooperation Administration. A double taxation agreement has been negotiated between the United States and India. Another factor of considerable importance is the Indian government's impeccable record for providing foreign exchange for the remission of corporate earnings.

On the other side of the coin, corporate tax rates in India are indeed very onerous. However, against this consideration can be placed the very substantial tax reliefs available in the early years of the operation.

To invest in manufacturing facilities in India requires the obtaining of an industrial license from the Ministry of Commerce and Industry, approval by the Ministry of Finance of the financial plan, and an authorization by the Reserve Bank of India in regard to the foreign exchange provisions.

The most important of these is the industrial license. Principally, the Ministry of Commerce and Industry examines the proposal to see if it contains a basic manufacturing program or at least provides for the phased development of one. Of vital interest to them will be whether the products to be manufactured will save or earn foreign exchange or make some other significant contribution to the economy.

Another very important feature will be whether the plan provides for partnership with local Indian capital. I may add that our corporate experience has been that a partnership with good sound Indian interests can be of the greatest benefit to the enterprise. There have been many other American corporations which have established happy and satisfactory relations with Indian partners.

We, like many others, found our negotiations with various government departments to be a rather protracted affair requiring considerable patience. However, in our case, this was principally because of a difference of opinion over one issue. Partly because the government officials' attitude was very reasonable and accommodating, partly because we took considerable pains beforehand to prepare our proposal in as much detail as possible and to adapt it to accord with the government's policies, we experienced very little difficulty in obtaining approval of the basic proposal with a minimum of discussion over the details.

I would rather think that negotiating a proposal has become an easier matter now since Delhi has become more experienced in handling foreign investors and has more clearly defined the policies by which it is guided. I understand that it is now planned to establish several centers in countries abroad to expedite the consideration of foreign investment proposals.

There are several recommendations I would make to a prospective investor from our own experience. Firstly, prepare your proposal with great care and in considerable detail. Secondly, be flexible in your negotiations. As far as possible, adapt them to fit in with the policies and philosophies of the central government. Thirdly, if possible, conduct the important part of your negotiations with highly placed officials. Delhi is still a place where decisions are made by a surprisingly small number of competent men at the top of the various ministries.

There is one last point I would like to add. It has been our experience that though acceptance of the proposal must be the result of considerable negotiation, the authorities abide strictly by their agreements once made. As far as I am aware, no one else has had a different experience.

I think that far too many opportunities are being missed in India by American private enterprises. India is a large country, has an expanding economy, and represents a considerable market for a wide range of goods. While it is true that bureaucratic controls are a hindrance to the freedom of operation that we are accustomed to enjoy in the United States, this may be offset by the absence of competitive activity met in the United States. There are always problems in doing business anywhere. In India they are simply different problems. Too many investors have been deterred, in my opinion, not by the magnitude of the problems, but by their unfamiliar nature.

Antonie Knoppers. The case of Johnson and Johnson presented by Michael Webster is somewhat similar to ours, so I would like to limit myself to mentioning only some of the peculiarities, some of the developments in our experience that were out of the normal order. One striking peculiarity of our case that should be mentioned at the outset lies in the fact that we are active both in the public sector—in the form of technical assistance—and in the private sector—through a joint venture with Tata Sons Private, Ltd. Our activity in the public sector is confined to technical assistance for Hindustan Antibiotics, Ltd., a government-owned company which we have licensed to produce streptomycin and dihydrostreptomycin.

The case study which I shall present is of our joint venture. I would like to describe that development by dividing it up in a number of steps.

Step No. 1. For about five years we were in the process of discussions with the Indian government—off and on—about the possibility of producing streptomycin and dihydrostreptomycin in India. Since malaria has been brought under control, tuberculosis is the most important disease in India. We knew from publications by the Indian government that drugs, especially antibiotics and other essential medicines, belong in the category which can be handled both in the public sector and the private sector. We were aware, too, that the Indian government definitely prefers to handle antibiotics in the public sector, mostly because of the central importance of those drugs for Indian health. We came to the conclusion that we would be prepared in principle to license the government-owned Hindustan Antibiotics, Ltd. Further, that if possible, we would like to establish a company ourselves in India to produce and sell other drugs arising from our research in the private sector.

Step No. 2. In this project a thorough and careful study of the problems involved was a necessity. We interviewed, for instance, many, many people who had actual experience in India.

Step No. 3. In 1957 and 1958, negotiations were held with the Indian government. We had become aware of the fact that the U.S.S.R. had offered the Indian government a plan of broad assistance in the drug field. One part of that plan included the production of streptomycin and dihydrostreptomycin. Let me state emphatically that our deal with the Indian government to give technical assistance to Hindustan Antibiotics, Ltd. was motivated by reasons of business alone. But the tempo with which this deal was achieved was certainly influenced by the facts just mentioned.

Step No. 4. During these negotiations concerning streptomycin, we also discussed separately a possible investment in the private sector. Although the negotiations on this subject were kept completely separate from those of streptomycin and dihydrostreptomycin, we feel, in retrospect, that the positive atmosphere of the negotiations on streptomycin was helpful in expediting entry into the private sector.

We are very grateful that the Indian government acted so rapidly and gave us the license to operate in the private sector by approving our plans to build a chemical and pharmaceutical plant.

Step No. 5. At this point we had not decided whether we would like to start such a plant alone or in the form of a joint venture. In the beginning of the negotiations the Indian government suggested that they would have no objection to our starting with 100 per cent ownership if we would take in partners inside of a few years. However, when the license was definitely issued, the Indian government insisted that we should take Indian partners or investors in immediately, though there was no objection to Merck having a 60 per cent majority. As by that time we had come to the conclusion ourselves that a joint venture should be our first choice, we accepted this condition of the license without grumbling.

Step No. 6. This step was certainly one of the most important: the selection of a partner in our joint venture. We felt that it would be most important to discuss with prospective partners the problems thoroughly and in depth, since many difficulties can be averted when these problems are frankly discussed before making the deal. Many excellent and respectable firms had approached us for a joint venture. One of them—Tata Sons Private, Ltd.—offered many advantages. A number of our goods had been distributed for about thirty years by Volkart, a company in which Tata had acquired a minority interest. Our ties with that firm were excellent and had withstood the test of time. We had many lengthy discussions with the representatives of that excellent firm. I cannot emphasize enough the importance of such negotiations. They are real preventive medicine for potential trouble in the future.

Our total initial investment will be about $5.8 million. A chemical and pharmaceutical plant will be built producing steroids, vitamins, diuretics, and other products of our research.

Step No. 7. In the spring of 1959 I was in India and both projects in the public sector and in the private sector had made substantial progress. In the private sector the relationship with our partners has deepened; we really are making headway. The streptomycin and dihydrostreptomycin project in the public sector has made substantial progress as well. It is with some pleasure that I report that the progress in the private sector seems to be somewhat faster than that in the public one.

What happened when *Arthur J. Phillips*, general counsel of Godfrey Cabot, Inc., sought to establish a carbon-black factory in India provides an omnibus case history of the many real or imagined obstacles sometimes confronting the investor in India. Mr. Phillips' account is the starting point for a wide-ranging discussion—on the possibility of nationalization, rates of profit, and Indian licensing policy on raw material imports— which evokes the participation of Washington lawyer *Jerome Levinson*, who has studied aspects of United States private investment on a Fulbright fellowship in India; Professor *Wolfgang Friedmann*, Delhi industrialist *Bharat Ram, Matthew J. Kust*, and *C. S. Krishnamoorthi*. Mr. Krishnamoorthi, who is Counsellor in the Commission General for Economic Affairs for India in Washington, was previously responsible for screening foreign investment applications in the Finance Ministry, New Delhi.

Arthur Phillips.   We at Godfrey Cabot manufacture, among other things, a rather unglamorous but essential chemical called carbon black which results from the incomplete combustion of hydrocarbon, and when added to tires increases their life from, say, 3000 miles to as high as 30,000. Up until the second World War, all carbon black was made in the United States from natural gas, but because of technological breakthroughs during the war it became possible to make it out of heavy residual oil which made the carbon black industry mobile; you could put the oil in tankers and build plants anywhere in the world near deep water. This mobility permitted us to launch a program of foreign expansion and we now have carbon black plants in Canada, England, and France and we are building in Italy, Australia, and Argentina.

The Indian market for carbon black is approximately 20 million pounds a year for which India has to spend very valuable foreign exchange to the extent of about $2 million a year. This is really a very small market and will support only a small and rather inefficient size plant, but if India reaches the real take-off stage, the demand for tires in India, and hence for carbon black, will grow enormously. Recognizing that this material is essential and that its local production would save important amounts of foreign exchange, India in the Second Five Year Plan has given a high priority to the establishment of a local carbon black facility.

Now in 1957 we met in London with Mr. Kasturbhai Lalbhai and after two or three days of very pleasant negotiations, we arrived at an agreement under the terms of which we would set up a carbon black plant in Bombay, to be owned 50 per cent by Mr. Kasturbhai Lalbhai and 50 per cent by ourselves. One of the initial stumbling blocks was the apparent reluctance on the part of India to grant what we consider normal royalty and other fees, so to obviate that difficulty we agreed to transfer all our India patents and patent applications to the new company in exchange for 20 per cent of its stock and to purchase the other 30 per cent of the stock for cash in dollars, that being more than sufficient dollars to take care of the necessary imports of machinery and equipment with which to build the plant.

That was about two years ago. We asked, in addition, before making the investment, for certain assurances from the Indian government and I would like just to run through them—there are only seven of them, they are quite mild.

The first and most important one would be permission to import the raw materials with which to make the carbon black free of duty, there being no local raw material available in India suitable for making carbon black. Second, the right to import machinery and equipment not readily available in India. Third, the classification of the parent United States company as a nonresident company for tax purposes. Fourth, freedom of entry for technicians subject to security restrictions. Fifth, waiver of capital gains taxes upon nationalization. Sixth, obtaining freedom from supertax on dividends under Section 56A, and seventh, permission to use compulsory deposits to expand the plant rather than inject fresh capital. Now the assurance in connection with compulsory deposits, I understand, is no longer of any particular importance as the government has since abolished the program.

On the question of no capital gains tax on nationalization, we were told that would be unconstitutional. But we were also told there was absolutely no danger of our being nationalized, and here I must take a little issue with Professor Friedmann, who seemed to imply that you might be able to obtain from the Indian government an agreement not to nationalize for a period of years. He mentioned Cal-Tex and Stan-Vac as having obtained that in 1953. I can only assure him that from our own experience it is utterly impossible to get such a letter from the Indian government today; they bitterly regret having given such a letter to Cal-Tex and Stan-Vac. So we have to, more or less, take it on faith that we will not be nationalized. Of course, there is no I.C.A. program to cover this. It is just one of the risks that you have to take.

On the other four assurances, we received, I think, rather vague answers, rather brief; in fact, I can quote them in full. "Government agrees with you in principle"—that was the answer on four of the assurances.

Last, but not least, is the question of import of raw materials. At first we were told we could not import raw materials at all, that there were adequate raw materials available in India. We happen to know from our contacts in the oil industry that there are no adequate raw materials in India for making carbon black. In the fall of 1958, Mr. Manubhai Shah, the Minister of Commerce and Industry, gave us permission to import raw materials provided the cost of importing the raw materials and the necessary recurrent supplies for running the plant would not exceed 50 per cent of the foreign exchange savings achieved by the local plant. But we have not been able to achieve an agreement from the government on the waiver of duty on the raw materials. We have been told that the duty will be varied anywhere from zero to 40 per cent. This question of duty we consider extremely vital for three reasons.

First, if the duty on the raw materials is 40 per cent, that will add a burden of approximately $300,000 a year to a plant which is quite small because the market is comparatively small. Second, an import duty might force us to use local raw materials with which we would make, we are quite sure, inferior black and alienate our customers in India. And that alienation might spread to headquarters in London and Akron with disastrous effects. Last but not least, this variation of the import duty might be an indirect method of price control to restrict our profits to what is considered a reasonable level. We feel that the Indian concept of reasonable profit is a percentage of somewhere between 6 and 12 per cent of gross bloc, pretax, and if this duty is imposed, that we will be restricted to that level which is hardly an adequate return on the investment.

In conclusion, to sum up where we stand now after two and a half years, I think a lot of our original enthusiasm has been dissipated. I think we are somewhat frustrated—I think we must insist on a waiver of import duty, and frankly, I just don't know where we stand. I think we would be very reluctant to go in with such an unknown as this import duty on the raw materials which is such an essential part of the entire project.

Wolfgang Friedmann. I am quite sure of the Government of India's reluctance to give assurances against nationalization to all companies. One reason, of course, is that the promise given to the oil companies has given concern. Oil is, of course, one of the industries basically reserved to the public sector and it was probably necessary to give an additional assurance in that field so that there was no fear that the government would come, or the Congress Party would come, and say, "well, this is not according to basic policy and will have to be operated nationally." I think that Mr. Phillips and I, being lawyers, are probably more aware than many others of the limitations of the assurances against nationalization. My main point was, and I think it is important, that in this field the essential is confidence that in the future you will not have a violent overthrow. Because in that case, of course, the new government won't care two rupees about the agreement of the prior government.

Jerome Levinson. You are quite right in saying that the decision on the oil companies has given concern. Within India there is a great deal of feeling, especially among the younger people, that the oil companies, at a time when the Indian government was not sure of itself, got terms which, in retrospect, the younger people feel are unfair to the economy of India and the Government of India, and as a result, there is a great deal of emotional bitterness and agitation to rectify, without overturning these decisions.

Matthew J. Kust. I would like to get back to another important point Mr. Phillips has raised. In order to have a mixed economy such as India is pursuing, where you have a private and a public sector under one economic plan, you obviously have to have some kind of coordination of those two sectors. That's where all this licensing comes in. One of the most novel institutional innovations that has come out of economic planning in India is the Industries (Development and Regulations) Act. This Act gives the government the power to license industries and it has set up a number of criteria on the basis of which they are to be licensed—such as foreign exchange savings, proper allocation of the resources in the country, and the objectives of industrialization. Obviously when you get something like that into your legal and administrative framework, it's pretty rough on private enterprise to contend with.

Mr. Phillips has indicated to us that it has taken them two and one half years and they are frustrated and they don't know where to turn. Mr. Hitch gave us a slightly different picture. We get the idea that this is a mixed thing and that there might be some way to cut through the delays. I think it is a justifiable complaint on the part of foreign business.

C. S. Krishnamoorthi. We have been going through a process of development and a clarification of our own ideas of the respective roles which private enterprise in India and foreign private enterprise could play, not primarily for their own betterment but for our betterment as a country. Parliament and its agency, the government, have to draw up plans and mark the place where not only private business but also public sector business, or government business, or agriculture, all these things, can draw upon the resources that the community as a whole produces. The government does not itself regulate the relationship between the Indian participant and the foreign collaborator. What it does is to set certain criteria and watch that there is no adverse effect of such investment on the economic plans.

For instance, it has to watch that the setting up of new industries does not, in the long run, add foreign exchange commitments rather than help the economy in earning foreign exchange. One may feel with Mr. Phillips that this watching can be very trying and very far from brief. We are trying our best to see what can be done to get over these difficulties.

I myself have been very much alarmed when, sitting back in Delhi, I got files three months old, four months old, five months old, with a great deal of nothing on points which didn't affect the issue either way and which finally got a "yes" or "no" on the strength of much the same data that was available in the very first ten pages or so of the file. These are difficulties which we have to get over and we are trying our best to expedite the consideration of these various issues in government. At the present time, there are about three or four various departments concerned and each department takes some time considering the application and these reviews are not always simultaneously done and therefore it takes more time. We are trying to shorten this process. We are also trying to set up an investment information center with headquarters in New Delhi, possibly branches abroad, which could help both Indian private business and foreign private business to get together and, even more important, to get on quickly with the government departments concerned.

Matthew J. Kust. You must remember that the Government of India gets a large number of applications: in 1956 the Licensing

Committee reviewed over 1000 applications and granted some 850 licenses to new industrial undertakings and expansion of existing enterprises.

Bharat Ram. In the early fifties we used to count on two to two and one half years to get a very small tax matter settled. Now it's between two and three months.

Matthew J. Kust. It is improving. And in any case, the Industries (Development and Regulation) Act has been passed by Parliament and the government is charged with the responsibility of allocating these resources. Mr. Ram, what is the attitude of the Indian businessmen to the Act; do they accept it as a necessary evil and do they find it interfering with their business?

Bharat Ram. From time to time we find in industries and particular fields there has been, according to us, a wrong decision. Through our various chambers of commerce we put pressure on the government and in various aspects the Act has been from time to time changed by the pressure which comes from the industrial and trading communities. I do not think that we have necessarily always to go to the Parliament. The administration in many fields has got the flexibility to be able to change some of these things.

Matthew J. Kust. Bear in mind that the Industries Act brings in private business through the administrative process for setting these allocations.

Bharat Ram. In Mr. Phillips' particular case, I am not aware of the reasons why the Government of India is not allowing the import of raw materials. As far as I know, the Government of India usually says you will be allowed to import the raw materials for manufacture, but of course if it is an article which at no time can be manufactured in India, the Government of India would be stupid not to allow it to be imported.

C. S. Krishnamoorthi. Mr. Phillips, has it been that you have not been able to get a decision on the question of import duty on raw materials or has it been a difference of opinion as to whether you should have it? The one is an administrative problem of getting it to the right person to make the decision and the other is a matter of your knowing who can make this decision but he has disagreed with you and you can't go ahead. So, which is it?

Arthur Phillips. We've been to the right person.

C. S. Krishnamoorthi. Then this problem is not of administrative delay; it is a problem of substance as to whether you should get this particular. . . .

Arthur Phillips. Well, not on that particular point. . . .

Bharat Ram. On your possible duty, couldn't you still manufacture carbon black at a price below the present price?

Arthur Phillips. No. We would have to sell at the current price of black plus the current tariff in India and the plant such as we're supposed to establish to handle all of India's current needs would be an inefficient sized plant—large capital investment, rather low production.

Bharat Ram. In other words, your basic production price is higher than it would be in the United States, Persia, or some other place?

Arthur Phillips. Oh, much!

Jerome Levinson. May I ask Mr. Phillips if he encountered any difficulty with the government in capitalizing your patent and know-how at 20 per cent?

Arthur Phillips. Yes, but we finally had an agreement on that. We would normally not do that at all, we would normally prefer a royalty arrangement but since we were not able to get normal royalties, we did agree to transfer the patents. We haven't encountered any really serious problems.

Matthew J. Kust. It seems to me from all I've heard and from the experience that I have had that the best way to break through this administrative delay, which undoubtedly costs money to an American concern, is to do two things. First, pick the right partner in India, one who can do the job for you and I think he can do it much more easily than an American can, and secondly, I just think you have to make up your mind to be persistent, that you have to send someone there to help along. I don't know of any simple formula by which to lick this problem. Mr. Krishnamoorthi has told us that the Government of India plans to centralize the screening of foreign investment. This is a great step forward. After all, we must remember, this Act has only been on the books a few years and there is a lot of groping in setting up the administrative process.

INDIAN SOCIALISM

The possibility of politically-inspired labor trouble is a particular worry voiced by some United States businessmen. *Van Dusen Kennedy*, Professor of Industrial Relations at the University of California (Berkeley) and author of many studies on problems of Indian trade unionism, discusses the general setting of labor relations in which foreign businessmen operate, and *Charles J. Myers* of the Massachusetts Institute of Technology, author of *Labor Problems in the Industrialization of India*, considers the specific implications of India's compulsory arbitration procedures for the United States investor.

Van Dusen Kennedy.   From the American point of view, collective bargaining is one of the underdeveloped features of the Indian industrial scene. Three basic manifestations might be mentioned.

First, there is relatively little systematic and genuine joint determination of the terms and conditions of employment. There are, of course, exceptions which one could cite. The Ahmedabad textile industry, Tata Steel, Indian Aluminium, Bata Shoe, Dunlop Rubber, and Imperial Chemical are cases in which continuing collective bargaining does go on. But taking industry as a whole, genuine joint determination of most terms and conditions of employment is not the rule. A second feature is that what joint dealings do exist tend to exist, it seems to me, more on employer sufferance of one kind or another than as the result of propulsion from strong majority-based unions. Thirdly, collective bargaining in India does not have the fullness of content and scope of subject matter that we are accustomed to in American collective bargaining.

Now, more specifically, apart from these broad features of under-development, what are the characteristics of Indian labor relations? One finds very little use of comprehensive written agreements with such notable exceptions as the Aluminium Company and Tata Steel. The agreements or the memoranda of understanding which the parties draw up over a period of time tend to cover a fairly narrow range of subject matter. The most frequent subjects are wages—basic wages or cost-of-living adjustments—and the annual bonus problem which is an integral part of the wage problem in India.

Likewise, there is some negotiation or bargaining interchange over issues that we would call grievances, issues dealt with in India more often on an *ad hoc* general collective bargaining basis with strikes as possible recourse.

In this country an integral part of collective bargaining is, of course, grievance administration—the day-by-day interchange between unions and employers about the interpretation of contracts and the complaints of workers. One finds even less development of grievance procedure in the Indian situation than of contract negotiation. In part this is because of the lack of comprehensive written agreements to be interpreted and implemented and carried out. Partly it is because of lack of rank-and-file organization in unions, particularly at the plant level, and the presence of outside leaders who are not closely involved in local plant situations. It is also because management lacks experience with grievance administration and has not developed the attitudes necessary for good work level labor relations.

The lack of this work level development of day-by-day settlement of the minutiae of job security and employment conditions means that there is a notable absence in India of what we call industrial jurisprudence in this country—an accumulated body of common law and regulations governing the employment conditions and rights of workers on the job.

Given the existence of a fairly active trade union movement, given the existence of employment problems, given the imperfect development of collective bargaining and the bias in public policy against strikes, some method must be employed to resolve disputes. As a practical matter the method used in India is adjudication by public tribunal, which is to say in terms of our practice, public arbitration. Under Indian labor law, the government has the authority to refer any labor management dispute at its discretion to compulsory settlement by a government-appointed tribunal. And this is the system by which many more employment conditions and disputes are determined in India than by collective bargaining.

Charles Myers.   If one bears in mind that there is a divided labor movement in India, and that one of the strong sectors of that labor movement is a Communist-dominated sector, it is easier to understand how the Indian government feels about the necessity to have compulsory arbitration.

When I first went to India in 1954 I went with what I think was an American bias against government intervention in labor management relations. After considerable time there, in talks with some of the leading government officials, as well as employer groups and trade union groups, I came away feeling that compulsory adjudication was likely to continue. I think American companies are bothered by this. It is said that it is more than we have here in this country except in periods of real national emergency. The Wage Stabilization Board and the War Labor Board did represent direct intervention in the settlement of the terms of a labor dispute—that is, wages and other conditions in employment similar to compulsory adjudication. But mediation as we have it now is not similar.

I think the difference is that the Government of India (and I think rather rightly) considers itself to be in an emergency. It is in a hurry to develop. It cannot afford the interruption to production that serious, wide-scale strikes as a test of strength between employers and unions might involve. And so American employers operating in India, I think, have to accustom themselves to a different pattern for some time to come. I was glad to see in the case of one company which I came to know fairly well, the Standard-Vacuum Oil Company, that they have been able on the basis of the tribunal decisions that have been made earlier to negotiate the size of the bonus directly with their union. They did not have to go through these long delays which go a year or two years sometimes to do this. But it took, on their part, a willingness to try to reach an agreement.

I think there is all too much in India of this attitude that is still prevalent in this country, that a union is something to be avoided, or that you would rather see a long-drawn-out negotiation before you reach a settlement. The availability of alternative methods of settling a dispute does tempt either employers or what many people think is an unreasonable union to hold out. But in the case of some American companies and some Indian companies there has been a genuine effort to try to reach an agreement with their union. While this system discourages direct collective bargaining, it does not mean it is totally impossible, as an increasing number of companies, both Indian and American, are showing.

Herbert Harig is an Ohio small businessman who went to India in 1958 as head of a trade mission appointed by the United States Department of Commerce. He sees a big future in the "joint venture" approach urged by *Matthew J. Kust* and *Wolfgang Friedmann,* and he suggests that joint Indo-United States small business ventures offer a field of special promise, a suggestion supported by one of the biggest of India's big businessmen, *Bharat Ram,* who gives an encouraging word of over-all advice to new United States investors in his country.

Herbert Harig. Something that we have to face is America's non-competitive position in world markets, what with our high standard of living and the relative cost of producing goods in this country. What with the world becoming smaller and the need for having trade with other nations to maintain our position, we have got a job on our hands. I think one way for us to help ourselves is to help India, specifically by going into more joint ventures. I think that that is the real answer to what India is looking for. Money doesn't give them the help they need. They want people, with technical know-how, and the equipment that can be sent over as part of the joint venture. They can, as their part, supply the necessary buildings, land, and working capital to work out a satisfactory arrangement.

The size of our company is 125—we are very large in our industry, yet a small company as far as industry in general goes. I am so sold on the idea that we can be of tremendous help to India that I have attempted to set up a joint venture with a company in Calcutta.

We have to find some way of getting American industry to recognize the job that they have to do, because while much of what we do is based on government relationships, government help, I have seen enough of the small businessman in India to know that he is going to have to get his help through private enterprise. The best way that he can get it is for a counterpart of American industry to get over there and get into business with him.

Bharat Ram. I should like to make two practical suggestions which might be of value to our friends.

One is that so far most of the collaborations have been by the big people of India with the big people of this country. There is in my view a great scope for collaboration between the smaller industries of this country and the smaller men in our country who do not get a chance, as freely perhaps, as some more fortunate people get, of coming over to this country and being able to discuss various matters. And I notice here in this country there are agencies who help in bringing forward—preparing schemes for people, even giving them the know-how to get financial collaboration with smaller people and so on, and I think it would be a very good idea if some of these firms could send out their people for maybe a couple of months, letting the people in India know that here are these people who have come to discuss various schemes with the smaller people. I'm sure we would be flooded by smaller people who would like to take their assistance and a good deal of two-way traffic would build up. I know that there are a lot of people in my country who have the enthusiasm, who have small capital, but who just do not know how to go about the whole process of collaboration.

Now, the second suggestion which I would like to make, and I would like Mr. Krishnamoorthi to close his ears, is that you please do not take the Government of India too seriously. For example, they say you've got to produce these things within a certain period, after which we will not allow you to import certain things. If we say five years and you think it can be done in seven years—you accept five years. Experience shows that the Government of India does not want an industry to stop once it's got started. Sometimes they say, well, we'll allow you to manufacture—go into this manufacture, but after a certain period you must manufacture the whole of this in India. I know that very often it isn't possible to meet this condition, and yet those industries are still going on—folks are still coming in—and the Government of India realizes these things.

Matthew J. Kust.   There is a lot of give and take.

VI / "THE SLOWLY SIMMERING STORY"

Journalistically speaking, the intensity of the Indian-American encounter during the Eisenhower visit in 1959 can be measured by the volume of news cabled back to the United States—an unprecedented 650,000 words in five days. But the India which suddenly became so vivid and real to Americans does not normally get this kind of press attention, and if it did, would the readers be interested? An International Press Institute Study, *The Flow of the News*, shows that Americans read on an average five and one-half words about India per day, usually in the form of a single item per month. And the editors who decide what news reaches the readers do not even use most of what they get: only 14 per cent of the foreign news provided by wire services found its way into the I.P.I. sampling of 105 newspapers. Clearly our journalistic communication with the developing countries is far from adequate, and this inadequacy will become more and more apparent with the increase in economic and cultural contacts.

Misunderstanding begins, we are reminded by *William L. Stringer*, Washington Bureau Chief of the *Christian Science Monitor*, when we do not have the factual basis for understanding.

William L. Stringer. It seems to me that when we deal with misinformation, it is often one consequence of a lack of information. Good information drives out bad, faulty, and mistaken information. For instance, there was a flare-up recently on the problem of Pakistan and Kashmir. Well, I immediately discovered by talking with some of the Indian leaders and American Embassy people in the area that India's position on Kashmir is not merely a question of wanting to hold down a certain territory. It is a question of internal public security because if the Indians should surrender Kashmir, the Hindu majority in India would, it is expected, turn on the 40 or 50 million Moslems in India, and you would have some more communal riots. Therefore, when you understand that, you understand a little better India's position on Kashmir. All down the line you can find areas where more reporting in the American press of the events and the reason for the Indian positions in these events would bring a larger realization of why some of these positions are taken.

ASIAN-AMERICAN COMMUNICATION THROUGH JOURNALISM

The elements of the problem of Asian-American journalistic communication are reviewed by *Price Day*, winner of a Pulitzer Prize for his reports on the transfer of power in India, who addresses himself, as Associate Editor of the *Baltimore Sun*, to the nature of reader receptivity to foreign news in his community; *Albert Ravenholt, Chicago Daily News* correspondent in Southeast Asia; *Robert Eunson*, former Associated Press Bureau Chief in Tokyo and now San Francisco Bureau Chief, discussing the control points through which the news passes on its way to the newspaper; and *John Thompson*, the National Broadcasting Company's Pacific Division News Manager at Los Angeles, where NBC news is processed en route from the Far East.

Price Day. My assignment is merely to try to state one aspect of our problem—to look at it from the point of view of the local newspaper in the United States—both the handling of news and editorial writing and policy.

A newspaper reporter who has worked abroad and returns to a city of, say, medium size in this country finds himself now and then asked to speak before certain groups—civic organizations, library gatherings, perhaps a university audience. If his subject is a portion of Asia, he discovers—except sometimes with a university audience—that most of his listeners seem to be hearing for the first time the simple and fundamental information upon which any understanding of Asia must be based. Their knowledge of Asia is limited to a few prominent names and general impressions. Yet a group of people attracted to a talk on an Asian subject may be supposed on the whole to be interested in Asia. Their questions show that they are. The questions are intelligent. These people want to know more; and they are the sort of people who, if they did know more, would influence the thinking of the community on Asian matters.

They are also newspaper readers: and one wonders to what extent the newspapers are responsible for the community's limited knowledge of Asia.

The International Press Institute has found that the average newspaper in the United States carries about 45 words of news per day on the largest country of South Asia, India; while the average English-language paper in India carries about 1250 words daily on America, and the average Indian-language paper about one-third that much; and they suggest from this that those who are reached by the Indian press (only about 1 per cent of the population) are reached more intensely than is the much larger American newspaper public. It is true that if an Indian and an American meet in London, neither having visited the other's country, the Indian will almost certainly know more about America than the American knows about India. He will not be free of misconceptions, any more than the American is, but the questions he asks will be more pertinent.

For this there are many reasons, most of them not relevant here, but one reason surely is that the average American newspaper gives to Asian news a coverage inadequate for any real understanding of Asia on the part of its readers.

American newspaper editors are not unaware of the inadequacy; but they are faced with conditions. One condition is the rigid one of space. With few exceptions indeed, we must ration space in our news columns. From the mass of material that reaches us each day we must try to give our readers a balanced presentation of that day's news.

To an extent it is true that we sometimes give the reader things he wants to read, at the expense of things we think he ought to read—but not to the extent that is sometimes supposed, and by no means to the extent that some of us used to.

A further limiting condition on our coverage abroad is our inability to undertake thorough coverage of our own, by our own reporters. We do not have the staff or the money. Some of us try, but only the mighty *New York Times*, with its space and its resources, is able to do an adequate job. Nor can even the *Times* do everything. It has no correspondent permanently assigned to Burma, or now to Karachi, to take two examples only. Some of its Asian reporting—distinguished reporting, we all agree—is and must be on a regional basis.

There are other and yet more modest approaches, such as that of my own newspaper, the *Baltimore Sun*. Perhaps a brief look at our way of trying to give the reader a balance of foreign news will contribute at least to a clarification of the problem, merely as an example of what one newspaper has done.

We have, to begin with, a method of displaying the news that may be peculiar to us. Local news, except in the case of elections and, rarely, municipal or state disasters of some magnitude, go in the second section of the paper, moving—or jumping—inward from the back page, which is in fact a local front page.

This leaves page one, and the pages immediately succeeding it, open exclusively for national and international news. Thus we are able within a comparatively limited space to present, or try to present, an orderly and carefully weighed picture of news throughout the country, and abroad. Obviously, we can in this way give more space—more prominently—to international affairs than would be the case if we used an orthodox make-up.

In the past, before World War II, our interest in international affairs—that is, our interest in dealing with international affairs through our own reporters—was confined almost entirely to Europe, and there it was limited to a one-man news bureau in London, and for a while, a similar arrangement in Paris. In World War II we expanded, as did all newspapers which could expand—but it was a special and temporary sort of expansion, in war correspondence. After the war we had to draw in again. It was clear, however, that we could not draw in to our earlier position, and still pretend to give satisfactory coverage for our readers. Accordingly, we did two things.

We established a few more permanent, and one-man, bureaus abroad, spotting them, we believe, with some care. Here again our first concern was with Europe—Bonn and Moscow. But meanwhile we were looking more and more toward Asia, and becoming increasingly convinced of the necessity of better coverage there. A Tokyo bureau, or a bureau centered in Tokyo, is in prospect, also another in Hong Kong. Quite recently we have opened a Rome bureau—actually a Mediterranean bureau—more precisely, in fact, a news post for covering the Middle East or, if one prefers, West Asia.

In addition to permanent posts, we have also since World War II tried to keep one or two men rather constantly in motion, on assignment to particular regions, sometimes to particular countries, for periods of four or five or six months at a time. More than half of such assignments have been in Asia, from Pakistan to Japan. It has been a matter of bringing us from time to time up to date, rather than of continuous coverage. In example, we had a man in India and Pakistan in 1947, again in 1951, again in 1955.

Our interest in Asia as evidenced by this kind of coverage carries over to an extent, of course, into the day-to-day news columns. Yet it is true that, in the intervals between the reports, our news from Asia tends to fall into a more ordinary American news pattern; nor do I see how it could be otherwise. What I am attempting to say is that at times we devote an extraordinary amount of space, considering our limitations, to Asia; and that our coverage of Asia otherwise is necessarily what must be called intermittent.

The writing of editorials on Asian questions is still difficult for us, as I believe it is for any American newspaper. In part, again, the problem is one of space. A few hundred words is quite enough for an editorial dealing with a subject on which one has a strong opinion that can be simply stated, and a subject about which the reader is well informed as to background. But how do you discuss, for example, Kashmir, in a few hundred words?

Editorials nevertheless have to be written. Important events in Asia have to be discussed on the editorial pages of American newspapers. In cases where a staff editorial writer possesses special knowledge, from personal observation, the discussions may be supposed to have value to the reader, even though the writer's knowledge may not be wholly up to date. Too often, I fear, editorials on Asian matters are written rather with an eye to not being wrong than in a conviction of being right. I can say this because I write them myself, about parts of Asia that I do not know well.

Many suggestions are made for correcting the dearth of Asian news reporting on America, and American on Asia. One proposal is that groups of several newspapers each join cooperatively in the sponsorship of foreign correspondence. To a degree this is done now, insofar as subscription to syndicated material may be called cooperative. It would be hard to do in a much wider way. Most newspapers, I believe, see no satisfactory middle ground between their own correspondence and the increasingly excellent correspondence of the news associations.

Another suggestion is that foreign correspondence to serve papers unable to maintain their own coverage be underwritten by private foundations or even by agencies of the United Nations. Private foundations can play a large role in creating Asian-American understanding as can agencies of the United Nations; but their role lies elsewhere than with news. Any newspaper looks askance at any reporting sponsored or underwritten outside the profession: and should look askance. In some cases it would be wrong in mistrusting such material; but the chance is a kind it cannot take.

Albert Ravenholt. It is my conviction that our profession of working as observers and writers abroad is in a rather bad way.

The modern world in which we live imposes demands for performance upon members of our profession abroad such as we have never really known before. These are demands not only in the nature of a growing awareness of the rest of the world but they are also demands in the sense that, to a very significant extent, the quality of information that we accept in our society regarding the areas of foreign concern also enters into the equation of war and peace and the type of conflict that ensues. While the physical sciences have advanced with really spectacular speed, I feel that our profession is about where the medical profession was a hundred years ago. At that time it was possible, in a good part of the United States, for almost anyone who chose to do so to hang out a shingle and call himself a doctor, and by a process of trial and error you and your relatives and your friends found out, sometimes, whether he knew his business. Today, it is my impression that the American people are almost as confused about where to look for worth-while insight when it comes to an assessment of problems abroad. There are no simple yardsticks by which to judge the competence of the individual who writes and analyzes, and a result of this is, I believe, a considerable measure of confusion and disenchantment in the minds of Americans.

There are several developments in the postwar period that have complicated this. One has been the tendency for sources of foreign information to become ingrown. I think an interesting comparison could be made between the sources of foreign information between World War I and World War II on the one hand and since World War II. My own conclusion after making a cursory investigation and my reason for being concerned is that we find that, while following World War I, the faulty reporting frequently came from capitals and had to do with the heads of states, etc., still it came from abroad. Today, if you make such a tabulation, you'll find that a very large proportion of the foreign news published in this country originates in Washington, D.C. And I think it leaves the American people open to what I consider an insidious process.

Essentially, I am satisfied that what we have accomplished by going to Washington, D.C., for news of events abroad is to narrow the actual base from which the information is drawn. I have watched this process at the foreign end of the line, so to speak, and what happens is in a large measure a product of the arrival of the airplane on the scene. Twenty years ago important officials of our government didn't go abroad unless they took time to learn a fair bit en route and to stay a considerable period when they arrived. Today, admirals and generals and special congressional investigating committees come abroad and drop in for twelve hours or thirty-six hours as the case may be. And this is also true in the provinces when some other VIP's arrive from private secretaries to scientists.

Let's take the case of Formosa. The Chinese Nationalist government has a single regiment whose chief assignment is to hold reviews for visiting American VIP's. It's the same regiment. This same regiment has been putting on reviews for a couple of years. The arriving admirals—most of them go out, there's a grandstand, the whole thing is set up—and I can imagine (in fact I've talked to some of them) the attitude of these Chinese soldiers when they hear that an American VIP is arriving—it means another review. The technique for briefing American VIP's has been highly perfected, not only by the Chinese Nationalists on Formosa, but also by the American official representatives abroad, by our ambassadors, by the heads of our economic and military aid missions, and they have regular briefing procedures—staff members who are assigned to do this job. They have charts—they have all the modern paraphernalia that we have found in the United States for conveying effective impressions. So these individuals arrive and they're given routine treatment. In the case of Formosa, for example, if they're really first-rate, they rate dinner with the Generalissimo and his Madam. And in the case of the less important ones, the Governor of Formosa gives a dinner for them. But be that as it may, they get the full treatment also from the chiefs of the American missions on Formosa. And mind you when I say Formosa I could duplicate this also in the

Philippines, in Bangkok, and in a number of other communities in Southeast Asia.

Essentially, as far as I can determine, what these visitors do is to return to Washington and reinforce the assumptions upon which United States policy is already operating. That is, reinforce the premises that have been reported to Washington through the official channels by the chiefs of the United States diplomatic missions abroad and their assistants. So we have a narrower base, in effect, rather than a broad one. Once they get to Washington, I think we have all recognized the proclivity of American politicians to leak to the press almost everything they have acquired in the way of information. For one thing it's a way of getting their own names in the newspapers, something which in my experience few politicians can resist the opportunity of doing. This news then is reported out of Washington by often well trained and hard-working newspapermen to the American people.

To be sure there are obvious economic advantages for a newspaper or a news agency in covering a fair bit of the news from Washington, D.C. It enables them to milk the State Department, the United States Information Agency, to some extent, C.I.A., Defense Department, and the numerous foreign embassies that are established in Washington. It's a center into which flows an enormous amount of information, or to some extent it is information; there are factors which condition it. And, as a consequence, it's feasible for a newspaper or radio station, or what have you, to place a man or several men there, and to do a job for a fraction of the cost of placing correspondents in the field where these things actually happened. Now, the fact that the news that these men get in Washington is, after all, sifted—at least, as it often is from some of the official agencies—or the fact that it comes from an inadequate base originally abroad, I think is the corrupt, pernicious consideration. Because, basically, as I view it at least, our society has to have a multiple number of sources of information in order to encourage effective competition of ideas in the examination and formulation of policy. And, if we're operating all on the same set of assumptions, I think there's a real danger that we won't have this kind of effective competition at the point where it counts; which is, fundamentally, in looking at the actual event as it takes place and the factors which affect it.

How do we actually begin to produce men who have had the

benefit of an adequate opportunity to prepare themselves realistically and in terms of background for service abroad? We know that it's no good taking a man who is simply an academician and sending him to this assignment. I'm persuaded that you have to start with a newspaperman who has a feel for what makes news. And even with proper training, he cannot do really high quality reporting until he has lived for an extended period in the same area. American editorial executives in this country tend to take their image of Europe and transplant it to the Far East. For example, to assume that it's just as easy to send a man from Hong Kong or Manila to Kuala Lumpur as it is to send a man from Rome or Berlin to Paris. If you look at the map for a minute, measure the distances (and the distances are far greater in terms of changes in society and attitudes than they are in geographic distance), you begin to appreciate the enormous burden under which a man works who is trying to get around such an immense area with its great differences in culture, in language, and in attitudes of the people. I'm persuaded that we have not fully come to appreciate the work of giving the correspondent abroad an opportunity to build those personal friendships with the citizens who live in those societies that is absolutely essential, in my view, to significant reporting.

Robert Eunson. I would like to continue on briefly the last thought expressed by Mr. Ravenholt, on the question of people being present and living in a country to be able to report it. We were always amused during the years I spent in Tokyo when the trained seals would come through from New York, especially if they were writing for a syndicate that was published in the *Nippon Times*, now the *Japan Times*, so we could all read it. I remember one fellow came through. We could tell the first day he had been at the Embassy talking to the press attaché, he was speaking the Embassy gospel, and the next day it sounded as though he had been talking to a taxi driver, and the third day I was sure he had met a Japanese girl in a geisha house.

In a more serious vein, let me discuss briefly the technical setting of the problem of communication, and in particular the manner of the movement of copy in and out of Asia, the screening of the news as it takes place at certain key points such as, in the case of the AP, the Foreign or Cable Desk in New York and until recently the

Far Eastern desk in San Francisco. This business of desk men versus the writer in the field is an old one. During the Korean War many of our correspondents who came out to cover the war were brought through San Francisco first where they were schooled on the Cable Desk here, and given an idea of the type of copy that they were expected to file, how it was handled once it got to San Francisco and put on the trunks. These men would invariably come out to Tokyo and to the Press Club there and then on to Korea where they'd meet the other correspondents in Seoul and they'd say, "Why do you fellows all hate the desk men in San Francisco so much? They're really *good* guys." And in a week this same correspondent would say, "*Doggone*, those guys back in San Francisco. They ruined my story!" Invariably they'd change in a week. I don't know— it's a fight that goes on and proverbially men like Hank Lieberman are very fortunate in that the cable desk doesn't touch their copy. However, I must say that during the thirteen years I was overseas for the Associated Press, in both Europe and in Asia, the copy desks helped me more times, I'm sure, than they ever harmed my tone poems.

Right now, the Associated Press has centralized all of its cable desk operations in New York City. We've moved it out of San Francisco, sent most of the fellows back there with the operation. We believe in strong central control of the foreign report, both as it comes into the United States, and the world service report that goes out to the world services. The reason for this is first of all, the foreign report has to be tailored. It has to be tailored to fit the needs of the editors. Price Day has told you here today that, as an associate editor on the *Baltimore Sun*, it is necessary for them to give their readers what they want. And so, the foreign report has to be tailored to fit these needs of the member papers throughout the United States. Another thing, a very important item is responsibility. There must be a responsibility exercised somewhere over the flow of copy as it goes through the wires to the member papers and the member radio stations of the United States. For instance, yesterday an opposition service carried a story from Moscow which said in the first paragraph that the Russians had displayed a ballistics missile in the Red Square. Nowhere in the story was that statement backed up. Nowhere was any source given. The story completely fell apart at the seams. It was not reported by the Associated Press.

It was not reported by *The New York Times,* or the *Baltimore Sun,* or the New York *Herald Tribune* who were all present. There was no responsibility anywhere for that statement. In a story like that, if it had come through the cable desk of the AP, it would have been halted and the writer queried immediately and asked what was his source, and then that source would have been definitely established within the first three paragraphs of the story.

Many times, since I've been back in America, I've been asked why the Korean War never produced the type of reporting World War II produced. First of all, I think it is a true assumption, and second, the answer is the lack of communications that we had in Korea. This was a very tough baby to handle from the start because we were never able to get commercial communications established in Korea so that we could file directly to the United States. Copy that moved down from the front had to be telephoned over Army Signal Corps lines to Seoul and if there's an army major present will he forgive me when I say that the communications system of the Army hasn't improved any since Verdun. The telephones still sound just the same as they did in World War I, I'm sure, and once you have screamed a story all the way back from the front to Seoul and then taken that same piece of copy and screamed it over another telephone line to Tokyo, if you have the facts straight you're lucky, and God knows you won't have much color. However, we tried seriously to get the Army to let us put a commercial trunk in, especially after the talks started at Panmunjon. We were unable to do this. The Army said that the Koreans didn't want it. President Rhee told me that the Army didn't want it so we lost all around and we were never able to have a setup such as we had in Europe during World War II when each Army headquarters had either a Press Wireless or a commercial facility of some kind and we could file directly from the field into New York.

I would like to conclude by telling you about the Rube Goldberg setup we had to file the flash that the war in Korea had come to a halt. The night before we drew for positions. It had been decided that all the correspondents who cared to would be able to attend the ceremony. However, we had to pool. So we had a telephone line from inside the signing tent out to a small tent where a censor and a reader sat. We drew for position. The UP drew the telephone inside the tent; the AP drew to sit outside and take the report and type it. So, Leroy Hansen of the UP sat inside; AP drew the outside post; I was sitting outside at the typewriter. Leroy was giving me a running description of how all the delegates looked—stern-faced, glum. I was sitting outside with a headset on and an old rattly typewriter, typing as Leroy talked. Behind my right shoulder stood a censor, a colonel in the United States Army; behind my left shoulder was a reader for me, an ensign in the Navy, and he had a telephone. We had made this arrangement, that unless I typed something the censor didn't like, he would let me continue. So, we were going along and the censor was being quite cooperative and this boy was reading into the phone. He was reading by radio-telephone into Tokyo where an Army captain sat with another headset on taking it down, passing it on to a teletype operator, who sent it out over the Army teletype network to the five major news agencies of the world, to their Tokyo bureaus. So, we were going along like this and we had decided that when Harrison's pen touched the paper—General Harrison, the United Nations' chief delegate— when his pen touched the paper we would say "Armistice signed." So, in the midst—at 10:02 it was—Hansen says, "Harrison signs!" So I typed, "Flash, Panmunjon Armistice signed 10:02." The boy read it into the phone, it went to Tokyo, retyped out on the teletype network to the bureaus, retyped, radio teletyped to San Francisco, retyped and reteletyped. It went through four typewriters and three teletype machines in two minutes. It was timed off at 10:04 in the United States. And that's moving copy. I have a great deal of respect for my colleagues here who can write the "big picture" stories and I tried my hand at it myself a few times in the two wars I covered. However, my greatest thrills were in ending the wars and seeing how fast we could get it in there and I think that that is probably why I'll always be an agency man and always a fire horse.

John Thompson. Today the National Broadcasting Company is broadcasting and telecasting more news and news-based programs than ever before in the history of our corporation, and this is a believe-it-or-not statement because this includes the days of World War II with the enormous public interest and the days of the Korean War. I need to follow that statement with the immediate qualification that our news from the Orient, from the Far East, which comes to the networks through the West Coast, is relatively speaking at a low point. The answer to this, of course, ties in with the editorial decisions that are made at a high level in our corporation.

The number of correspondents that we have overseas and how much they broadcast to the networks to be put on the air is controlled by economics. During the Korean War we had six full-time staffers working in the Orient, five of them in the combination Tokyo and Korean War operation, and another one in southern Asia. We are now, in 1957, down to the low point of having exactly one full-time correspondent in the Orient, and that's quite a beat he has to cover [Ed. Note: This had increased to two, one each in Hong Kong and Tokyo, in 1960].

And this pattern is identical to that of our major competitor, CBS, and our other competitors, ABC and Mutual, on the radio side. We supplement this extensively with stringers who are local newsmen, usually newspaper men, who in places like Manila and Singapore broadcast for us upon occasion when in our opinion the news from these areas warrants it. This situation in the Orient contrasts with that in Europe where we maintain ten—the Europe-Mediterranean area—we maintain ten highly skilled, highly trained, very well paid correspondents, in places ranging from Moscow to London to Cairo. And so the ratio between this area of the world and the Orient is obviously ten to one.

The mechanics of what we call the editorial transmission, that is, news by word, as against that by picture, which I'll get into in a few minutes, is that these men in overseas capitals broadcast to the United States receiving points at NBC, which are in San Francisco and New York—New York for Europe, San Francisco for the Orient —voice reports, which are either recorded or put on the air live for our radio and television network news and news-based programs. This broadcasting is done through commercial facilities by short wave. The reports break roughly into three categories. The basic kind is a direct report, running from 150 to a maximum of about 250 or 300 words, which is a spot news report and in many cases has nothing more to offer than a similar story that we might get from the Associated Press, though it does have a personal touch and first-hand reporting and the voice of the man who was there and saw it or has directly interviewed somebody. The second kind of a report we do is somewhat more lengthy—it's what we call a report in depth. Upwards of 700-800 words are devoted to painting what I believe Bob Eunson called the "big picture," if you can do that in 700 or 800 words. Many times in these reports we are able to use by tape recording the actual voices of some of the people who are involved in the news. The third kind of a report that our correspondents and our stringers handle are feature reports or color pieces that are not strictly speaking news and sometimes they run very far afield from news but do give some of the color of the country or the particular happening in the country of the type that would never make the news agency wires or the pages of 99 per cent of the newspapers in this country. Reports on a rally or a meeting in one of the capitals of the Orient or of Europe, or such things as a band concert with music. These reports might vary in length anywhere from three to as high as seven or eight minutes on the air. This type of reporting from overseas is something that we have just dug into within the last few years and it is done on our radio network because we are getting more into real live programming all the time on the radio side in some of our programs such as "Monitor" and "Night Line" in which we can use a vast amount of editorial material from all over the United States and all over the world, covering the widest possible range of interest.

In these things we have no high-flown objective to educate the people of the United States about everything under the sun. We are trying to present things to them that will interest them, very frankly. I'm sure that there's quite a bit of an educational process that goes along with it coincidentally. But believe me, this is not our basic objective. We're very frank that we're trying to get an audience and hang on to it with every device that we can and if something is not successful, why it gets dropped.

Now to get to the picture side: on television we may staff news cameramen at various points in Europe, and we had exactly one in the Orient, but we have an enormous number of arrangements with local film photographers that we engage by the day or the week or whatever to cover stories for us that you see on the network news programs. They always used to give us those regularly scheduled riots in Tokyo—though I think we've stopped covering them now—the Japanese students on a certain day of every week seem to be demonstrating. After a few weeks that got boring. So we have our special reports, digging into subjects much more deeply, and able to tell about them with greater impact, we think, than any other medium, by the use of motion picture film transmitted on television. We have gone into this very deeply twice in Asia at a very considerable cost, in excess of a quarter of a million dollars. We produced an hour-long study of India which involved sending a camera crew from this country to India together with skilled editorial people to shoot an enormous amount of film, both silent and sound, on film, including an extensive interview which in its raw form ran close to two hours with Mr. Nehru, and boiling this down into an hour-long study of India. Our attempt in this area was to take the problems of India, their past and their future, tell the thing in an hour of picture and text, to come up with the profound truths such as *The New York Times* would discover, but to present it in a form that the kind of people who watch television extensively would accept and understand. And believe me this is quite a job and that's why the quarter million dollar figure. We are presently working on a second one of these because the first one was so successful—successful from every standpoint. It was not condemned by the intellectuals of this country and yet it was accepted by the general public, and so that is success. Projects such as these have to be blocked out and gone ahead with on the company's own money and you can't plan these things based upon a commercial sale. There are too many complications involved then, because they take from six to nine months to do, ordinarily, if you do them right. The editing job, after you get the raw material back in New York is so enormous, for one thing. It's one of these things where the company expects to spend the money and get no return on it other than good will for the network, but if we can make some money or even break even or recapture some of it, so much the better.

I would like to point out that so far as not only NBC but the other networks are concerned, the entire business of gathering and broadcasting news is a money-losing business. And this is true of all the corporations. I'm not sure that all our competitors would make the same admission but we know it to be a fact that in the possibly twenty-five years that NBC has been broadcasting news intensively, never have we made any profit. But it's corporation policy to continue to do the best possible job within certain limits and the economic limitations are always to keep the deficit from getting too big—from sticking out too big when the board of directors sees it.

The news from the Orient, not only on NBC, but on CBS and the other networks, is handled by men who, to the best of our ability to obtain them, are qualified to handle it. The one full-time man that we now have in the Orient on the editorial side has lived there a large part of his life. He spent—he got a major part of his education in China, he is married to a Chinese lady, he is still under forty, young enough and vigorous enough and—with enthusiasm enough to make him an excellent reporter. He knows the Orient, not only China where he has lived, but other capitals and countries where he has worked. And this kind of a man is basically unfamiliar with the problems of those of us in the United States who are comparable to the desk men that I have heard referred to here lately, who have to decide what actually goes on the air. It is our opinion that it is better to have this type of man in the Orient and then place control over him and to attempt to guide him in his coverage; and that's what usually works out. What actually gets on the air is many times completely influenced by him; at other times we reject completely material that he thinks is important and should go on the air and our view prevails. But it is always subject to discussion. On short-wave we can deal with these people directly and hold, if need be, extensive conversations that would be similar to a telephone conversation in this country, to work out how things will be handled and covered. We have a few commentators who have spent some time in the Orient—one who has traveled extensively in the Orient on a regular basis every few years. He's one of these hit-and-run guys, but we have faith in him and believe that he's learned quite a bit while he was in the Orient. We have some others who have actually worked as resident correspondents in the Orient for extensive periods though I hate to admit that one of our very best, who has worked in the Orient the longest time, we now have covering Berlin for us. Now *that* one I can't figure out myself.

As for the future, I think the extent of our coverage in the Orient is probably at its peak right now, unless there should be some kind of an involvement that would make the news more interesting and more important to the American citizen. I'm speaking now of something in the nature of the Korean War. The reason, of course, that the Korean War was so interesting to the American public was not just the stake that this nation as a nation had in it. From a news standpoint it was the large number of American troops that were over there. And we have found this has been pretty much of a rule of thumb—the more directly involved individual Americans are with a foreign area, why the greater interest there is in the news. And we in television and radio have to be guided much more, of course, by our broad potential audience than newspapers do.

WHAT IS THE "NEWS" IN INDIA?

Television increasingly emphasizes the special reports cited by Mr. Thompson—Ghana and Iran were the subject of hour-long documentaries within a single month in 1959—and to some extent this provides the broad picture which is missing in the day-to-day fragments of the news. How can newspapers convey what *Henry R. Lieberman* calls (with special reference to India) "the slowly simmering story" within the limitations of their formats and, one might add, of their conventions? Mr. Lieberman and *Price Day* discuss possible methods. *Albert M. Colegrove,* former managing editor of the *San Francisco Daily News* and now West Coast representative of the Scripps-Howard Newspaper Alliance, echoes Mr. Thompson in observing that any method, to be successful, must initially overcome a massive sales resistance to foreign news on the part of the American public. *Clifford Weigle* is a Professor of Journalism at Stanford University.

Henry R. Lieberman. The chief question we are dealing with really is: what is the nature of news? Is it the spot news, the particular event that occurs at a certain time, or is it the slowly simmering story? I think that what is happening in India now, uncovered to a large extent, is probably the most important story in the world, according to my evaluation of news. My evaluation is based upon what I think is important in long-range terms, in terms of its effect, of things that will eventually catch up with us. India is in the midst of an acute financial crisis that has all kinds of political implications. If Mr. Nehru fails in his economic program, well, you are quite aware that waiting to take over are the Communists as the only opposition party that means anything on the Asian scene. I was in China during the Civil War period and I got the feeling in India that this was China in 1946 or 1947 all over again.

Now news organizations, whether press or your television, have a tremendous responsibility to tell this story. I recall the great surprise in many quarters when China fell. China was falling for years before it actually fell. I would like to say that I hope I'm wrong.

I'm worried about this situation in India. Now how do you tell this story? This is a very important dramatic story when put in these terms. Is this news, or isn't it news? In my book, it's news. However, looking at the problem from the technical standpoint, I can see it is very difficult to tell this story so that the people aren't just going to get bored to tears with it because you've got to tell the same story over and over again. Today the government has got $22 and tomorrow $21 and I mean you can't have two, three, and four stories chronically with small and rather unimportant changes. Now that is in essence the outline of the news problem as I see it.

How can we get across stories of this kind? I think that there's too much bong-bong-bonging—the "lead." It's become traditional, although I think it's outmoded in terms of what you actually have to say about the kind of thing you see in Asia. You can't get a zippy lead about something that is essentially unzippy but nevertheless important. The most effective technique that I know of in telling a story of this kind happens to have been developed by a magazine— that is the Letter thing in the *New Yorker* which provides the means of telling a situation in civilized terms, without getting all riled up by it, and getting across the essential information. Perhaps a newspaper could have on its editorial page, for example, a column whereby correspondents in different parts of the world could sit down and write a letter home, so to speak, without being required to write a story with a "lead" that would get a commanding headline. This would provide an opportunity, as I see it, where correspondents abroad could summarize, informally and without the necessity to get the headline lead, a situation which is important. It may be the putting together of a whole complex of facts and impressions, or it may be a restatement of what has already been filed, you see. In other words, this would be what is commonly known in the newspaper business as a "situationer."

You have to do this. Basically, your job is to make sure that nothing that ever happens in your area surprises your reader. You have to prepare him, and you need the relaxed sort of format I have described to do so most effectively.

Perhaps correspondents of NBC could be represented from different parts of the world one night a week, or one afternoon a week, one evening a week on something—Letters from Abroad, or Fireside Chats from Abroad, or whatever you want to call it. With all due honor, that half or a quarter million dollars that NBC loses on this thing could be spent more effectively. If you're going to lose it anyway you might as well do something effective. Applied over the long range it would have greater impact. All right, you present a spectacular. The reaction of the average guy is: "My, those people eat lots of rice, don't they?" I mean that's no great contribution to—it's the quaint that people light on. . . . "My, isn't it interesting —did you notice this, did you notice that? . . . " The important thing is not that the people are half undressed, that they eat lots of rice, but how is what happens there going to affect us? I think some formula—or formulae—have got to be evolved so that this story can be told continuously in meaningful terms.

Price Day. Something that Mr. Lieberman said is the core of the whole problem. He said, you've got to write so that nothing that happens there will ever surprise. That is the problem. Don't let your reader be surprised. You're supposed to have prepared him for anything and this is all, I think, part of developing a new kind of reporting. There's almost no such thing as flat news coverage from abroad. Once in awhile there'll be one, but you always have to put into the story the background of the story. There is a degree of interpretation always. In any story that you can comprehend at all there is this interpretation, to put it into context, and you have to learn to do it in a small space. A flat news story, a strictly spot story, is no news story at all any more—it's inadequate. And as this becomes more and more so, you need more and more to have your people trained for the job. I'm not convinced in my own mind that initial training in a school of journalism is worth very much.

Clifford Weigle. When you boil down as far as you can, "What is news?" all you can say is, "What the editor decides is news!" Many of them are men who are interested in foreign news, who know that what is happening in India is news. But the real crux of the problem is the sixteen hundred plus newspapers, daily newspapers, whose editors and publishers and news editors do not think that the Indian financial crisis might be today the biggest story in the world. On any single day the story about the Indian financial crisis will always give way to the "cat up the telephone pole."

Albert M. Colegrove. We go on a false assumption if we decide that—if we say that editors decide what is news. Readers are the people who decide what's news. I'll take an example; the biggest sale that the *Call-Bulletin*, during this past month, has enjoyed was not the day that the satellite was launched, but the day that Bing Crosby married Cathy Grant. Now, the editor decided that was the best story of the day, and obviously it was. It's what the people want. That's what they're interested in. We have got to—we can't decide what is news. We've got to let the public decide that, and if there's any doubt on that score, I'll be glad to introduce you to any number of former editors who are now looking for jobs. They failed to get what the public wanted.

There's an old saying which applies to newspaper readers: "You've got to get them in the tent before you can preach the gospel to them." We've got to get the readers into our tent before we can give them any foreign news. We've got a hundred and twelve columns of news a day. Probably five columns of that, at the very most, go toward foreign news. But, if we didn't have the other hundred and seven columns of Alley Oop, national problems, Hollywood problems, and so forth, you wouldn't be getting that five columns of news.

The problem in getting better and more foreign news in the papers is a terrific challenge to editors and to correspondents. Some way, somehow, correspondents have got to find more and better ways of writing news so that we can sell it to the public. I agree very much with Mr. Lieberman when he said he didn't go for the bong-bong-bong type of "lead." On the other hand, if you don't get them in the tent with the bong-bong-bong "lead" you'll never preach them the gospel. So that these reporter guys themselves have got to find more and better ways of making good news copy. It's one thing to say that editors cater to the public, but putting it another way: editors give the public what it wants or they don't survive. The gentleman said something about, "It would shock you that India is now in the stage that China was in in 1946–1947." This shocked me, because I did spend a little time in China, not too much, but I had a concentrated dose of it; I was the only American with four hundred and fifty Chinese guerrillas during the war for a while. And the thought of India going Communist is very shocking to me. Possibly one approach to this story—only one of nine hundred and ninety-nine—but to me, if I could get inside a native Communist mind and tell the story of one man who's sitting back there, waiting for the right day, and we get that story, the financial crisis, what he knows, and what he's aware of, and what's going to happen, and what he plans to do when it does happen; the story of one man, I think that would be easier for my readers to understand and to be gripped by than the story of five million men. It's personality, self-identification. I can believe what I read about one man, but I have a hard time understanding what I read about millions and millions of people.

Henry R. Lieberman. Mr. Colegrove has spoken the gospel, all right. I agree with him in general that presenting news is not just a function of the editor. Let's talk about that for a second in terms of what the practical problems are. There are just so many columns you have. There's the little story to come in each day, and you know pretty well instinctively what the lead story is, what the second-lead story is, and so on. However, the fact is that newspapers still have a responsibility to the public quite apart from the business of selling newspapers, otherwise they certainly have no claim to freedom of the press, and cheap mail service, etc. Now it struck me—I mentioned the *New Yorker*—and I was looking for an opportunity to take off from there. It seems to me that a considerable amount of information about foreign affairs could be imparted to the American public in less space than what these little snippets add up to each week. If, for example, each Monday morning on your editorial page or somewhere, there would be a report from a correspondent, say; this would actually be the broadcasting technique, calling in your correspondent in effect. For example, you say, "What's happening in India?" On Monday morning there is this two columns or three columns on your editorial page which is not taken up with stuff from a syndicated fellow, but devoted to pertinent observations about non-bong-bong-bong type stuff, which would in effect be as interesting as a letter that you had received from a friend of yours who happened to be in Rome, or in Paris or in Hong Kong. This would help to provide continuity and at the same time, more meaningful information, this form of presentation. I'm not suggesting that this is the only way to do it. I bring this particular suggestion up to drive home the point that I think presentation is the responsibility of editors as well as correspondents.

Albert Ravenholt. Now, we're getting really to the heart of this matter. It isn't just what the reader wants; it's what the editor is able to present to him in such a way that he thinks he wants it. I realize that there are a lot of editors, ex-editors, looking for jobs because they didn't give the media what it wanted. On the other hand, if you learn your business well as an editor, you can present significant world news in such a way that people will want it, and they'll read it.

I think that newspaper editors, and newspaper publishers, and newspaper executives might very well adopt the policy that has been adopted by many industrialists who go to Aspen, Colorado, once a year, or up to Arden House in New York and learn their business better. Foreign correspondents usually are much more intelligent than the editors who handle their stuff. Now, the usual practice is—a sensitive, articulate young man goes overseas and it takes him about two years to learn his country. As soon as he learns something about the people and something about the problems, the things he sends in begin to annoy the editor because they raise intellectual and other questions in his mind that he doesn't want raised. And so they send out the parachute troops to ride over, around him, and above him, or they cut his copy to pieces, or they bring him back, or they fire him. Now the same thing happens in the State Department. They send an intelligent political reporter out and as soon as he learns what he's talking about and begins to send back an intelligent report, he's yanked out of that country right away because he runs into high policies made by people by the process that has been described; big people who go around and get the snow job from the embassies of foreign governments. That's the whole problem wrapped up right there.

THE LANGUAGE BARRIER

Perhaps the most often discussed specific barrier to Asian-American communication, a barrier looming inordinately large to the journalist, is the lack of specialized linguistic competence. American contacts in India are restricted on the whole to the numerically large but proportionately small number of literate Indians whose literacy extends to English. *Henry R. Lieberman* and *Robert J. McCarthy, S.J.*, a Marquette University journalism graduate and a veteran of Chinese Communist prisons, consider how important language training actually is for journalists as well as what constitutes adequate training. The writer then joins Mr. Lieberman, *Mr. Eunson*, and the Assistant General Manager of the Scripps-Howard Newspapers, *Jack H. Lockhart*, in a discussion of possible ways to help equip Asia-bound United States correspondents with linguistic and area background.

Soviet diplomat *Valentin M. Ivanov* is inspired by the discussion to interject a reminder of his government's emphasis on language training.

Henry R. Lieberman.   I don't think that language can be over-stressed as a problem, but I also want to stress the point that I think if you have to choose between a man who speaks the language and has no other qualifications, and a newspaper man who is a good absorber and knows how to get the story across, I would take the latter in preference. That does not mean, however, that a man who is a good newspaper man should not also have the opportunity to learn the language of the area that he's covering. Now, we're on tricky ground here because I'm not altogether convinced, although I was at one time the recipient of a fellowship to improve my knowledge of the area I was covering—I'm not entirely convinced that that is the solution to the problem. I think that some formula has to be worked out so that a man can learn the language while he remains actually under the direction of the newspaper or news agency or television company or radio company for which he is working. I think perhaps outside aid or foundation aid, or something of that sort, might be dovetailed with training programs established by newspapers and news agencies themselves. In other words, let them select the men they want to train and if this agency or organization lacks the resources, then perhaps foundation aid could be made available. But the point I want to make now is that I think this aid should be funneled into programs established by the institutions themselves, that is, by newspapers, by radio stations, by news organizations.

Robert McCarthy, S.J.   I've been in the Orient for sixteen years, and I think a two-year course in the language is minimum for anyone who wants to converse in the language. I've had a lot of experience with that among my missionaries. We speak about getting some human interest into the news. For human interest you have to have human sympathy with the people you are dealing with and you have to be able to manifest that sympathy, and language is an extremely important element in doing that. If you are able to speak the language you'll be able to speak to those people there who feel and who have a difficult time expressing their feelings, perhaps—but nevertheless their feelings are very important for understanding them. I also wanted to mention the often-heard emphasis on the need for more correspondents, on the number of correspondents. Such an emphasis would be wrong. Correspondents should have integrity, should have intelligence, and should have technical ability. And it's far better to have a few with those three qualifications than to have many men without them because such men will do more harm than good, in telling the truth of the situation there and establishing understanding.

Henry R. Lieberman. I think that in talking about language and area studies we've got to be fairly practical—very practical I should say. A newspaper sending a man abroad is hesitant about letting a man take two years off to study a language. An editor—ideally, that should be the way to approach it, I suppose, but people of the caliber required are usually people who are needed in whatever spot they're already working in. Therefore, I think it might make more sense if provision were made for people being sent abroad to do this studying while they're continuing to work. If they're sufficiently interested in becoming properly equipped to cover an area, then I don't see why it would not be possible for them to study the language in whatever city they happened to be in. After all, most of the big news organizations operate in cities that have university facilities to provide language training. So I'd like to suggest the possibility of on-the-job study as one way of convincing editors that perhaps this might be feasible.

Selig S. Harrison. I should like to dwell on this thought of Henry's briefly because I think a number of us who have experienced some of the existing fellowship programs have eventually come to something like this—that to augment the existing programs, ways should be developed so that newsmen chosen through the internal processes of their own organizations to go abroad can receive some specialized background before they go. I wonder what you think of this, Bob, in the case of the AP. The choice of the man would rest inside the organization, not with outside selection committees. Suppose Foundation X were to say, "We're going to make available a certain amount of money each year. Organizations can come to us as they wish and work out programs in consultation with a committee of leading newspapermen which would help to coordinate available facilities so there will be a suitable language course in such and such a city if a man wants to take it." Would this offer a way to fit in with the actual staffing programs of the organizations as distinct from the broader aims of programs like the Nieman and Council on Foreign Relations fellowships?

Robert Eunson. I think that would be a very noble idea. As you probably know, the latest procedure that we follow overseas is for correspondents to study in the country in which they're operating and it's considered work-time. *Time* and *Life* did this originally. *Time* and *Life* correspondents in Japan all studied Japanese. Now all the American staff of AP in Tokyo is studying Japanese; one of them, Gene Kramer, is proficient enough now to make a speech. But if you could work out a program whereby these foundations could help, I'm sure the larger news agencies would be delighted to go along with it.

Selig S. Harrison. Would you be able to plan the staffing? I know, for example, many times a man will be told that he's going to India this week or possibly four weeks ahead. Do you think this would serve to promote long-range planning?

Robert Eunson. I thought you meant a facility to study the language would be set up in New Delhi once a man had arrived there. . . .

Selig S. Harrison. Well, that's another question, of course. I was talking about funds and coordinated planning to make it possible for the AP or UP foreign news editor to know that if he wants to send a certain man to Ghana or Indonesia, a year before he's going to go, six months before he's going to go, he can begin to get him into a part-time language training program, which somebody else is going to pay for. Often there just isn't the money in the budget to do this. Do you see any kinds of objections?

Robert Eunson. Not at all. As you know, now they bring fellows into the New York cable desk prior to an assignment like that. The old days of pulling a man out of Phoenix and saying, "You go to New Delhi," are over. Now you can go to New York and work on the cable desk for experience.

Selig S. Harrison. You go there to learn how the cable desk works, not to learn about New Delhi.

Robert Eunson. Yes. But if in addition to that you can beat a little New Delhi background into him, that would be wonderful.

Jack H. Lockhart. I, personally, disagree with you, Bob. I think that the wire services and the publishers would be somewhat leery of affiliating with any foundation, I don't care how pure or how purposeful, for the training of their men. We would be very suspicious of any man whose training we didn't pay for. Now, we may have been remiss, we may not have done the proper job in training our people, but I don't think *The New York Times*, and I don't think the AP or UP or Scripps-Howard, is going to welcome any foundation coming in, however generous, and saying, "Look, we will give you a quarter of a million dollars to train a certain man to speak Chinese (or something else) and then you send them overseas." It has implications.

Selig S. Harrison. My thought was, you're planning the program and who is going to go. It's your own program that you planned anyway. All that's contemplated is that if something were economically impossible, if it didn't make any sense in terms of the economics of an organization, this was a way for the economic obstacles to be overcome.

Jack H. Lockhart. I don't think there is an economic problem. I think that any organization which can maintain its own foreign correspondents can pay for any training that needs to be done, and I don't think that we need a program except a program that's within the organization. And there's another thing that disturbs me a little bit about this conversation. A newspaper does not train a man for a career in a certain area. You train a man—you don't train him; he trains himself, becomes trained—so that he can go to any one of a number of places. There are very few newspaper people who would be willing to devote themselves to a career in Asia. There are some. They're on the staffs of very large newspapers. And to give two years, say, at what would be the most productive period of a foreign correspondent's life, to give two years to training him in a specific area, unless there is sufficient opportunity in that area, sufficient incentive for him to spend his life there, I don't think you're going to find there are many people willing to do this.

There's not as much as there used to be—but there's a lot more of Phoenix and the next day New Delhi than there should, perhaps, be. But, there's always going to be. You're not going to have two years to learn a language; you're going to have to be there day after tomorrow and start working. It's simply, practically, the way it works. If you have a competent man, you send him wherever you need a job.

Selig S. Harrison. There's no way—there's no way to plan that in six months that you're going to send him there?

Jack H. Lockhart. Well, sometimes, and sometimes no.

Henry R. Lieberman. I think there are many ways that this could be approached, and there's no reason why the publishers themselves can't provide the funds for this foundation. I mean, it doesn't necessarily follow that the man's name has to be Ford who puts out the money; it could be the publishers and it could be done another way. On most newspapers, I think, big newspapers (and I restrict myself to newspapers because I think I know a little something about how they operate) you'll always find some young men who are interested in becoming foreign correspondents. This one fellow will want to go to Europe; another fellow will want to go to Asia. The newspaper may be undecided in its own mind as to whether it's ever going to send this fellow anywhere. Well, shouldn't it be possible for a newsman to qualify himself in a language even though he has no immediate foreign assignment confronting him? The time always comes when a "spot job" comes up, and you need a man for this place, and if you've got a fellow who can speak Russian, who can speak Chinese, who can speak Japanese, he's chosen quite often. I know a number of newspaper men who have gone out on their own to qualify themselves in languages. Now it might be possible for a young newspaper man, or an old newspaper man, for that matter, who is interested in becoming a foreign correspondent, might not it help for such a man to be able to get his training even though he has not got an immediate foreign assignment?

Valentin M. Ivanov. I am Ivanov, first secretary of the Soviet Embassy. My government provides a program for studying foreign languages. Not only in newspaper and magazine publishing, but just in general. We try to induce our people, to create an interest on their part, by giving them a certain bonus. For instance, I myself get a 10 per cent increase in salary for my knowledge of English. More than that, our bonus depends upon the degree to which you can handle foreign languages. If you're studying a foreign language for one year, you get 5 per cent, if you're studying for two years or more you get 10 per cent or 15 per cent. And more than 25 per cent of your salary depends on how many languages you know. Let me also give a little more propaganda here. This year, 25 or 30 per cent of, let's say, students in my country study English. Around six million Russians are studying English, while a far smaller proportion of Americans, some thirty thousand, study Russian. It is embarrassingly in favor of the Soviet Union.

VII / THE PROSPECTS
FOR INDIAN DEMOCRACY

In making the case for economic assistance to India, American leaders of both parties have arrayed India against Communist China and in so doing have attached critical significance to the contrast between India's parliamentary institutions and repression in Peking. Indeed, the case rests so squarely on this contrast that United States assistance to New Delhi has been virtually conditioned on the perpetuation of the present Indian Constitution. Thus President Eisenhower in his 1960 foreign aid message to Congress asserted that the Indian people were "deeply committed and irrevocably determined to develop and maintain institutions of their own free choice, and to raise their standards of living to levels of decency. The force and drive of this great effort is unmistakable; it warrants the full and warm support of the free world."

Would the commitment of the free world cool if the Indians should shape new political and economic institutions that do not conform to Western definitions of freedom? If, for the sake of national freedom, India limits some existing personal economic and political freedoms, does this negate the Western stake in her stable growth? *B. K. Nehru,* cousin of the Prime Minister and India's Commissioner General for Economic Affairs in Washington, is a distinguished spokesman of a generation of Indian leadership which most certainly feels a deep and irrevocable commitment to free institutions. And still he speaks frankly of these institutions as a "problem," an "obstacle," a "limitation" which "complicates infinitely the task of economic development." The possibility that the revolution of rising expectations will in time compel Indian leaders to modify present institutions drastically and that this modification might produce a political hybrid new to human experience emerges in most serious discussions of the Indian scene. *Averell Harriman* points to this possibility in affirming his own dedication to a program of Western aid.

Averell Harriman. There's an aspect of the Indian situation that I think we ought to do a little pondering about. I think we're a little bit inclined to feel that if there's improvement in economic conditions that then democracy is assured. I for one am, of course, completely dedicated to the conception of economic growth in the underdeveloped countries and it is our task to give a helping hand, but I think we must be careful not to assume that because there is economic growth that will assure democracy. Actually, I think there is a good deal in what some of the dictators of the world have felt— that it is safer for them to keep the people in ignorance and in poverty. After peoples get over the first end of misery and begin to have a chance to attain some of the better things of life, there's a demand for more. And when people get educated and they don't get what they hope to attain promptly, there is frustration.

In India there is a group of people, the educated unemployed, who are very dangerous. I believe we should give greater thought to what we can do in the way of giving a helping hand in advancing understanding of the values of democracy and the dangers from communism in Russia and in China. I'm not sure that it wouldn't be better for us to talk about Russian and Chinese imperialism rather than to argue over the values of communism. I found in India that many Indians thought they could get better technical assistance from the Soviet Union than they could from us because they have found, they've seen, the extraordinary results that have been achieved rapidly in the Soviet Union. The taking within forty years of an illiterate people and making it one of the best, most educated, they think, people in the world; a health program has been developed which they have great admiration for, the program of industrial expansion, of course, has been phenomenal. And I found that they are anxious to find out how these things were done. But I didn't feel that they were ready to give up the freedoms which they have so recently won, either personal or as a nation.

B. K. Nehru. The biggest problem of India is its size. We are a nation of almost 400 million people; we are one-seventh of humanity and nearly 40 per cent of the population of the non-Communist underdeveloped world. I emphasize this because one tends to regard India sometimes as just one more underdeveloped country. It is not always appreciated that India is equal in population to the whole of Latin America and the whole of the continent of Africa put together. The immensity of the population is, therefore, one of our basic difficulties. Any operation in India to be meaningful must be of colossal size; otherwise the entire effort tends to get lost in the vast desert of need.

The second problem of India is its extreme poverty. Even when judged by the standards of the less developed countries of the world, India is among the poorest of them all. The average per capita income of the non-Communist underdeveloped world is a little over $100 per annum. The India per capita income is only $60 per annum. There are only a few countries in the world poorer.

The third problem of India—and I speak of it as a problem because it complicates infinitely the task of economic development—is the fact that India has chosen for herself the democratic method of government with all the checks and balances that that method implies and with all the individual liberties that are inherent in a system that respects the rule of law.

When current consumption is less than a dollar and a quarter a week it becomes extremely difficult to squeeze out of this miserable pittance even the smallest amount required for investment. In this effort to raise resources democracy, to which we are fully and wholeheartedly committed, is an obstacle, for no democracy can afford to enforce that degree of hardship which alone can raise investible capital in a poor economy to any significant amount. Nor do we have the power which is available in other systems to regiment labor and to compel it to perform arduous tasks without any material reward. There are countries in the world where millions of peasants can be made to part with a sizable part of their crops in exchange for little or nothing, where millions of people can be transplanted hundreds of miles from their homes to work in forced labor camps at subsistence wages. But such methods are rightly anathema to free societies. Democracy must necessarily rely more on the carrot than on the stick. The difficulty with India, as with all poor countries with low levels of production, is that it does not have a large enough carrot to offer.

This then is the problem and these are the limitations within which we must work. When the odds are so heavily against us, we have, in societies such as ours, to develop certain guidelines along which the entire process of economic development must take place. The shortage of capital makes this commodity so precious that we cannot afford to allow it to be wasted in unproductive activity or frittered away in achieving objectives of a low priority in national terms. The limited trained, technical, managerial, and administrative manpower that is available also has to be conserved for the tasks of the highest priority. The determination of priorities in a free enterprise system is left almost entirely to the mechanism of the market and is dictated by the choice of the consumer. In rich societies, it does not really matter if, for a short time, the consumer prefers lipstick to hospitals or Cadillacs to schools or color television sets to roads. There are already within a rich society sufficient roads, schools, and hospitals to permit that society to continue to live and develop at a very high rate. But where capital and skilled manpower are scarce, there has to be some ordering of priorities; and in particular, there has to be some policy for the transference of resources from consumption to investment.

The method we have adopted in India to combine the essence of democracy with the need for development is the instrument of the planned economy. Indian planning is done by a Planning Commission which is outside the main structure of political government. The Planning Commission is assisted by a large body of experts in all fields of the country's growth. The plans they draw up are submitted to genuine popular criticism, are discussed throughout the country in popular forums, are examined and criticized by the governments of the states and finally, after such alteration and amendment as this democratic process justifies, are submitted to the Parliament of India for adoption.

Indian planning differs very considerably from planning in the totalitarian states. I have already mentioned that a poor society wanting rapid development cannot rely entirely on the dictatorship or the sovereignty of the consumer. Nevertheless, Indian planning operates almost wholly through the market mechanism. There are controls at various points of the economy such as import control, exchange control, capital issues control, and the like; but within the framework of these controls the processes of the market are allowed free play and the incentives are the same as in the more developed free economies.

Another characteristic of Indian planning is that the guidelines laid down for development in the plan cover both the public and the private sectors. The agency for the execution of the plans in the two sectors is different; in the public sector, it is the ministries of the Government of India or the State governments; in the private sector, it is the private entrepreneur within agriculture or industry.

But there is a fairly close interrelationship between the two sectors both in the matter of exchange of personnel and in the coordination of activities. And a significant part of the developmental activity of the State consists of programs of assistance and encouragement to the private sector. The Indian economy, contrary to popular belief in this country, is still a predominantly private enterprise economy.

In India, as in postwar Europe, the trained manpower, the managerial, administrative, and organizational capacity exist and the only factor limiting economic growth is capital. The Marshall Plan operation took 3½ years and cost $13 billion. At the end of it Europe was an independent and self-generating economy, with the strength to help economies less fortunate than her own. India is on the threshold of such an economic take-off. A similar operation in India will take a longer time but will cost less. At the end of it India should be in a position to cease to require abnormal external aid on a government-to-government basis; and should be able, in fact, appreciably to increase the help it gives to its less fortunate neighbors. The figure for such a plan of external assistance may in absolute terms be large; but it is a very small fraction of the annual increase in income of the Western world. The stakes are so high that it seems to me the sacrifice is well worth making.

TRADITION AND CHANGE

The temptation to employ the big stick in the absence of "a large enough carrot" becomes peculiarly acute for a politically conscious élite struggling against the drag of ancient tradition and custom. *H. V. R. Iengar*, Governor of the Reserve Bank of India, reports that the fatalism built into Hindu psychology is giving way, that there are "growing islands in which people are beginning to feel that something must be done."

H. V. R. Iengar. In this country and generally in the Western world one hears talk to the effect that there is a problem of poverty and that steps must be taken to raise the standard of living, or somebody will do something about it—the people will do something about it. Now that has been the basic fundamental problem in India—namely, to get the people to realize that poverty is a disease that ought to be fought, fought by them. We have been taught over centuries, by religion, by mythology, to believe in the doctrine of destiny. There is a great deal in that doctrine that is philosophically correct and justified, but by a perversion of this doctrine in actual practice, people have been led to think that if there is poverty, or any other disease, it has been foreordained by destiny, and there is nothing that can be done about it, and the results are pretty useless when you try. And therefore, people have been accustomed in our country just to shrug their shoulders and do nothing about it.

The great central problem that the Indian planners had to face in the beginning was to take steps to change the whole national psychology, the whole attitude of the people toward economic effort. It is a tremendous undertaking. I suppose if I were to put it in reverse, it would be very much as if the Government of the United States took on the job of telling the people of this country that they had better give up automobiles and television sets. Indeed in retrospect, I think it will be found that perhaps one of the most significant events of the contemporary world is the attempt on the part of the Government of India constantly to make efforts to change the whole national psychology. There is great and dramatic social change taking place in our country, so great, indeed, that even fundamental problems like the law of property and the law of marriage are being changed and no one bothers about them. You may have noted that we decided to tidy up, merely as incidental, the Hindu law of marriage and we men decided to deny to ourselves by formal parliamentary statute the very dubious privilege—one which was very rarely exercised—of marrying more than one wife.

In this process of changing national psychology the United States has played a very considerable part; a much bigger part than is realized even in this country. We are trying to do this job of making the people feel that they must get up and do something about this themselves, through the plan of "Community Development." And I must mention some of the great Americans who worked in India at the time this program was initiated. If I may say so without making any invidious distinctions, Chester Bowles, who was Ambassador at that time, played a very big part, indeed, in assisting the Government of India at the inception of this program. The Americans have left a mark in everything instituted at the time that the "Community Development" program was put on its feet.

I regard the problem of our national psychology as absolutely basic to the success of the whole plan, and I think it is interesting to know exactly what has happened in this field. Now it is quite clear that it would be folly for anyone to pretend that along the length and breadth of the country suddenly an enthusiasm has sprung up for economic improvement. This would not be correct. But it is astonishing how the thing is catching on. I'd put it like this. There are growing islands in which people are beginning to feel that something must be done, and that something can be done and that it can be done by themselves. I can give numerous instances in which the whole face of the countryside over small regions—it may be a group of 200 villages, or 300 villages, or 400—have been changed as a result of the community projects that we have started. Very shortly before I came to this country I visited a region not far from Bombay where we had taken some irrigation water. It used to be the practice in that place for the peasants to lease their lands, on which sugar cane is grown, to the sugar factories, to the big corporations from Bombay, and for many farmers to become laborers in the factories. Now what these people started asking themselves was why not, instead of leasing their lands and becoming ordinary workmen in the factories set up by the big fellows from Bombay, why not set up a sugar factory themselves and run it themselves? Remember, these are people who have never been to school. Most of them couldn't even sign their names to a document. It took them four years. They got together, they collected a little money, they went and bullied local representatives in the assembly, and to cut a long story short, there is today functioning a sugar factory operated by these people. Undoubtedly they get a certain amount of assistance from government, or rather, they did in the beginning, but they don't now. When I visited them, I met the board of directors, all of them farmers, and after a whole lot of questions about the investment, about the possibility of this, about the loan repayment program, and the like, I had all the answers pat. The chairman of the board of directors, who was himself a farmer and could not sign, told me very proudly that no one was going to cheat him about the price of sugar because he had installed a telephone in his house and he knew half a dozen brokers in Bombay, and he was absolutely certain that he always got one price more than the Bombay factory running next door to him.

Similar changes are taking place in various other places. I remember going to another place where cotton is grown and where it has been traditional for the last seventy-five years for three or four families to lend the money to the farmers for the production of cotton. They gin it, they press it, they send it down to Bombay—I mean, these four families, and it has been traditional for them to go every summer to Europe. They go to the Riviera, and places like that. Well, the heir of this family took me out on the river, when I visited him. He had just given a tea party, at which a number of the farmers were present at his house. And I remember—I don't want to sentimentalize about this—I remember it was evening and the sun was going down. The young man, who was heir to a great fortune, told me that he would not give himself more than another five years. I said, "Five years for what?" He said, "I will be out of business in five years, because what has happened is that in the last two years these people have learned how to band themselves into cooperatives; these cooperative societies are financing the production of cotton. They are taking over ginning factories very fast and ginning the cotton and pressing it. They have a marketing society and they are on to the brokers in Bombay, and I am being run out of business." The only thing that was wrong about this was this—I learned subsequently that the process took not five years but three!

When the eminent Sanskritist W. *Norman Brown* of the University of Pennsylvania asked five students of the Indian social scene whether tradition helps or hinders desirable change, he got answers ranging from K. A. *Nilakanta Sastri's* judgment that change, "under proper leadership," has an integral place in Indian tradition, to B. B. *Misra's* flat assertion that a caste-based social order is completely antithetical to change. Professor Sastri, author of A *History of South India* and other works, and anthropologist *Milton Singer* of the University of Chicago, contest Misra's contention that the persistence of caste, which is simply being "communalized instead of being weakened," both impedes economic development and imperils democratic institutions. *Flemmie Kittrell* of Howard University and *Richard B. Gregg* express admiration for India's efforts to retain what is of value from the past. Gregg pleads that the Gandhian tradition has greater contemporary validity than has normally been acknowledged by "modernist" Indian opinion.

W. Norman Brown. As a basis for discussion, I have asked each participant in advance the same question, and this question was— Is tradition helping or hindering desirable change in India? This assumes awareness of the fact that India has one of the oldest and one of the most highly developed traditions in the world. And it assumes also awareness that change is in the air in every part of India.

I have not asked for a definition of tradition. It certainly includes such matters as religion, social structure, language, law, rules of inheritance of property, women's rights—there is an unlimited range of topics which may be included under it. I asked that the question be answered in something like twenty-five, or at the most fifty words.

Mr. Gregg, who is as we know a student of Gandhian philosophy, says, "Some teachings of tradition such as caste and the literal sacredness of the cow are hindering desirable change in India. But people differ on what changes are desirable for India. I believe that chief emphasis should be placed not on industrialization, but on reforestation, soil composting, the weaving of homespun cloth, and birth control."

The answer which I received from Dr. Singer is as follows: "Although some traditional aspects of Indian life are widely considered to be obstacles to desirable change, tradition in India is so varied and adaptable that it can support practically any form of desirable change with institutional precedent, scriptural sanctions, and old vessels for new ideas."

Now let me read you Dr. Kittrell's answer. She says, "People resist change as a rule because of fear of the unknown. When individuals, a group, or a community have been nurtured in certain types of folk ways, religious beliefs, food habits, et cetera, these form a type of security and it isn't until the individual or a group has seen a new way demonstrated and explained in detail that he is willing to take the final step in a new direction. There is a quotation from a Basuto proverb as follows: 'If a man does away with his traditional way of living and throws away his good customs, he had better first make certain that he has something of value to replace them.'"

Dr. Nilakanta Sastri's answer is as follows: "Change under proper leadership is an integral part of Indian tradition. Popular practices and beliefs, superstitions, are the real obstacles. The spirit of Indian tradition is neither world-making nor opposed to material progress, only it insists on constant allegiance to the higher moral values, *dharma*."

That is, he quotes the Sanskrit word for those higher moral values.

And finally the reply of Professor Misra: "Tradition in India hinders desirable change in that its religiously ordained social system restricts education to the upper castes, recognizes no natural rights of man, obstructs social mobility, prejudices industrial and technological developments, makes for population growth, and narrows down human sympathies by an encouragement to thinking in groups."

I am going to let Dr. Misra's statement stand until I have had it commented on by somebody else. That is, I am not going to ask him yet to defend his statement. First I want others to comment on it. I shall ask Dr. Singer to make the first comment.

Milton Singer. Dr. Misra's position is one which was familiar to me before I went to India. I must say that after I went I changed my mind.

There are many specific traditional customs that are obstacles to change in India as everywhere else. I suppose we mean by tradition something that is handed down from generation to generation and is taken for granted. And when any change comes along it's bound to step on the toes of some particular traditional custom or other.

But this is different from saying that Indian tradition as a whole—the caste system, Hinduism, the joint family—is massively opposed to all those things required for desirable change: individual initiative and social or geographic mobility, greater enterprise, and the like.

With all due respect to his much greater experience and knowledge of things Indian, I think Dr. Misra has somewhat exaggerated the opposition between tradition on the one hand, and industrialization, agricultural improvement, on the other. One can systematically select factors in each institution which seem to oppose change. On the other hand, if one looks at the positive side, one can find sources of support in some of these traditions for desirable changes.

For example, take the much maligned caste system. Even that in some of its aspects can serve as a kind of springboard for new effort in industrialization and in other kinds of desirable change. Let me cite the studies by Mr. James McCrory and Father James J. Berna of newly developing small industries in North India and South India. Their studies show that one important source of skill and enterprise for the development of these new industries has been the traditional craftsmen and merchants. It was not very difficult to get these people to develop and experiment with new methods of manufacture in these industries. And their attitudes, their approaches are based pretty much on their traditional hereditary occupational outlooks. It is easy to forget that before British rule retarded the indigenous forces of industrial development in India during the nineteenth century, there was a very strong indigenous tradition of trade and craft within the framework of the caste system.

Another example showing how the caste system is not altogether a negative force is the case of the Brahmans. I think many historians would agree that westernization and modernization in India under the British depended to a large extent on the Brahmans and other literate, educated castes coming forward to take advantage of the new opportunities provided under British rule. They furnished the literate and educated groups who helped build up the very distinguished civil service in India, as well as many other clerical, supervisory positions.

A recent study by Richard Lambert of five factories in Poona showed that although Brahmans were represented in all levels of the factory population, from the lowest to the highest, they predominated in the clerical and supervisory skills where their relatively greater degree of literacy and education qualified them disproportionately for those jobs requiring those skills. This tradition of respect for knowledge and learning, I think, is now being broadened to absorb many new developments.

As for the farmers and peasants, they too, I think, traditionally have had a very practical outlook, a very shrewd outlook. They have skills and knowledge about agriculture based on practical experience. And I think the Community Development program has shown how they too are willing to respond, slowly perhaps, occasionally, to new opportunities; they want new roads, new schools, new wells, and new methods of production.

I give this just as one example of how, by taking one of the oldest and most traditional institutions in India—the caste system— and by looking at it in terms of its potentialities for providing skills and precedents for modern developments, you can draw, I think, a far more optimistic picture than the one that is more familiarly drawn and which is, to some extent, reaffirmed in Dr. Misra's statement. The caste system has cultivated traditions of learning, of trade, of craftsmanship and agriculture which provide a reservoir of important skills and motivations for modern economic changes.

K. A. Nilakanta Sastri. The impression that Professor Misra's comments made on my mind was that these comments were very common and were very familiar to me in my younger days. I was also in a little way a student of economics. In fact, I taught economics to the honor standard before I switched to history.

But much of this tradition historically stems from the Christian missions that criticized Hindu society. And it is a sort of handover from somewhat old world scientific "progress." Quite a few in India still tend to think on those lines, but personally, I think that it is taking a very obsolete and, as Professor Singer has pointed out, a too pessimistic view of present ways and tendencies.

Indian tradition, as such, has not been unchanging or petrified. It has been changing through the ages.

Take caste, for instance. Professor Singer has already commented on it. I'll give you one concrete example. Caste, you know, is closely bound up with handicrafts and hereditary skills. An attempt was made by a Madras leader, greatly respected everywhere, to make the traditional hereditary skill of the caste system the foundation for rural elementary education. He suggested a scheme by which children do not have schooling for the whole day, but only a part of the day—the rest of the day being left free for them to learn their hereditary skills from their parents.

Well the need for reviving handicraft and getting it a respectable place in the Indian economy comes inevitably, for even as advanced European countries have found out, there is really no conflict between handicraft and machine industry. They can co-exist and even mutually benefit each other.

But there was opposition to a man against this scheme: they said it was a scheme on the part of this scheming Brahman to keep the non-Brahmans in their respective positions of subordination. This scheme has been given up. Now why do I cite this?

The spirit of the times today in India is not the traditional caste spirit but something directly running against it. That is what I want you to realize.

It is true that these skills have to be taught, not in homes but in public schools run by either government agencies or nongovernment agencies.

This system has also been criticized on the score that school education is not tantamount to domestic education under the father's benevolent guidance, and there is some loss involved in the change. This is inevitable but the change is coming.

In another field, marriage changes affect the essence of custom.

Old restrictions are overlooked and breaking down. Each caste, which is an endogamous group, is now widening its scope. The scope of endogamy is becoming wider. What I mean is that castes are going and only main, big divisions stand. Probably the castes are changing into classes. We do not know. It is too soon to say what the situation is.

Even in a field like religion, where you expect the highest amount of conservatism to prevail, what you find today is that sectarianism, very strong in the recent past of our country, is giving way to the discoveries of common ground among different sects.

Just a few months before I left my country, the spiritual leaders of three different schools—the heads of important sectarian maths—joined together and issued a joint manifesto calling upon all of their disciples and followers to combine in certain desirable lines for common religious practice and worship.

So that what I want to say is this—the old traditional society has felt the impact of new conditions and under these conditions it has changed.

Richard Gregg.   The first time I went to India was the winter of 1913–1914, the winter before the first World War. I was again there for nearly four years from the beginning of 1925 to the end of 1928, again briefly in 1930, again briefly in the winter of 1949–1950. And then I have spent eighteen months there in 1958 and 1959.

The changes that have taken place since 1914 are just unbelievable, perfectly tremendous. And even the changes since 1928 have been enormous. The old phrase about the "unchanging East" is no longer valid at all. The East is changing, if anything, faster than the West.

In a sense I'm not so much interested in the question of whether tradition is a hindrance to change as I am in the question of what things out of the past, what elements out of the past, are valuable and worth keeping. We cannot, any of us, either as individuals or as nations, suddenly cut ourselves off by the roots and make an utter change. We have to live on the shoulders of our past selves.

Now in relation to Gandhi's program, his way of handling conflict could, I think, be called traditional in that it was spoken of in the Upanishads perhaps 800 years B.C., was emphasized again by Buddha, and has been an element in Indian culture all along. Gandhi organized it and made it possible for great numbers of people to use it in organized fashion to settle very large-scale conflicts.

Again, his hand-spinning program, which in the West seems like nonsense, that also is an element in the old village traditional way of life. That, I think, is another element of the past which should be adhered to and kept as a proper kind of conservation. It is modern in that it is a remarkably useful and effective attack on the tremendous problem of rural unemployment brought about by the Indian climate, where at the end of nine months of the dry season, there is nothing that the peasants can do, and they just sit idle for at least three months of every year. The moral and economic burden of that vast unemployment of at least 110 million people every year is almost beyond understanding.

Not only is there this economic effect of reviving this old tradition of the Indian villages, there is the moral effect of it. We are too apt to think of implements and machines as being devices only for producing material goods. We have overlooked the fact that the use of the hands has a profoundly moral effect. It affects people's characters and their minds. All through the history of mankind we have used our hands in order to enlarge our minds. The association between hand and mind throughout human history is of immense value. Madame Montessori showed how creative, healing, and stimulating is the effect of the use of the hands for underdeveloped children, handicapped children. The military use the bodily skills and practices, partly of the hand and partly of the rest of the body, in order to discipline people and develop in them worth-while habits. The ruling group of almost every nation goes in for teaching their children, before the age of ten, how to ride horseback and how to control the horse with the use of hands. And that hand skill is considered by the shrewd ruling groups of the world as being enormously important in developing courage, self-reliance, self-respect, the ability to make quick decisions, and other moral and intellectual factors that are important to any democracy and to any individual. When a person gets into a dreadful state of despair and has to go to a mental hospital, they give him what they call occupational therapy. Here again, by the use of his hands, such a patient climbs out of his troubles and reestablishes his moral poise and ability to deal with the outer world.

And so I believe that Mahatma Gandhi's program is of great value. It's the sort of tradition that should be conserved.

Flemmie P. Kittrell. I have a very profound respect for the fact that India is moving ahead so rapidly. And they are being very careful that the truths they have found, if you please, are not going to be thrown aside for something that hasn't already been tested.

India doesn't change rapidly but I think it changes very securely as it moves ahead in a rather smooth traditional way. I'll be specific to the area of home and family living. We call this subject "home economics" in this country. The people in India, that is, in particular the people at the university level, had observed that science, physical science, had made for the very great changes in the Western world. They were especially concerned that this science should be applied to the home and the family. They were concerned also about the contribution the West had made in the social sciences and they knew that the social sciences had not kept up with the physical sciences.

They needed a great deal of help in nutrition and when we began to work on that program for research, the women especially were not only eager but they tried out some of the foods that they had been working with over a period of years. They had not yet analyzed these foods from the point of view of what was in them. They brought in food to see if this was good. This is what they had been eating. Is this rich in vitamin C that you've been talking about? And when we worked with the women and worked with some of their associates —men, too—we found that what they had been using for hundreds of years was very rich in ascorbic acid. So we tried to formalize it for them by putting it on paper.

Now in our thinking together, they wanted to see how we could apply science to the art of living and how we could help with the family structure, which they had depended upon for their real security and which, incidentally, is a security for any country. They wanted to see what they could do to improve their home and family living. Basically, the family group in India is a joint system.

I would think as we talk about change in the case of India that we probably could learn a great deal on how to change through stability. Some of the things the Indians had learned in the joint families, they didn't want to lose, such as sharing, or such as having children feel adequate in the family group—they didn't want to lose that. But, at the same time, they wanted to see what could be done to help the children move ahead in good physical strength and all-round development.

B. B. Misra. I am at present engaged in a work called *The Growth of the Indian Middle Classes*—a study of India's social development in modern times. This study has led me to a conclusion that although popular forces like Jainism, Buddhism, or devotional cults tried to break the orthodoxy of the Karma-ordained and caste-ridden Hindu society, they could not leave a lasting impression. They were in fact assimilated by the established Brahmanical order except in modern times when the growth of capitalism and English education created new classes, I mean the middle classes, who brought their political influence and power to effect liberal reforms and changes that are becoming more and more sustained. Western education and modern economic development became the basis of change in India, not India's own tradition, which preserved the Brahmanical monopoly of knowledge and the political power of bureaucracy. Priestly intellectuals and the king's officials always combined to crush the merchant who in the West became the torchbearer of liberal democracy.

It is true that India had a great intellectual tradition. But this great intellectual pursuit of which historians speak so highly was limited to a very small class of people called Brahmans, and to some members of a few other upper castes called Kayasths or Kshatriyas. There was nothing like a national system of education in India. Moreover, the nature of education was formerly literary. It was not related to manual skills, which were deemed socially inferior, even degrading. Those who were educated possessed no manual skills. Those who had skills remained uneducated. Education and skill did not go together. Prior to modern times there was no occupational mobilization. As I have suggested the whole of India's tradition has been based on what is known as *Karma*, or the Theory of Deed, under which a man is assigned a position in this life according to his past *Karma* or deed. Each individual is assigned an occupation and a social rank that goes with it. And that assignment is made not by any human agency or institution but by God Himself.

My friend, Dr. Nilakanta Sastri, says that caste is being weakened. I do not think so. It is being communalized instead of being weakened. As recently as 1942, when on the arrest of Congress leaders people in Bihar, for example, revolted against the British, and law and order became paralyzed, it was rumored that India had become independent, and that the traditional principle of caste would be restored—a principle more violated than observed by the British Administration. In one of the villages of my subdivision the upper caste men declared that since India had become free, the social system based on Hindu religion must be brought back into practice. There were certain low-caste people who used sandals, as they called them, to protect their feet against the cold. The Brahmans and other upper-caste people insisted that the use of sandals by low castes being prohibited by the ancient law books, especially in the presence of superior-caste men, they must not use those sandals. But because these low-caste men had earned a lot of money in Calcutta where some of their number worked, they paid no heed to the objection so raised. The situation grew tense and led to a breach of the peace. The result was that two of the low-caste people lost their lives. That was in 1942. It was not 1842, not 1742, not B.C.— but A.D. 1942.

Therefore, what I want to suggest to you all is that in a caste system based on *Karma*, theoretically speaking, there is nothing like the natural rights of man. The individual is not free to climb up the social ladder according to his talents. The Indian social system obstructs social mobility. Even a very small, petty, poor, and indigent Brahman would never agree to give the hand of his daughter to a very highly educated, wealthy, and enlightened person belonging to a low caste. And that is especially so in the State of Madras, from which my friend Dr. Sastri hails. Caste is still alive.

Another thing that I want to suggest is the way in which this social system hinders economic development. In a society which obstructed occupational mobilization, trade and industrial crafts remained tagged on to traditional castes with little or no education. The political and social systems both being authoritarian, they discouraged capital investment for production purposes, for there was little or no security of private property. The king or his officials could enter the market whenever they wanted to. Unlike India, the Western merchant had his charters of liberty, his control over town governments. He fought for limited government. He led the movement for constitutionalism, and contributed to the development of democracy in the Western world. In India the merchant was suppressed by priestly intellectuals and the bureaucracy except in mod-

ern times when the literary classes came closer to the bourgeoisie—
to fight against the British, who thwarted the interests of both.
In free India there is a tendency for the revival of the old relationship in which the Brahman dominated the Bania.

Please bear in mind that the middle classes which grew up under
British rule were for the most part professional and literary in
character, not commercial or industrial. The intelligentsia rather
than the bourgeoisie dominated the public affairs of the country.
That signified the continued predominance of the traditional literary
classes, though in a changed form. The Indian industrial and commercial interest was also there, but in a subordinate position. The
class which had the leadership in the fight for freedom was not a
class of merchants or of industrialists. It was the class of the intelligentsia, consisting for the most part of upper-caste men who
even now constitute the dominant strand in politics as well as administration. The British being a nation of shopkeepers recognized
the legitimate claims of the mercantile community. The new
rulers of India, though influenced by the liberal traditions of
English education, show a tendency to lapse into traditional authori-
tarianism.

The most powerful class, the civil service, to which reference has
been made, is a class consisting mostly of the upper-class Hindus,
most of them Brahmans. In Madras, as in Bombay, most of the
high positions in the civil service were occupied by Brahmans even
under the British. In Bengal they are held partly by Brahmans and
partly by another class, called Kayasths. In other provinces, too, it
was more or less a case of Brahmans and Kayasths in addition to
Mohammedans. So those who were higher up in society before have
continued to be higher up even in modern times. That is the force
of tradition in India.

The competitive system introduced by the British made the civil
service peculiarly powerful. Our modern civil service became not
only an instrument of authority but a class of intellectual aristocrats
combining with it the social influence belonging to it by tradition.
To this has been added the extended function of the State, especially in free India, and with the march of socialism. Today the civil
service can become a threat to democracy if the pace of industrial
development in India is not accelerated according to principles of
private and free enterprise, regulated though it may be to avoid
class antagonism. I personally believe that the safety and security of

democracy lies in the extension of free enterprise in India. Otherwise you have the possibility of the intelligentsia combining together with the bureaucracy to establish a form of government which we may call totalitarian. This happened in Pakistan recently.

"AFTER NEHRU, WHAT?"

The political scientist has a striking case study in the contrast between the rise of a military régime in Pakistan and the continuing viability of representative institutions in India. Professor *Richard L. Park* of the University of Michigan assesses the Indian parliamentary system. He believes that Indian institutions will exhibit "a great deal more staying power than many people give them credit for" in absorbing the shocks of social change. To *Frank Moraes'* suggestion that indirect elections would have been more appropriate to Indian conditions, he responds that such a system would only aggravate local patriotisms. *Asoka Mehta*, Chairman of the Praja (Peoples) Socialist Party, makes no attempt to minimize the disruptive forces in a body politic unsupported by a "social infrastructure." But he believes that Indian nationalism will triumph in the end.

Richard L. Park. Clearly it is important for us to assess the general stability—over time—of the kinds of political institutions, and the values underlying those institutions, that provide the political and social channels for the dramatic attempt at rapid economic development that is now taking place in India. For without an adaptable and relatively efficient political system within which such development can progress, it may be questioned whether serious political obstacles will not arise to render the economic impact less powerful than it might otherwise have been.

This problem of the political means for encouraging economic development becomes even more critical because, as successes are reached economically, political and administrative responses must necessarily themselves become more effective and more efficient. The people of India, as they become more aware of the opportunities presented to them to better their lot, will not be satisfied with tidbits; they will want more and more economic betterment. And politics will have to provide the buffer for unfulfilled expectations.

That being true, it will not be adequate for a government to be only *generally* satisfactory; government must be adequate to the particular situation, and in India's case that means improving internal institutions steadily and imaginatively as the economy grows.

It is quite clear to most observers of Indian politics that the Congress Party is now overwhelmingly in power throughout the country. It is true that there is one state that is held under precarious control by the Communist Party—the state of Kerala—and there are some states in which the margin of Congress power is modest, to put it mildly. But the power facts of politics are that the Congress Party holds dominant weight throughout the country.

There are a lot of reasons for this, including nationalist history. The Congress Party is heir to at least a good portion of the Indian National Congress' movement for independence; and the Congress is the party of Gandhi and of Nehru. Secondly, the Congress Party happens to have the majority of India's powerful leaders in its fold. The Congress possesses a powerful, if tired, organizational apparatus. It is an enormous apparatus that covers the country, and it is the only party organization that umbrellas the country right down to district levels and below. And, not unimportant, so far the Congress has been able to obtain the kind of financial support necessary to carry on this kind of Big Politics, attempting to appeal to more than one hundred million voters.

Analytically, if not formally, India is, in effect, a one-party state. There is a reason to explain this. It is what I call the *sarkar* effect. The *sarkar* is government or power. In the situation of India's past eleven or twelve years, people voting, particularly illiterate or unsophisticated persons, will tend to look on an election as a sort of referendum. One either favors the power (and thus the party) that is in power, or one doesn't favor it. And one will normally favor the government in power (the *sarkar*) unless one is overwhelmingly opposed for some reason. The impact of the sarkar effect is to give considerable strength to the party actually in power, in terms of a general affirmation of that enormous structure of government that can either give or take away important favors. Thus the Congress has been sustained partially by the fact that it *is* in power and that there is no really substantial opposing force.

But one does find "politics" if one looks on politics as being the open expression of a variety of points of view. In the first place, the Congress may be monolithic in certain ways, but it is not a monolithic party in terms of competing points of view. Within the Congress and between its factions, one finds some of the most vital politics of the country. Politics take place, of course, under circumstances in which discipline can be exerted over opponent elements within the Congress at crucial moments. And thus this kind of "inner politics" within the Congress is not as significant, perhaps, as genuine opposition politics. But nevertheless, one does get a good deal of discussion of issues, even without significant opposition. More politics take place, for good or ill, at annual sessions of the Congress Party, or at meetings of the All-India Congress Committee, the controlling body of the Congress, or more particularly, within the élite leadership group of the Working Committee of the Congress, than take place when national elections come onto the scene.

A second point that I'd like to make in terms of Indian politics is that fortunately, despite the fact that there is little substantial opposition politics in the country, there happens to be an affection for discussion on the part of the Prime Minister, and generally of the leaders of his party, which encourages opposition views to come forward. That is to say, there is a will among certain of the leaders of the Congress Party—certainly the Prime Minister on most occasions —and by the more sophisticated leaders of the Congress Party to seek out opposition views in order to add responsibility to the kind of treatment that is given to major issues in Indian politics. In a sense this is creative, and it's also a bit dangerous because one can't be sure that future leaders will allow these kinds of "opposition" views to be expressed in the forums of Parliament.

And finally—I'll state this point briefly—there are various groups within India that do not give their full agreement to the ideas of Indian democracy that have developed to date. There are groups within the Congress Party itself who oppose parliamentary government. The Communist Party of India pays lip service to established institutions, but in all theoretical and practical ways the Party obviously is opposed to the whole principle of democracy. There are groups, such as those in the Dravidian movement of the South that Selig Harrison has analyzed in his book, and others, that are opposed; some would rather see an idealized form of Hindu *raj* or something approximating a traditional Hindu "golden age" era instituted in India.

In my opinion, and differing with Selig Harrison, I don't believe these antiparliamentary (antidemocratic) movements are as powerful as he sees them to be.

There's another cleavage in Indian politics. That is the cleavage between the urban, educated population, and the vast rural population of the country. Rural people are by no means ignorant. They are, as a matter of fact, highly sophisticated in many ways, and knowledgeable, too. Their perspectives—their horizons—are more limited because their experience is more limited. But differing from many urban people, few villagers have as yet any kind of strong sense of commitment to any particular form of government for India. It is still possible to take a poll in India in rural parts of the country and ask questions as simple as "Who is Mr. Nehru?" and get blank answers. In other words, there are lots of people in India among the 400 millions who are relatively untouched by organs of public opinion, such as those that have been with such dignity administered by Mr. Frank Moraes and his colleagues over many years.

So far the full expression of India's political genius is yet to come and I think that much adaptation and new experimentation will take place over the coming decades. However, I take the conservative view that Indian constitutional institutions will probably have a great deal more staying power than many people give them credit for. I believe that it will be possible for radical social change and economic development to take place within the general pattern of presently-established institutions. Such continuity would be in accord with India's experience over the past couple of hundred years.

Frank Moraes. There's a very old story told, that in the old days an Englishman went out shooting duck. He was a very bad shot and he got a very small bag. And the Indian who accompanied him said, when he complained about his small bag of duck, "The sahib shot well, but God was merciful to the birds."

You see that despite our lack of literacy there is a certain subtlety in the Indian mind which one cannot overlook. I think we have in this discussion to start straightaway with the premise that India is not a democracy. India is a growing democracy. India is a developing democracy and India may express this democracy in institutional forms that are different from the rest. In fact, the American system of democracy is different from the British parliamentary system of democracy. And so is the French. You go further off. Therefore, there should be no superstitious attachment to the institutional forms of democracy so long as the spirit of democracy is there—the right of every individual to express his opinion and the right to form an opposition party. I think if you apply that acid test, it does not matter how democracy expresses itself.

I think in Asia, particularly in India, it should express itself in a different form. A great mistake we made was adult franchise. Gandhi was right when he talked of an indirect system of elections, pretty much like the Soviet system, in which the village council, let's say, elects one man to the nearest town council. And the town elects somebody to the district, and the district to the state, and the state to the center.

I think if we had adopted that indirect system of election we might have escaped from many of our difficulties. But there is no going back. Today we have adult franchise with the population 80 per cent illiterate and we have to make do within those limitations as best we can.

You know, when the British came they found an India of peasants and princes. And it is the British who created the middle class—the self-educated middle class—which they hoped would be a prop for their system of government. And in the end, that middle class destroyed them.

Gandhi, in turn, then created a new class. He created a *corps élite* which he thought would serve as the basis of the government when India became independent. But that new class, because it has taken office, has become a very closed preserve. I think you could apply the parallel of which Djilas speaks from Yugoslavia to India. Just as Djilas says in his book: "The class did not create the party; the party created the class." And as the class gets stronger, the people entrenched in power, in this case the Congress, get stronger. The party weakens.

In Asia if one is given the choice between democracy and freedom, we will, because of our colonial past, compromise with democracy. We will never compromise with freedom. And, therefore, you can have such things as guided democracy or controlled democracy.

Democracy and freedom are very large terms, very loosely used. But in Asia and in Europe, the terms mean something different because you have been used to freedom for a long while. We haven't. And, therefore, when the choice comes, we would rather compromise on democracy than on freedom.

Asoka Mehta. I must confess that I often wonder as I confront the forces of social reaction in our political affairs whether this logical

concept of democracy is precisely what India needs. I remember
talking to Prime Minister Nehru and telling him that the forces of
opposition in India were weak. He smiled and said to me, "Do you
really think so?" He said, "The forces of opposition in India are
really the ignorance and obscurantism among our people." And he
said, "Thank God that they have no well organized spokesman in
the country today."

And there is a great amount of truth in what he said. Because
what, after all, is the fight in which India is engaged today? It is
the fight to transform the old traditional society into a modern state.
It is a fight of modernism against forces of medievalism embedded
in the very fabric of our society.

My country is very different from yours. You have many differences but by and large it's a homogeneous society. In my country,
on the other hand, a social scientist can discover many layers—a
kind of social geology, a society with many layers and many structures. You can witness at any time in my country a cavalcade of
centuries because you can find side by side people living and belonging to different centuries—the men of the twentieth century as
well as the men and women of the nineteenth, eighteenth, and
fifteenth centuries. Fifty-five million people—the *harijans* or un-
touchables—were condemned for centuries before we embarked on
their social rehabilitation to a fixed position at the bottom of the
social scale. Twenty-five million people belong to the tribal people—
men who were driven centuries back into the recesses of the jungle
and into the hills. The more virile people moved forward and pushed
these ancient people of my land into the darker regions. One is
reminded of your countrymen also.

So these forces exist and they are powerful and we have to fight
them. These forces lend themselves to organization, to destructive
political groupings canalizing all protest, and yet to fight them we do
not have enough constructive groupings or enough constructive
political leadership. Now the modernists in India, the so-called élite,
is very small. We do not have enough élite to go around. We have
to develop and create the leadership and the institutions to bring
about the change that we desire. You do not realize what it is to
function in a politics where a social infrastructure does not exist.
You already have your organizations, your Chambers of Commerce,
your Lions and Rotarians, your League of Women Voters, your
clubs, and all manner of organizations. My God! Every American

belongs to all kinds of organizations. And the longer the list of clubs to which a woman belongs, the more important is her position in the social register.

In my country, Mr. Moraes—Frank—may belong to a number of clubs but I don't think the people in the villages have heard of them. We have to create this structure of voluntary organizations to provide a basis for democracy.

Frank said that he is not happy that we have adult franchise. Well, my view is that's the one wise step that we have taken. But for our democracy to work, in view of all of our social fragmentation, we have to realize that while differences are important we must also discover our points of agreement. If we only focus attention on the controversies, on the points of argument, we shall then undermine the very republic that we tried to create.

Of course, it does not help a politician to emphasize points of agreement.

In India today, as far as the union Parliament is concerned, there is in practice a kind of a democracy without an alternative contender for power. And as I look ahead, I see for the next ten years the likelihood that democratic forces will be brought closer and closer together. I see some kind of a national front coming into power in my country in the next several years. Imagine organizing cooperatives in a period of a few years in more than a half million villages. Think of mobilizing internal resources for economic development in a country the size of India. This is going to demand a new measure of popular participation and identification, a government that has the backing of 90 per cent of the people, and not 43 per cent of the people as is the case today.

Now you might say that to minimize party conflict would be the very negation of democracy. I say that is not so. What has happened in times of crisis in other countries which do have, as we do not, a framework which is able to hold the country together through a period of crises? What happened in England? For a time the game of democracy was either suspended or played in a manner it is not normally played. You must realize that we live in a country of crisis, that we are in the very heart of a great national emergency and, therefore, our democracy has to be conditioned by the national emergency that confronts us.

One special danger we face is that while at the national level democratic forces can be seen in action and effectively so in our country, at the state level we are fast becoming something like a French parliament. With each new local crisis political parties are formed and re-formed. What we might call nuclear politics are at work in our states—in some of our states—and the precedent of a British pattern of democracy is slowly getting transformed into a French pattern. Ultimately at the state level there could be a breaking down into very dangerous instability. But I believe that with all that our Constitution gives us the weapons to assure the triumph of the strong forces of nationalism. We have welded our people together in the crucible of nationalism for half a century. It is this that is going to help us.

And I would say that even the Communists, now that they have got into the parliamentary game, find that they are influenced even while they try to undermine us. Because as a great French philosopher said in the nineteenth century, between two members of a Parliament, one of whom is a revolutionary and the other not, there is more in common than between two members of the revolutionary party, one of whom is a member of Parliament and the other not. I think there is a profound truth in this observation. The Communists sit next to me and I sit next to them in the Parliament and I know the sobering influence that parliamentary institutions are exercising over them. It is rather unfortunate that you have not put one or two Communists in your Congress.

Asoka Mehta's prophecy that the emergence sooner or later of a national front government is a "political compulsion" of India's planned economy raises the broad question—"After Nehru, What?"—as well as some specific questions concerning the component forces envisaged as part of such a coalition. Mehta spells out his conception of a government having as its political core centrist Congress and Praja Socialist elements, grouped around Prime Minister Nehru in support of the progressive economic program necessary, in Mehta's view, to mobilize public support for a bigger than ever Third Five Year Plan. This implies a submergence of party conflict hardly characteristic of parliamentary politics. As *Charles Burton Marshall* observes, however, it is a "politics of policy" rather than a "politics of protest" carried over from anticolonialist years which is needed if the underdeveloped countries are to succeed in development and self-government. Mr. Marshall, author of *The Limits of Foreign Policy*, served on the State Department's Policy Planning Staff (1950–1953) and was Adviser to Prime Ministers of Pakistan (1955–1957).

Asoka Mehta. What will happen after Nehru depends, of course, very much on when such a contingency might arise. Secondly, I think it is still not being recognized by people in India and inevitably abroad that the Third Plan is going to have a tremendous impact on the politics of the country. The imperatives of the Third Plan are going to be very different from the imperatives of the earlier plans. That means that within the Congress Party, even under Nehru's leadership, there will be in the next few years a considerable polarization.

There are many men in the Congress who will find they can no longer get along with the Prime Minister. There has been a kind of uneasy partnership with the Prime Minister providing progressive leadership and some of his colleagues, some of his followers, indulging in erosive tactics. But I do not think in the conditions in which the Prime Minister will find himself when he undertakes a Third Plan of the dimensions that he wants to, that he can permit this kind of erosive tactics to go on. Nor will it be possible for those who want to indulge in these erosive tactics to reconcile themselves to the kind of plans and policies that the Prime Minister is now being compelled to enforce because of the needs of a big plan.

To some extent this polarization has already been reflected in the formation of a conservative party—on the argument that the choice of the people is now between Tweedledum and Tweedledee because everyone claims to be Socialist. But I am afraid that a conservative party is not likely to succeed because the mood of the people is radical.

The central fact in our situation is that the leadership of the Congress is committed to what is, taking the over-all picture, a progressive position, so that it is true no worth-while democratic opposition in India can today offer a completely alternative set of policies. And it is interesting to notice that even the Communist Party's claim is that it is trying to implement the Congress Party program better than the Congress Party. So it really—the situation is that our politics offer variations on the same theme because the Congress Party program today is the program that they took away from us only yesterday.

Charles Burton Marshall. I thought your premise is that protest is the essence of democracy.

Asoka Mehta.   You misunderstand me.

Charles Burton Marshall.   Protest is a part of it but there is a great deal more to it than that. And if protest were the main part of it even, I would say that the politics of colonial régimes is the politics of democracy because that is the politics of protest. But I think that the going into nationhood and responsibility in any one of these countries is regrowth into something besides protest. It is the growth, let's say, of the politics of policy as well as the politics of protest. And the combination of these two things is a very, very difficult one. A very knowing Pakistani once remarked to me that in Pakistan, for instance, they had only two kinds of men who got interested in public life at all—those who believed in discussion without decision and those who believed in decision without discussion.

And I think the problem is the problem of getting the protest part—the discussion part—welded with the decision part, which is the politics part. I say again, there's more to democracy than protest.

What about the Hindu revivalist forces at one political extreme and the Communists at the other? Are they to be part of the national government?

Asoka Mehta.   The right-wing Hindu parties are very strong and will be a factor in all of our political life. As for the Communists, I think you will find that as a result of the developments on our northern borders, the Communists will be isolated. These developments might provide a kind of crystallization of national unity on the part of the non-Communist forces. The Communists no longer belong to the community of India, and I am inclined to doubt whether the Communist Party can have any place in such a configuration.

Is military intervention a possibility in India as in Pakistan and Burma?

Asoka Mehta.   The situations in Pakistan and Burma and the situation in India are not at all comparable, but I will not go into that. At present the Indian Army is completely outside politics and does not seem to have any political ambitions. The organization of our armed forces is also such that it is not easy for it to exercise that kind of initiative.

But, as Mr. Frank Moraes pointed out, if it is a question ultimately of the nation surviving or the nation going to pieces, I think the people would support, even in India—though I do not think the contingency will arise—but if it were to arise, the people of India would be willing to rally around a military government so that the freedom of the country is protected.

Frank Moraes is asked about his earlier statement that India would in a showdown sacrifice "democracy" to save "freedom."

Frank Moraes. It is quite obvious that if one compromises with democracy, ultimately one compromises with freedom—freedom in the democratic sense, individual freedom. But what I was trying to distinguish between was that—well, the West, Western countries, are used to freedom. They've had years, possibly centuries, of independence. But Eastern countries have only newly gotten their freedom, that is, their independence. And, therefore, when it comes to a choice between compromising on democracy or national freedom, they would rather compromise on democracy.

Will an either-or compromise become necessary? Or will India find a way to keep both national freedom and democratic institutions? When it comes down to it, warns *Charles Burton Marshall*, it is much easier to throw over democracy than to find an adequate substitute.

Charles Burton Marshall. When I was in Pakistan I never talked much about democracy. I talked about other things, such as the principles of accountability, the necessity of discussion, and confidence in the system of justice. When I heard Pakistanis make the point—as some of them, especially those connected with the executive establishment and the viceregal tradition, were wont to do—about the country's not being ready for democracy, I always raised this question, "What are you ready for?"

Now there are certain things, it seems to me, that a state has to have in the situation of modern times in order to fulfill its mission as a state. Let us see what a society has to have—at least if it is not going to take the oppressive course.

It does have to apply the principle of accountability. It has to have some function of discussion. The word has to get around so that there is a common understanding, a rapport, an identity between the régime and the people who live with that régime. Then there must be a principle of legitimacy. A franchise is one way of forwarding the principle of legitimacy, though indeed not the only way. If there is a system of monarchy, or if there is a tradition of aristocracy, then well enough, for these might serve well. If these things, a tradition of kingship or a competent and well established élite, are not at hand, then one must ask what there is to turn to except some system of franchise. It is no real answer to the problem to say that the country concerned is not ready for a democracy.

I should like to emphasize what we may call the concept of the public. I mean by that the idea that there must be a determining number of people in a society—not necessarily all, nor even a majority, but a significant portion, enough to count—who can think about things beyond their vocational ambit, who can exercise criticism beyond matters in the immediate span, and who can think beyond the mere conditions of their daily work and beyond the limits of the neighborhood. I mean, by using that term, the public, also that a society be suffused with a sense of belonging, a sense of responsibility to something. Edmund Burke referred to this as a sense of responsibility to the generations that have gone before, to the generations that will follow, and to all one's notional contemporaries, meaning those who do not come directly within one's span of personal knowledge but of whose existence one is nevertheless aware.

It is when we know that others whom we do not personally know and whom we cannot identify are affected by our acts and that we, in turn, are each affected by their acts, and that we have a responsibility to all of them and they to all of us—then it is that we begin to develop a grasp of the public aspect of our lives. Without that sort of comprehension, it is impossible to do the work of the modern state—unless, of course, one turns to the totalitarian alternative of having a dictatorial régime at the top and under it a mass following. I stress in this connection the basic distinction between a mass following and a public following, because the public is based upon the concept of obligation and a function of criticism whereas the mass is not.

The necessary thing in any one of these new states—and in a way in this respect, India does serve a great function as a leading light—is the problem of creating a public, with a set of public values, a set of principles of public life, a notion of public service and public principles. I do not think that there is any answer to this in the purported alternative of personalism. I put no stock in this notion that the new states can free themselves of the requirements of developing a public life merely by setting up and vesting all authority in some figure who will be here only a while and who must die and go on some day as all mortals must.

Many Americans fancy the idea that the economic approach can lead to a solution of all of the problems of these new states. They treasure the dream that it is necessary only to bolster production, to dredge out some harbors, to sink some wells, to improve the quality of seeds and the methods of plowing and that, in consequence, everything else will fall into line and the conditions of a healthy national life be established.

Many of us are preoccupied with economic development and with stability. We believe that the one necessarily leads to the other. These things are just not true. There may be some truth in them, but they do not encompass the whole truth. The fact of the matter is that dictatorships in these countries have proved to be just as productive of mischief and even sometimes of instability as have experiments in democratic processes.

I hear often of the efficacy of dictatorial régimes in this country or that country or the other country. This is often presented in the metaphor of a new broom. It is supposed to sweep the country concerned in such a way that everything falls into place and all problems are put on the road to solution. The trouble with the new broom is that after it has swept a while, it becomes an old broom and loses its reputed efficacy. Moreover, a trouble with the dictatorial approach is that it hinders the development of an answer to one of the most important needs of the fledgling countries—namely talent, which requires a wide participation in the conduct of affairs.

I stress all this to our Indian friends. I reject the idea that the institutions and practices of a free system are only for Westerners and that something less desirable is good enough for Orientals. I do not think that these are matters of difference between East and West. I think that they are matters of the conflict of impulses that are common to all human experience. The Indians have not done perfectly in these matters—nobody has, for that matter—but they have not given up the attempt, and this is commendable.

Appendix

INDIA AND THE UNITED STATES—1959

A CONFERENCE SPONSORED BY:

THE COMMITTEE FOR
INTERNATIONAL ECONOMIC GROWTH

May 4 and 5, 1959

at the Mayflower Hotel, Washington, D.C.

CO-SPONSORS

The National Planning Association
The Asia Foundation
The Stanford Research Institute
The Center for International Studies, Massachusetts Institute of
Technology

CONTRIBUTING SPONSORS

K. A. Export Corp.
The Bank of America, NT&SA
Kaiser Engineers Overseas Corp.
Merck Sharp & Dohme, International
Standard-Vacuum Oil Company
Pfizer International, Inc.
Koppers Company (International)
Isthmian Lines, Inc.
The Carborundum Company
Willys Overland Export Corporation
Kaiser Aluminum & Chemical Corp.

Central Gulf Steamship Lines
Checchi & Co.
Union Carbide International Company
Johnson and Johnson International
Bunge Corporation
States Marine Lines
Pan American World Airways

May 4

THE MORNING SESSION

Opening by the Chairman... The Honorable Eric Johnston
Welcoming Remarks...The Honorable Richard M. Nixon, Vice President of the United States
Response...His Excellency M. C. Chagla, The Ambassador of India
The Bases of United States Interest in India ... The Honorable John F. Kennedy, United States Senator from Massachusetts
India's Development: Problems and Programs . . . His Excellency B. K. Nehru, Ambassador at Large and Commissioner General for Economic Affairs, Government of India

THE LUNCHEON SESSION

Hostess . . . Mrs. J. Ramsay Harris, Co-Chairman, The Committee for International Economic Growth
Remarks and Introductions by the Chairman . . . Mr. J. Russell Wiggins, Executive Editor, *The Washington Post and Times Herald*
The Free World Stake in India's Future . . . Lady Barbara Ward Jackson

THE AFTERNOON SESSION

Host . . . Mr. Erle Cocke, Jr., Co-Chairman, The Committee for International Economic Growth
Opening Remarks by the Chairman . . . Dean Harlan Cleveland, Maxwell Graduate School of Citizenship and Public Affairs, Syracuse University
India, China, and the West . . . Mr. Frank Moraes, Editor, The *Express* Newspapers of India, Bombay
    Discussion:
        Mr. Henry R. Lieberman, *The New York Times*
        Professor Hans Morgenthau, Washington Center of Foreign Policy Research
India's Five-Year Plans: Results and Aims . . . Mr. H. V. R. Iengar, Governor, Reserve Bank of India

Discussion:

Mr. Leon Keyserling, Consulting Economist

Dr. Ansley J. Coale, Princeton University

PANEL: Role of American Industry in India's Development

Mr. C. B. Marshall, Vice President, The Standard-Vacuum Oil Co.

Mr. Michael Webster, Assistant to the President, Johnson and Johnson International

Mr. Herbert Harig, President, The Harig Manufacturing Company

THE DINNER SESSION

Host . . . The Honorable Eric Johnston, Chairman, Committee for International Economic Growth

Opening Remarks by the Chairman . . . Mr. John D. Rockefeller 3rd, President of the Asia Society

An Indian View of the U.S.A. . . . The Honorable Asoka Mehta, M.P., Parliamentary Leader of the Praja Socialist Party, New Delhi

An American View of India . . . The Honorable Averell Harriman, Former Governor of New York

May 5

PLENARY SESSION

Opening Remarks by the Chairman . . . Mrs. George H. Shaw, Executive Committee, The Committee for International Economic Growth

Imperatives of Understanding: The Conference in Perspective . . . The Honorable Chester Bowles, Member of Congress from Connecticut

PANELS:

INDIA'S ROLE IN WORLD AFFAIRS

Chairman: Dr. Phillips Talbot, Director, American Universities Field Staff

Professor Ross Berkes, University of Southern California

Professor Michael Brecher, McGill University

Professor Norman Palmer, University of Pennsylvania

Professor Quincy Wright, University of Virginia

THE POLITICAL SCENE IN INDIA

Chairman: Mr. Selig S. Harrison, Associate Editor, *The New Republic*

Professor Charles Burton Marshall, Visiting Research Scholar, The Carnegie Endowment

Mr. Asoka Mehta, M.P., Parliamentary Leader of the Praja Socialist Party
Professor Richard L. Park, University of Michigan
Mr. Frank Moraes, Editor, *Express* Newspapers of India

INDUSTRIAL POLICY AND PROGRAM

Chairman: Mr. Bharat Ram, Industrialist, New Delhi
Mr. Gardiner C. Means, Economic Consultant
Dr. I. G. Patel, Alternate Executive Director, International Monetary Fund
Dr. Antonie Knoppers, President, Merck Sharp & Dohme, International
Professor Wolfgang Friedmann, Columbia University
Professor R. Mishra, Indian Institute of Technology, Kharagpur

OBJECTIVES AND RESOURCES

Chairman: Professor Wilfred Malenbaum, University of Pennsylvania
Mr. Leon Keyserling, Consulting Economist
Professor Max Millikan, Massachusetts Institute of Technology
Mr. George F. Gant, The Ford Foundation
Mr. P. S. N. Prasad, International Bank for Reconstruction and Development
Mr. B. N. Adarkar, International Monetary Fund

AGRICULTURAL DEVELOPMENT

Chairman: Dr. Carl C. Taylor, Consultant in Rural Development
Mr. B. J. Patel, President, All-India Cooperative Union
Dr. Clifford Taylor, University of Maryland
Mr. Albert Mayer, Architect and Town Planner
Mr. J. S. Raj, International Monetary Fund
Dr. Sherman Johnson, United States Department of Agriculture

SMALL INDUSTRY IN THE INDIAN ECONOMY

Chairman: Dr. Eugene Staley, The Stanford Research Institute
Reverend James Berna, S.J., Georgetown University
Mr. James T. McCrory, Director, Community Relations, St. Louis, Missouri
The Honorable P. Govindan Nair, Economic Minister, Embassy of India

Mr. Kennard Weddell, Small Business Consultant
Mr. P. Chentsal Rao, Secretary, Federation of Indian
Chambers of Commerce and Industry

LUNCHEON SESSION

Host . . . The Honorable Eric Johnston
Remarks by the Chairman . . . The Honorable Hubert Humphrey,
United States Senator from Minnesota

ROUND TABLE: INDIA AND AMERICAN OPINION: MYTH AND FACT

Mr. Lawrence Spivak, Producer of *Meet the Press* (Moderator)
Miss Barbara Ward (Lady Jackson)
Mr. William Stringer, *The Christian Science Monitor*
Mr. Harold Isaacs, Author of *Scratches on Our Minds*
Mr. Frank Moraes, Editor, *Express* Newspapers of India
Mr. Clark R. Mollenhoff, the *Des Moines Register and Tribune*

PANELS:

TRADITION AND CHANGE

Chairman: Professor W. Norman Brown, University of Pennsylvania
Professor Milton Singer, University of Chicago
Professor K. A. Nilakanta Sastri, University of Chicago
Dr. B. B. Misra, University of Wisconsin
Dr. Richard B. Gregg, author
Dr. Flemmie P. Kittrell, Howard University

PRIVATE ENTERPRISE IN INDIA

Chairman: Mr. Matthew Kust, lawyer and author
Mr. Arthur Phillips, General Counsel, Godfrey Cabot,
Inc.
Mr. J. Delano Hitch, President, The Dorr-Oliver Com-
pany
Mr. C. S. Krishnamoorthi, Counselor, Commission Gen-
eral for Economic Affairs of India
Mr. Bharat Ram, Industrialist, New Delhi

EXTERNAL ASSISTANCE TO INDIA

Chairman: Professor Max Millikan, Massachusetts Institute of Tech-
nology
Professor Arthur Smithies, Harvard University
Mr. I. G. Patel, International Monetary Fund
Mr. Frederick L. Holborn, Legislative Assistant to Sena-
tor Kennedy

Mr. Hart Perry, The Development Loan Fund
Mr. Geoffrey Wilson, United Kingdom Treasury and Supply Mission

THE COMMUNITY DEVELOPMENT PROGRAM
Chairman: Mr. Albert Mayer, architect and town planner
Dr. Carl C. Taylor, consultant in rural development
Professor Richard L. Park, University of California
Mr. Asoka Mehta, M.P., New Delhi
Mr. Jack Gray, Texas A & M
Dr. Arthur Mosher, Council on Economic and Cultural Affairs

PROBLEMS OF LABOR AND MANAGEMENT IN INDIA'S DEVELOPMENT
Chairman: Professor Charles A. Myers, Massachusetts Institute of Technology
The Honorable George Lodge, Assistant Secretary of Labor
Professor Van Dusen Kennedy, University of California
Dr. Subbiah Kannappan, University of Chicago
Professor Morris D. Morris, University of Washington
Mr. Harry Pollack, AFL-CIO

"ASIAN AMERICAN COMMUNICATION THROUGH JOURNALISM" . . .
A panel discussion at a conference on United States-Asian relations, sponsored by the United States National Commission for UNESCO, in San Francisco, November 7, 1957.
Presiding: Jack H. Lockhart, Assistant General Manager, The Scripps-Howard Newspapers, representing the American Society of Newspaper Editors
Chairman: Selig S. Harrison, former Associated Press correspondent in South Asia
Price Day, Associate Editor, *The Baltimore Sun*
Robert Eunson, Chief of Bureau, The Associated Press, San Francisco
Henry R. Lieberman, Assistant to the Foreign Editor, *The New York Times*
Albert Ravenholt, Correspondent, *The Chicago Daily News*
John Thompson, Pacific Division News Manager, The National Broadcasting Company
Clifford Weigle, Professor of Journalism, Stanford University, rapporteur